Also by Michael Fellman

Inside War: The Guerrilla Conflict in Missouri during the
American Civil War

Citizen Sherman: A Life of William Tecumseh Sherman

THE MAKING OF ROBERT E. LEE

The Making of
Robert E. Lee

MICHAEL FELLMAN

 RANDOM HOUSE · NEW YORK

RANDOM HOUSE and colophon are registered trademarks of Random House, Inc.

Library of Congress Cataloging-in-Publication Data

Fellman, Michael.
The making of Robert E. Lee / Michael Fellman.
p. cm.
Includes bibliographical references (p.) and index.
ISBN 0-679-45650-3 (hardcover : acid-free paper)
1. Lee, Robert E. (Robert Edward), 1807–1870.   2. Generals—Confederate States
of America—Biography.   3. Confederate States of America. Army—
Biography.   4. Gentry—Southern States—Biography.   5. Lee, Robert E.
(Robert Edward), 1807–1870—Political and social views.   I. Title.

E467.1.L4 F45 2000
973.7'3'092—dc21
[B]   99-044062

Random House website address: www.atrandom.com
Printed in the United States of America on acid-free paper

2 4 6 8 9 7 5 3

First Edition

DESIGN BY MERCEDES EVERETT

For Laura

Contents

Robert E. Lee, 1838

1868

Preceding pages: *(left) Robert E. Lee in the Dress Uniform of a Lieutenant of Engineers,* by Benjamin Edward West, ca. 1838, Washington/Custis/Lee Collection, Washington and Lee University, Lexington, Virginia; *(right)* Photograph of Robert E. Lee by John C. Boude and Michael Miley, 1868, the Valentine Museum, Richmond, Virginia.

Introduction

Struggling for Self-Mastery

> "Erase fancy; curb impulse; quench desire; let sovereign
> reason have the mastery."
>
> —Marcus Aurelius[1]

*I*n 1867, the president of Washington College, a small
men's institution in Lexington, Virginia, was asked by the
Educational Society of his state to serve on a committee of three
that was to prepare an address to the parents of the sons of Virginia, urging on them a more hearty cooperation with teachers
in matters of discipline and instruction. The Civil War had left a
legacy of wildness among young men, and authority needed reinforcement.

President Robert E. Lee, former commander of the Army of
Northern Virginia and former commandant at West Point, was
as expert on education and discipline as any man in the state.
Upon his appointment, he wrote a lengthy position paper in the
form of a letter to the other two members of the committee—
one a professor, the other an Anglican minister—to outline the
basic purposes and goals of education, which were also the
markers of a proper gentleman's character. In many ways, he

also painted a picture of the man he hoped he had made of himself.

Education, not nature, made the man. "Education embraces the physical, moral and intellectual instruction of a child from infancy to manhood," Lee wrote. "Any system is imperfect which does not combine them all, and that is best which, while it thoroughly develops them, abuses the coarse animal emotions of human nature and exalts the higher faculties and feelings." Repression of the brute beneath was a sine qua non; therefore, "obedience is the first requisite" in family training as in school, the two central sites for the struggle to inculcate order in the unruly child.

But education was not to be the simple dictatorship of the teacher: The appropriate control of others had to stem not from sheer force but from example. "Neither violence or harshness should ever be used and the parent [and teacher] must bear in mind that to govern his child he must show that he can control himself," Lee stressed. The essential need was for "firmness mixed with kindness." Not merely should the child's "mind be expanded," but "his heart must be affected, his feelings moved." The "sentiments of religion" had to be inculcated by "systematic instruction." Likewise, learning to love labor, to develop independence and quash animal idleness, must be "pursued by earnest and regular exertion." But, as with the teaching of religious sentiments, all drills had to be coupled to demonstrations of piety and industry by parent and teacher.

If all went well, the heart as well as the head of the student would become attuned to self-control. "The love of truth is equal in importance to habitual obedience," Lee reiterated. Nobility of character was the chief end of education—careers would follow—and any choice would be socially responsible and individually fulfilling if made by the dutiful man.[2]

These calmly stern teachings came without hesitation or doubt from the pen of the sixty-year-old Lee, who had seen so much of the affairs of men, including the most base. As he wrote this letter, two books sat on his desk: the Episcopalian *Book of Common Prayer* and a well-worn *Meditations* of Marcus Aurelius, the Stoic Roman emperor.[3] These sources and values, inherited from the milieu of the Virginia slaveholding gentry in which he was bred, explain much about the persona of Robert E. Lee, the Lee who was an exemplar, in his own eyes as well as those of others, of the best of his class, his place, and his time. Perhaps more than any other American, with the exception of George Washington, whom he consciously emulated, Lee has long been taken as a moral hero, the greatest Southern white gentleman, the Marble Man.[4] Lee was complicit in this creation because he held himself to a life of endless discipline and selfless virtue in a very determined way.

The struggle for self-mastery—the effort to repress every potentially disruptive impulse and emotion—was perpetual.[5] The Christian virtue of humility instructed this moral wrestler that he would, of course, never reach his goal, but the older Stoic virtue of pride—one of the seven deadly Christian sins—kept him marching along the stony path of control and denial.

Such a character ideal had been typical for the eighteenth-century Virginia slaveholding gentry. But Lee lived in the mid-nineteenth century, in a society still defined in part by such traditions but also deeply influenced by Romanticism and the warm piety of Evangelical Christianity. In middle age, to be true to his religious striving, Lee felt obliged to open himself to soul-searching and spiritual passion during a conversion experience. Once he had reached upward, however, Lee turned toward an even more distant and chilly sense of duty, as if in flight from the vulnerability his transformation had demanded.

As a young man, Lee often had been quite ebullient. One story Lee told on himself to a close friend demonstrated in a lighthearted way some of the tension between the less repressed side of his character and his endless drive for self-mastery and self-abnegation.

In 1846, when he was thirty-nine, Lee was stationed at Fort Hamilton in Brooklyn, engineering new fortifications. One winter's day, when a heavy snowfall blanketed the roads of New York City, several enterprising liverymen brought out horses and sleighs and offered rides up and down Broadway. Lee wrote to John Mackay, his closest West Point chum, about his experience on the sleighs. "The girls returning from school were the prettiest sight, piled on each other's laps, with their bags of books and laughing faces. Indeed there were no lack of customers at sixpence a ride, and you might be accommodated with a lady in your lap in the bargain." Temptation. "Think of a man of my forbidding countenance, John Mackay, having such an offer." Will the mask cover the desire? "But I peeped under the veil before accepting and though I really could not find fault either with her appearance or age, after a little demurring preferred giving her my seat." The gentleman dominates the man when he recalls the discretion demanded of a properly married gentleman such as he. "I thought it would not sound well if repeated in the latitude of Washington," where his wife's family lived, as well as many other young women of his acquaintance, "that I had been riding down BW with a strange woman sitting in my lap. What might my little sweethearts think of it, Miss Harriet H[ackley Talcott]," the wife of another West Point friend, "among the number. Upon reflection I think I did well, for though you know I am charmed when I can get one of the dear creatures on my knee, yet I have my fancies in this as in other things. I found however that I was looked upon as such a curmudgeon by my fellow passengers that I took the first opportunity to leave them." Hooted at for his punctiliousness, which some took to be prudery, the proper Lee conquered his desires by getting off that dangerous sleigh.

Although his primary purpose in telling this suggestive and playful tale was almost certainly self-mockery, Lee was also demonstrating his rectitude to the same old friend to whom he confessed his desires. The next day, he related to John Mackay, "I drove our ladies here several times and my little horses fairly flew over the road. I am all by myself—Mrs. Lee and the children have all gone to Arlington."[6] In her ninth month of pregnancy, Mary Custis Lee had returned to her paternal home to deliver the Lees' seventh and last child.

Southern men of Lee's class were trained to deny their selves and act correctly all of the time in a manner that strikes many modern ears as strained. The man of virtue ought to have no selfish desires and no demanding ego—just a pure concern for service—no feelings uncontrolled by reason and duty, no personal interest or subordination to self-serving groups or political parties. He should be utterly independent and passive, never behaving in a grasping or showy manner. He must train himself to respond perfectly to events imposed on him but never strive for power. And yet such passivity collided with the belief that the man of honor was to act forcefully in the world, in demonstration of his inner superiority of character. The desire to render utterly disinterested service masked the will to power; striving for independence meant going into the world to master it, even though one could never acknowledge such ambition.[7]

This stringent if internally contradictory code often went unobserved. Possessors of great wealth in land, slaves, and trade, which they considered their entitlements by blood and birth, Virginia grandees frequently behaved in willful and self-indulgent ways. Many, perhaps most, gambled, drank, fought, and whored their ways through life, taking their passions out on their slaves, their children, and their wives, as well as on each other and in the end on themselves. They were no worse than other powerful ruling classes, but their practices hardly matched their professions.

In contrast to the swashbuckling roarers who sporadically tried to be good and failed, Robert E. Lee really made a sustained effort to conform his actual behavior to that set of values all men of his class subscribed to in principle. Understanding and admiring Lee's enormous discipline and self-denial, others of his ilk could look to him as their one perfect representative, proving that their ideal might be made actual. It would be all too easy to debunk this idealized construct, but iconoclasm, though tempting, is far too simplistic and in its way as dehumanizing as worship at the shrine of the Marble Man. Still, Lee's ceaseless efforts to attain an impossibly austere manhood reveal a great deal about both the man and his society.

However completely Lee defended this ideal of himself, fortune, of course, intruded upon him, pushing him into relationships and situations he could not avoid, not just in war but throughout his life. In common with other Virginia gentlemen of his generation, Lee was cast adrift in a rapidly changing society in which men of his class were no longer as dominant. In the bustling nineteenth century, problems of aristocratic self-creation were compounded by rapid social and economic change. Even in Virginia, new men and new money—products of wildfire Jacksonian economic and political transformation—undercut traditional society: A gentleman could no longer count on his birthright for respect, deference, wealth, fame, or friendship. In response, in common with most of his class, Lee was deeply antidemocratic, fearing that unprincipled demagogues in alliance with the undisciplined lower orders were destroying his genteel world. And in Lee's case, family scandals in his youth had called the aristocratic Lee name into question even as they plunged him into poverty, forcing him to live on the generosity of his kin. A personally embattled member of a threatened class, Lee's inheritance gave him a lot to prove.

In many ways, family still provided the most important social grounding for Lee, even if his sort were losing social authority. And beyond his family, West Point and army hierarchy defined life more clearly for Lee than any other American institution could have, with the exception of the slave plantation. Yet the army, which was tiny and embattled and outside its own confines viewed with a certain contempt as an aristocratic backwater, normally played a marginal role in American development. Only war could bring him fame and fulfillment, the opportunity for self-creation beyond a mere existence.

In a very real sense, the Civil War rescued Robert E. Lee from marginality and obscurity. In it, he learned to focus his values, his talent, and his deepest feelings on the terrible martial problems at hand. Only in combat did Lee discover and express a well of anger and desire for action that allowed him to overcome his lifelong habits of self-abnegation and passivity. For one period in his life he was prideful and aggressive, developing a contempt for the enemy whom he was dominating, until Gettysburg brought him back down. For the remainder of the war, his gloom deepened, though he and his army remained the firmest force defending the Confederacy. Awareness of his fame strengthened his sense of self and of military and political importance: He began to think about the South in new and more conscious, even political ways, exchanging his passivity for a greater engagement, a sensibility that deepened after the war.

And yet, in many ways, Lee remained a man of convention and ritual, as his postwar educator's letter shows. Such codification demonstrated a great deal about the life he lived and the abstract values to which he continued to ascribe, even as other

attitudes and behaviors became more worldly. As his muted and
humorous recounting of the sleigh ride unintentionally had revealed, Lee always felt conflicts about trimming his energies to
fit his social role, conflicts that led him both to yearn for life and
to redouble his efforts to control himself and others.

The requirements of the gentleman's code corroborated
Lee's most intimate emotional experience of life, which led him
to fear engagement. The belief that duties were thrust upon him
from outside conformed to his inner desire for inaction and
avoidance of conflict. He guarded himself from the vicissitudes
of human commitment; his incessant demands on himself and
on others led to highly constructed barriers between himself
and them. Carefully fashioned, depersonalized individual and
social boundaries prevented him from experiencing much personal happiness and warmth, leaving him distant and enig-
matic, even to himself.

In the face of the frightful aspects of life, most especially
war, the collision of detachment and inactivity with striving and
ambition—and that is what it was, whether or not he could acknowledge it—provided the central dynamic of Robert E. Lee's
lifelong self-creation. In emotional terms, Lee's stoic perfection-
ism masked self-doubts and the often brittle urge to control. In
an endless emotional cycle, half-formed desires and anxieties always threatened to burst through the surfaces of his personal
and cultural conformity, which led him to dampen his fires yet
again. Whatever the personal and social ramifications of his efforts, the making of Robert E. Lee was, in the mode of Marcus
Aurelius, an impressive struggle.

The Making of Robert E. Lee

Chapter 1

PATRIMONY RECAPTURED

*D*uring a long, dull tour of military duty in Saint Louis in the late 1830s, Captain Robert E. Lee grew interested in his genealogy. He wrote home to his brother Carter and to several other kin, in search of a family seal and a copy of a family tree he believed he had once seen at the home of his cousin Edmund Lee. "In my old age"—he was actually thirty-one years old at this time—"I begin to feel a little curiosity relative to my forefathers, their origins, whereabouts, etc.," he wrote his cousin Cassius.[1]

Inquiry into the Lee family meant exploring the whole embattled gentry class of tidewater Virginia. In 1793, Robert E. Lee's father, Light Horse Harry, after being widowed, married his cousin Ann Hill Carter, fortifying ties to the single most powerful, widespread, and wealthiest Virginia family, the descendants of "King" Carter. In common with others of their class, the Lees continuously augmented wealth and power by marrying their cousins. Bankhead, Beverley, Bolling, Byrd, Custis, Dabney, Fitzhugh, Harrison, Ludwell, Marshall, Mason, Randolph, Stuart, Taylor, Washington, and many other famous names all were cousins to the Lees. Five of the seven Virginia signers of the Declaration of Independence were kin, including

Richard Henry Lee, Robert's grandfather, who introduced the resolution for independence at the Continental Congress in June 1776. Also related were seven governors and numerous other state officeholders, two presidents, and the most eminent chief justice. The Lees were embedded in what was already being called, by the mid-nineteenth century, the "First Families of Virginia."[2] We must understand Lee in this aristocratic milieu, the context in which he developed his senses of place and identity.

One marker of the deep ties of gentry kinship was the habit of using surnames as first names. Thus, for example, Robert E. Lee's elder brother was named Carter, after his mother's family, a practice Robert continued when he named his two eldest sons after relatives. Intermarriage and naming practices consolidated family landholding and other forms of wealth, as well as elite political power and social prestige. Virginians of the gentry class could look across the vast reaches of the plantations in their state and see a dominating network of cousins.[3]

Much of the wealth and power of this class derived from slaveholding, an institution conducive to developing habits of authority and control. Yet the realities of slavery also heightened owners' awareness that absolute mastery was an unreachable goal. Claims to authority were perpetually negotiated with recalcitrant slaves, which meant that each master was constantly monitoring his "self" while dealing with slaves. The drive for mastery, rather than its supposed attainment, lay at the core of the South's master class, and this continuous effort gave these men much of their energy as well as their anxiety.

In addition, planters held increasingly problematic control over the white lower classes. Sometimes the deference elites expected as their due was accorded out of admiration, fear, or awe. For example, in 1806, an upwardly mobile preacher recorded of his boyhood betters, "We were accustomed to look upon, what were called *gentle folks,* as beings of a superior order. For my part I was quite shy of *them,* and kept off at a humble distance."[4] The resentment latent in this statement, which was almost worthy of Uriah Heep, was one rather mild expression both of the power still held by those in authority by birth and of the growth of antideferential attitudes.

The ability to command as a matter of birth and rank long had been declining in Virginia. In the course of the eighteenth century, the first Great Awakening had not only disturbed ecclesiastical authority but challenged the very notion of deference. The Episcopal Church to which Robert E. Lee belonged was no longer the state-supported church to which all Virginians had to belong: Its membership already had shrunk to a small, elite core by the growth of the Baptist and Methodist denominations concomitant with the religious upheavals of the previous century.[5] And the American Revolution further released and amplified notions of democracy and equality.

In the material as well as the social and political world, the gentry were succumbing to long-term pressures as power shifted both to the new commercial elites and to a wider range of small farmers. Their population swelling, their soil exhausted, many Virginians of all social standings began to move west after about 1800, first to Kentucky and then to the new states of the Deep South and the Midwest. Wealth lost its firm base in the land, as Virginia began a slow shift to newer sources of wealth: Burgeoning industrialization and commercial agriculture in grains and meat, as well as tobacco, proceeded as rapidly in Virginia as in nearby Pennsylvania.

Over the course of the early nineteenth century, especially after the mid-1820s, the leveling and often angrily antiaristocratic politics sweeping the nation made a major impact on Virginia, too, where new men entered the electoral realm, pushing aside, often rudely, the less aggressive gentry participants, in the name of the people. Those aristocrats who wanted to remain in public life had to learn to adjust at least their public language, if not their inner thoughts, to more democratic times. Others retreated to the sidelines and bemoaned the good old days when men of birth and virtue held power, as if by nature. Here, too, as with slaves, mastery was being called into serious doubt, and men of high station had to adjust to stay relevant to new social and political conditions, even as they struggled to retain some core of gentility and control.

Although the dominance of the gentry was declining, its members did not lose their grip on power and prestige entirely. They could still exercise considerable authority, in part by making timely alliances with merchants and the more successful yeomen, and they had not lost their sense of command, much of which continued to stem from their roles as slavemasters, about which they dug in their heels, in defiance of abolitionism spreading in the North and abroad.

The Confederate nation would be led by new men and old in an uneasy alliance, with martial discipline strengthening the claims of aristocratic officers such as Lee to great power over their men, who proved to be both brave and unruly, thus continuing and even heightening prewar Southern social divisions. Asserting a calm and certain authority under such circumstances was a ceaseless and often losing struggle, which led to even greater effort and to increased self-doubt.

Like the relationships between the classes and the races, marriages among the traditional Virginia cousinage were supposed to make good common sense—the ties that bound were primarily economic and social. Marital love was intended to derive not from passion but from calm, rational, mutual commitment, not from coercion but from good behavior and genteel character. As Thomas Jefferson asserted so clearly when he contemplated romantic love with Maria Cosway, the head certainly ought to govern the heart. Yet affection was also important. The ideal husband instructed and guided his wife with kindness rather than force, eliciting her freely given acquiescence and respect. Husbands and wives were to love one another, but this did not imply equality between them. However warm the marriage, he led, she followed. What was this but patriarchy, a term quite acceptable to Virginians if not as much to their contemporaries to the north?[6] However clear this code was in theory, in practice many gentry wives were as unsettled and rebellious as the lower orders were.[7]

Robert E. Lee was a unquestioning member of the Virginia gentry, with all the privileges and problems that entailed. For example, on the subject of marriage, Lee instructed a younger, Kentuckian officer, John Bell Hood, when they were out on a horseback ride on the frontier of Texas in 1856, "Never marry unless you can do so in a family that will enable your children to feel proud of both sides of their house." Years later, Hood recalled that Lee feared "I might form an attachment for some of the country lasses, and therefore imparted to me his correct and at the same time aristocratic views in regard to this very important step in life."[8]

As a Stoic and Christian of the highest social order, Lee believed that he had to obey the timeless code of the gentleman—even if he doubted his social position, which connoted his right to command, he held himself to high standards of rulership in order to reinforce his standing. His credo of noblesse oblige, which deepened during his lifetime, reached something of an apogee during the Civil War, when he was in charge of the major institution of the Confederacy, the Army of Northern Virginia:

> The forbearing use of power not only forms a touch-
> stone, but the manner in which an individual enjoys

certain advantages over others is a test of a *true gen-tleman.* The power which the strong have over the weak, the magistrate over the citizen, the employer over the employed, the educated over the unlettered, the experienced over the confiding, even the clever over the silly—the forbearing or inoffensive use of all this power or authority, or a total abstinence from it when the case admits it, will show the gentleman in a plain light. The gentleman does not needlessly and unnecessarily remind an offender of the wrong he may have committed against him. He cannot only for-give, he can forget; and he strives for that nobleness of self and mildness of character which impart suffi-cient strength to let the past be but the past. *A true man of honor feels humbled himself when he cannot help humbling others.*[9]

Robert E. Lee's task was to attempt to recapture the author-ity and status to back up such a belief. His father and elder brother had squandered not only the family standing but the family honor—its very nobility of name—in serial catastrophes of gothic proportions. This spectacular collapse, played out hu-miliatingly in public, provided the deepest motivation for Robert E. Lee to do good, to do well, and to reclaim the family standing.

Lee was the son of one of the fathers of American Indepen-dence, probably the best cavalry commander of the Revolution-ary War. Yet in 1782, before the war ended, Light Horse Harry had resigned his army commission in fury and depression, fol-lowing a dispute with fellow officers over rank and command. Upon Richard Lee's death in 1787, as the eldest son Harry in-herited control if not title over the imposing Stratford Hall, with its 6,595 acres, as well as several other plantations, but his ambitions had just begun. Wanting to amass enormous wealth as quickly as possible, Light Horse Harry began to speculate in land and designed a visionary city to be built at the falls of the Potomac. The city was never begun, and most of the other speculations quickly soured. By 1800, Stratford Hall plantation had been reduced to about one tenth of its 1787 size. As if this were not bad enough, Light Horse Harry mortgaged and remortgaged the same lands and wrote checks he knew he could not cover. This was not a new practice for him. Earlier he had gone so far as to write a bad check to General George Washington, who had rebuked him in a humiliating manner and let it be known quite widely that though a fine soldier, Lee was not to be trusted in money matters.

The long slide accelerated, even while Light Horse Harry and Anne Carter produced a set of five children between 1798 and 1811—Robert, born in 1807, came fourth. After spending much of 1809 and 1810 in debtors' prison, which did not resolve his financial liabilities, and after being beaten within an inch of his life by a Baltimore mob for writing especially nasty anti-Jefferson pamphlets for the Federalist Party in 1812, Lee fled to the West Indies in disgrace in 1813. Everyone knew what had befallen Light Horse Harry. On March 25, 1818, he died on his way home from his exile, just after landing on an island off the coast of Georgia.

The sequel was even more macabre. Stratford Hall passed to Light Horse Harry's eldest surviving son from his first marriage. That same year, young Henry married a wealthy and well-dowered orphan, Ann McCarty, with whom he soon had a lovely daughter. Ann's younger sister, the teenage Betsy, came along with her sister and soon made Henry her guardian. Immediately after his marriage, Henry set about squandering his fortune by more or less continuing his father's financial practices. In 1820, his little daughter fell to her death down the long outside staircase at Stratford Hall. Ann McCarty then developed a heavy morphine addiction, while Henry took up with Betsy and impregnated her. Betsy soon fled to other relatives, underwent either an abortion or a miscarriage, and then sued her guardian to regain her estate, which Henry was in the process of wasting. By 1822, Henry, now known in Virginia as Black Horse Harry for abusing his sister-in-law, lost Stratford Hall, which was seized by the county and later sold to Betsy McCarty, now Betsy Storke, who lived for fifty years on the lands of her ex-seducer.

Still pursuing the main chance, Black Horse Harry turned to politics, writing a campaign biography for Andrew Jackson, upstart from the west and archenemy of the Virginia gentry, against whom Harry wrote polemical pamphlets as well. In 1828, Black Horse Harry pressed his luck when he persuaded Jackson to offer him the United States consul position in Algiers. Betsy then continued her revenge: She passed the lurid tale of her youthful seduction to the aristocratic Virginia senator John Tyler, who disclosed the whole story of this caddish social renegade in rich detail before the full Senate, which had to consent to Lee's diplomatic nomination. Black Horse Harry was ruined. Already in Algiers, Harry and his wife fled first to Rome and then to Paris, where, having destroyed both his fortune and, what was worse, his honor, he remained in exile until his death in 1837.[10]

In the meantime, Light Horse Harry's widow, the sickly Ann Carter, lived in genteel poverty with her five children, dependent on her relatives. Others found her brave, if pitiable.

Almost nothing is known of Robert's boyhood, although he apparently lived at least some of the time with Carter cousins, sharing their tutor.[11] Robert was two when Light Horse Harry was sent to debtors' prison and just six when he fled to the West Indies and so had few memories of his father, nor appropriate fathering, although he certainly came to know of his father's disgrace and, later, that of his half brother, Black Horse Harry.

The first descriptions we have of Robert E. Lee come from the impression he made in 1824, when, at age seventeen, he arrived at West Point, tall, stunningly handsome, bright, manly, commanding—a full-blown aristocratic beau ideal. Decades later, fellow cadets were still in awe of the Lee they had met then. Wrote one, "His personal appearance surpassed in manly beauty that of any other cadet in the corps. Though firm in his position and perfectly erect, he had none of the stiffness so often assumed by men who affect to be very strict in their ideas of what is military. His limbs, beautiful and symmetrical, looked as though they had come from a turning lathe, his step was elastic as if he had spurned the ground upon which he trod." Even at such a young age, Lee struck his fellow cadets as perfect not only in beauty but also in character. His classmate and close friend Joseph E. Johnston recalled decades later, "No other youth or man so united the qualities that win warm friendship and command high respect. For he was full of sympathy and kindness, genial and fond of gay conversation, and even of fun, while his correctness of demeanor and attention to duties, personal and official, and a dignity as much a part of himself as the elegance of his person, gave him a superiority that every one acknowledged in his heart."[12] There he was, the perfect Virginia gentleman, already, at seventeen, a natural leader of men.

Even allowing for the hyperbole of memory and the exaggerations stemming from their awareness of the unsurpassed fame of the general with whom these two Confederates later served, something genuine runs through their accounts. And performance matched promise. Lee was a brilliant student, finishing second in his class of forty-six, with no demerits for misconduct during his entire four years.[13] He then became a superb engineer; the best West Pointers gained entrée into the elite Engineering Corps, where they became the leading civil engineers in the nation. Neatness and order were the signs of the almost-perfect cadet and the meticulous, problem-solving engineer.

Whence came this paragon? Where were the wounds of a disruptive childhood, of a fallen and publicly scorned father and half brother? One not particularly analytic answer is that some young people from difficult backgrounds, the seemingly invulnerable ones, just turn out fine, for mysterious reasons. As Lee was not very introspective (perhaps in itself a useful coping mechanism) and as he almost never discussed his childhood, we can learn little about how he reacted to his "pillar to post" boyhood. However, Lee's fear of close ties with other men, his enormous reserve, and his desire to live through abstract principle rather than emotional engagement suggest the effects of an absent and disgraced father.

Lee revealed one indication of the long-term insecurity growing from his boyhood in a letter of congratulation to one of his own sons upon the birth of a grandson in 1860. He thanked his son "for this promising action of my scattered house, who will I hope resuscitate its name and fame." Although this might have reflected Lee's doubts at this point about his own rather ordinary military career, it could also be taken as his more general comment about the failures of the whole Lee line.[14] Lee's scars emerged in many ways, despite his strenuous regimen of self-control—indeed, sometimes through such effort.

Lee could not have sprung directly from his own head, but sources about sibling and peer relationships before West Point are nonexistent, and those concerning any surrogate fathering he experienced from older male cousins and uncles are few and obscure. However, the naming practices of the Virginia gentry provide some clues. Robert E. Lee named his first sons George Washington Custis Lee and William Henry Fitzhugh Lee, indicators of the most important male figures in his life, his father-in-law and one of his uncles.

When Ann Carter Lee and her five children were left with only a small personal inheritance by Light Horse Harry's death, she was thrown on the mercy of her kin, particularly her distant but kind cousin William Henry Fitzhugh, who sometimes took in her family at his plantation, Ravensworth. In 1824, when Robert was seventeen, Fitzhugh successfully appealed to the secretary of war, John C. Calhoun, that Robert be admitted to West Point, in a letter that the highly presentable Robert delivered in person. Fitzhugh's reference was grounded in the ideal of the gentleman, something he knew that Calhoun, the Carolinian defender of the planter class, would understand in his bones. Rather than evading the disgrace brought to the Lee family by the financial scandals of Light Horse Harry, Fitzhugh placed them in a wider context. "[Robert] is the son of Gen. Henry Lee, with whose history, you are, of course, acquainted; and who (whatever may have been the misfortune of his later years) had certainly established, by his revolutionary services, a strong claim on the gratitude of the country." If Lee's paternal line was stained by his father's failure, his maternal bloodline was not so blemished, Fitzhugh wrote, appealing to Calhoun's sympathies for the offspring of a genteel woman fallen on hard times not of her making. "He is also the son of one of the finest women the State of Virginia has ever produced. Possessed, in a very eminent degree, of all those qualities, which peculiarly belong to the female character of the South, she is rendered doubly interesting by her meritorious & successful exertions to support, in comfort, a large family, and to give all her children excellent educations." Fitzhugh spent less time describing Robert himself but assumed as paternal a stance as he could. "An intimate acquaintance, & a constant intercourse with him, almost from his infancy, authorize me to speak in the most unqualified terms of his amiable disposition & his correct and gentlemanly habits. He is disposed to devote himself to the profession of arms." Fitzhugh made no mention of Lee's intellectual aptitude nor of his educational background: Breeding and character were the telling points, plus a sense of martial vocation, which was suitable and traditional for a landless and impoverished young gentleman evidently interested in neither the ministry nor the law. In closing, Fitzhugh returned to the issue of diminished family means. "His own age (eighteen I believe [*sic*]) and the situation of his mother require that he should lose no time in selecting the employment to which his future life is to be devoted."[15]

Naming his second son after Fitzhugh was the clearest indication of how much gratitude Robert felt toward his unofficial guardian. But later, after Fitzhugh died, Robert wrote in a letter to his elder brother Carter, "I have grieved over the death of my good old Uncle Fitzhugh, whose kindness to me & us all, & our dear mother I shall never forget. I hope he is happier now than I fear he was in the world. Perhaps it is as well that his property will be distributed among all his relatives. It will leave a remembrance to each & not be too much for any. For myself I had expected none."[16] Despite all Fitzhugh had done for him, Lee did not feel like Fitzhugh's son, although the honorific title of uncle, of an extra special "good old Uncle," and the inheritance, however small, reminded him that this had been a special relationship. On the other hand, he was chilly and condescending toward a man he clearly believed to have been limited and unhappy. This letter appears to be the only reference Lee ever made either to Fitzhugh or to any paternal figure, with the partial exception of General Winfield Scott, Lee's much-admired commander during the Mexican War.

The links to the renowned George Washington provided an even more significant form of secondhand patrimony. Through his marriage in 1831 to his cousin, the wealthy heiress Mary Anne Randolph Custis, daughter of the stepson of George Washington, Lee improved his position by making an alliance with a family at the very pinnacle of the Virginia gentry class. Mary had been raised at the great plantation at Arlington, across the river from Washington, one of the three most notable plantations in Virginia, alongside Mount Vernon and Monticello. Although her father, George Washington Custis, was a down-at-the-heels manager, his fortune included immense landholdings and several hundred slaves. When Lee married into this family, he moved up socially and in wealth—a traditional aristocratic manner of regaining upward mobility. As the name of his first son, George Washington Parke Custis Lee, indicated, this tie meant a great deal not only materially but also in terms of the noblest of lineages—a strong bond to the father of his nation—even if that later seemed somewhat ironic in light of the secession to come.

George Washington provided Lee, as he did several generations of Virginia gentlemen, with an idealized paternal model of the most commanding and self-controlled Virginia gentleman conceivable. Dozens of sons were named Washington in his honor. But Lee fetishized this identification: Others sometimes noted his imitation of the nation's father. Former governor Henry Wise of Virginia, for example, remarked to him in 1862, "General Lee, you certainly play Washington to perfection."[17] His natural father was only a physical void and a bad reputation, and Lee was therefore free to imagine an alternative. The model he chose was already a legendary paragon, above normal human contradictions, whom the fates had chosen for immortality, the original Marble Man. Lee ignored, if he was aware of it, Washington's towering ambition, which he had cloaked in an aura of disinterested virtue.

In 1869, near the end of his life, perhaps trying to venerate his father's memory and to heal his own ancient resentments, Lee edited his father's Revolutionary War memoirs, adding his own biographical sketch and letters Light Horse Harry had written from exile to his son Carter, whom he had actually gotten to know before he fled. Here, Robert tied his father to the venerated George Washington. Washington had made a demigod of himself, Robert wrote. "It was not until the 'Father of his Country' had become the glory of the world that it pleased Providence to remove him to a higher sphere." And who was it but Light Horse Harry who had signaled this ascension into the pantheon during a funeral oration in 1799? "It must have been a consolation to General Lee, in his individual grief, to have been appointed by Congress the public organ of his country's sorrow, on which occasion he pronounced those memorable words: 'First in war, first in peace, and first in the hearts of his countrymen.' " Light Horse Harry would indeed long be remembered for those words, a sentence that would forever link him to the official memory of the Founding Father. Robert E. Lee returned to those lines again and again in his memoir of his father. "What a sublime eulogium is produced in this noble line," he wrote, "and yet how illustrative are they of the vast and matchless character of Washington; . . . words which will [be] graven on colossal statues of the Pater Patriae in some future age." Robert E. Lee could thus make the strongest possible case for his father's legacy and for his own noble inheritance.

But this was a legendary, not a personal connection with the memory of his actual father. When he had the chance, he showed little interest in visiting his father's Georgia grave site.[18] Indeed, the only time little Robert had appeared in a letter from the West Indian exile was when Light Horse Harry remarked to Carter, "Robert was always good, and will be confirmed in his happy turn of mind by his ever-watchful and affectionate mother. Does he strengthen his native tendency?" Robert E. Lee did not comment on this sad evidence of the paucity of connection he had with his father.

In his 1869 biographical discussion, Robert E. Lee sought to come to the defense of the memory of his father, seemingly to express some good about him for posterity. He blamed the Baltimore mob of 1812, actuated by "disgraceful . . . party spirit," for causing his father great physical pain, shortening his life, and preventing him from participating in the War of 1812, in which he might have reclaimed heroic military status. Ignoring the whole question of his father's dishonesty and financial disgrace, Lee argued that Light Horse Harry had undertaken his terrible voyage to the West Indies merely to restore his health from the ravages of the mob. He praised his father for having been, in certain respects at least, the best public man of his day: "In one particular Lee may be said to have excelled his illustrious contemporaries, Marshall, Hamilton, Gouverneur Morris and Ames [if not Washington, he might have added]. It was in surprising quickness and talent, a genius sudden, dazzling and always at command, with an eloquence which seemed to flow unbidden." Lee could not have known of his father's personality firsthand, but he tried to emphasize the best of what he had heard from others. He simply ignored issues of character and the pathetic later career, dutifully making the best case he could.

In 1782, when Light Horse Harry resigned his command in great anger, he wrote to his superior, General Nathanael Greene, "I am candid to acknowledge my imbecility of mind, and hope time and absence might alter my feelings: At present my fervent wish is for the most hidden obscurity; I want not private or public applause; my happiness will depend on myself; and if I have but fortitude to persevere in my intentions it will not be in the power of malice, outrage, or envy to affect me." Robert ascribed these paranoiac effusions to "sickness and sorrow. . . . The broken health produced by his long and arduous services depressed his spirits and caused the melancholy so apparent in his farewell letter." Seeking to praise his father, he also rather calmly analyzed his limitations and, by inference, his blemished reputation.

Lee then quoted, at considerable length, several letters of moral instruction to Carter. For example, Light Horse Harry told Carter to prefer "the practice of virtue to all other things; . . . you have often [been] told by me, that [lying] led to every vice and canceled every tendency to virtue." Light Horse Harry was fully aware that he himself was widely regarded as a liar, from Washington on down. Again, he admonished Carter, reflecting on his own experience from a curious vantage point, "avoid debt, the sink of mental power and the subversion of independence, which draws into debasement even virtue."

Here Robert E. Lee merely quoted such maxims, presented by a man who had failed to live up to them, yet he would himself spend a lifetime issuing similar aphorisms, thus demonstrating that it was not the code but the practitioner that had been at fault. What did the son make of these sentiments or of the following assertion? "A foolish notion often springs up with young men as they enter life, namely, that the opinion of the world is not to be regarded; whereas, it is the true criterion . . . of all things. . . . To despise its sentence, if possible, is not just; and if just, is not possible." Was Light Horse Harry acknowledging that he had failed and that he had deserved the punishment life had dealt him?

Light Horse Harry also wrote Carter that "the rank of men, as established by the concurrent judgment of ages stands thus: heroes, legislators, orators, and poets." Although he then argued that legislators, such as he had been on occasion, were the most honorable of men, he went on to discuss great Roman figures, only to conclude that their archenemy Hannibal, the great Carthaginian hero, was their superior. Alas, he wrote, one could learn of Hannibal "only from the records of his enemies, [from] Roman hatred and prejudice." Light Horse Harry appeared to be linking his fate and his historical reputation to that of Hannibal, with whom he identified against the victorious Romans; he seemed to be suggesting that he was not just an honorable legislator but also a failed hero, cast out by the new Rome.

Revisiting this correspondence in 1869, the son concluded that these had been "letters of love and wisdom," rendered almost holy by his father's "veneration for Washington and his fondness for expressing it, [that] clung to him to the last."[19] If his father had failed, he had failed at the most ambitious level and would nevertheless be forever identified as the author of the most fitting eulogy for the unblemished hero, that noblest Roman, George Washington. And Robert E. Lee had married the stepgranddaughter of the Founding Father and had named his firstborn son after the true Washington line.

Schooled in the classics, as had been his father and all men of their ilk, building his own reputation through a respectable military career and an advantageous marriage, Robert E. Lee constructed a symbolic patrimony that led him toward seizing the hero's mantle. When the opportunity arose, he pushed himself above other men to make the name of Lee honorable once more, to prove his fealty not to Light Horse Harry Lee but to George Washington, his ideal father. Self-control and duty remained his mottos, abstractions that masked the scars of his boyhood. He repeated his father's maxims—the received wisdom of the Virginia gentleman—and strove endlessly to live up to them where his father had failed abysmally. As he neared death, however, burdened by the knowledge that he had lost his war of independence, Lee attempted to reintegrate himself into the dominant Washingtonian—and American nationalist— mythography.

Chapter 2

MARRIAGE, EROS, AND SELF

One hot July day in 1835, lieutenants Robert E. Lee and Washington Hood of the Engineering Corps and a small body of enlisted men set out on Lake Erie to determine the northern boundary of the state of Ohio, which ran somewhere through the middle of the lake. Proper surveying techniques necessitated crossing over to the Canadian side of the border at Pelee Island. After the expedition, Lee wrote back to his friend George Washington Cullum (yet another Washington!), an assistant in the chief engineer's office in Washington, with a description of some little happenings—"an event of indiscretion," he called it—that transpired on Canadian soil that day.

To make the correct triangulation required climbing to the top of a lighthouse at the southern tip of the island.

> The door was locked & we could not gain admittance, but after some time succeeded in getting through the window in [the] rear when we discovered the keeper at the door. We were warm & excited, he irascible & full of venom. An altercation ensued which resulted in his death. . . . I discovered some glass lamp shades,

which we stood much in need of as all ours were broken. I therefore made bold to *borrow* two of his Majesty, for which liberty, as well as that previously taken, I hope he will make our apology to his Minister at W[ashington]. . . . I hope it will not be considered that we have lopped from the Government a useful member, but on the contrary—to have done it some service, . . . & we would advise the New Minister to make choice of a better subject than a d[amne]d Canadian *Snake.*[1]

In fact there was no such killing. The only resident of the island, William McCormick, lived eight miles away from the lighthouse he sometimes tended and usually ignored; he died of natural causes in 1840. The "d[amne]d Canadian Snake" Lee and Hood killed was in fact a snake, and the whole story was a mockheroic. Lee was sending up the hot-bloodedness ascribed to young soldiers, especially Southerners.

As a young man—he was twenty-eight when he wrote this letter—Lee often used such broad humor in his correspondence. Already quite reserved and honor bound, he was at the same time lively and playful, albeit in a somewhat heavy-handed fashion. It took years for him to clamp down on this lighter side. Over time, deepening religious sobriety as well as the Mexican War and, far more profoundly, the Civil War destroyed almost every lingering impulse to make fun of himself and of others. As he matured, Lee obsessively fled any hint of the irrational for the contained, play for duty, openness for control, ego for conscience.

Unusual for a man of his era and his station, Lee never smoke or drank, and he eschewed rough language and all forms of personal physical violence. Sexuality appears to have been the one arena in which he departed from what were by his lights nearly perfect habits. Although Lee married relatively young for his day and age, at twenty-four in 1831, his romantic interest in other women continued well after that, judging from his correspondence. Victorian-era letter writing between men and women was generally broad and warm in its expressiveness, and such conventions make it difficult to know for sure what acts did or did not accompany thoughts. Even in that context, however, Lee's correspondence is striking for its sexual content.[2]

At times, he used vivid metaphors otherwise uncharacteristic of his writing style to tell other men how much he desired women. Thus, one June day in 1834, he wrote to his closest West Point friend, John Mackay—"Delectable Jack" he called him—as he sat above a Virginia beach: "The Daughters of Eve . . . would make your lips water and fingers tingle. They are beginning to assemble to put their beautiful limbs in this salt water." At about the same time, he confessed to another old friend, "You are right in my interest in pretty women—it is strange I do not lose it with age." Lee was all of twenty-seven when he wrote this letter. And three years later, from the crude frontier boomtown of Saint Louis, which he described as a "desert . . . a desert of the heart," where no gentry belles swam by, he lamented to Jack that all was bleak save the pretty girls, "for I have met them in no place, in no garb, in no situation that I did not feel my heart open to them, like a flower to the sun." Seemingly struck by his indiscriminate taste for young women, he admitted the thought and then distanced himself from it: "It is true I have no preference, but this does not deprive me of a fatherly affection for the whole race." This assumption of paternal distance was not exactly convincing, but it allowed Lee to conclude that although he adored and desired women, such impulses did not imply that he was in danger of actual physical promiscuity.[3]

Marriage was, of course, the exclusive sanctioned outlet for sexual energy, and while Robert E. Lee admired the girls, he had also sought a wife with whom he could make a marriage and family appropriate to a man of gentry birth and breeding. While appropriate on these grounds, Mary Custis was also a financially valuable spouse, and she was attractive to Lee for her fine mind and character as well. Not terribly handsome, she was nevertheless bright, cultivated, extremely well read, of considered political opinions, and, most important to her groom, deeply religious. She was a pious Episcopalian, of the newer, more evangelical sort, committed to putting her faith into social action, particularly through the American Colonization Society, to which her mother also belonged. Not an abolitionist or an early feminist, neither was she a passive drone, and her husband always admired her greatly for her intelligence and social engagement, even if he did not necessarily agree with her projects. Indeed, throughout his life, Lee was fond of the aphorism that all the Lee women were fierce and all the men mild. A year after their marriage, Lee, describing the grief of the recently widowed Abigail Talcott Hale to Mary, expressed his notion of the wifely ideal in language that clearly referred to his wife: "I am sure you would have been delighted both to have nursed and relieved one so kind and good as she is & above all blessed with so strong a mind and true piety."[4]

Mary Custis apparently turned Lee down the first time he proposed, in 1830, as her father doubted that the impoverished son of the disgraced Light Horse Harry Lee would be of sufficient social standing or respectability to come into his family. On the other hand, Robert had a fine reputation and stunning good looks, the sort of qualities for which gentry *women* might marry upward, according to a convention that evidently sometimes could work inversely. Apparently, Robert had to pursue Mary and her father quite vigorously. Once, in 1830, Lee complained to his brother Carter, "Tell Cousin Mary that if she thinks that I am going to stay here, after you go away, without hearing anything of her . . . she is very much mistaken. So that she must write me, & if she does not I'll tell her mother."[5] Lee was frustrated—though he seemed to have found an ally in Mary's mother.

Courtship flowered over the course of the following year, however, and on June 30, 1831, Robert and Mary wed. Two weeks later, Lee wrote to his dear friend Andrew Talcott about the wedding and the honeymoon. "I am told I looked 'pale & interesting,' at the wedding ceremony, but I felt as 'bold as a sheep' and was surprised my want of Romance is so great a degree as not to feel more excitement than at the black board at West Point." He also bragged mildly to Talcott of the sexual pleasure the new marriage was giving the newlyweds. When all the wedding party finally left them alone at Arlington, "I would tell you how the time passed, but fear I am too much prejudiced to say anything more, but that it went *very* rapidly & still continues to do so." Yet as infatuation faded, the normal sorting-out process of the first few years of this marriage would be compounded by Mary's chronic illnesses, which contrasted so strongly to Robert's boundless physical strength.[6]

Mary gave birth to George Washington Custis Lee thirteen months after her wedding and had seven children in all over a fourteen-year period, a number that gave her husband male pride.[7] After her second delivery, Mary developed a painful pelvic inflammation that recurred with some of the later births. Even more seriously, her inherited rheumatoid arthritis worsened over the years, and she was in almost constant pain, in later years often confined to a wheelchair. When he was not absent on army duty, which he was most of each year, Lee nursed her faithfully, often taking her to hot-springs resorts in the Virginia mountains, which were coming into vogue as vacation sites for the better born. He worried and at times despaired, because in addition to her other illnesses Mary sometimes also became extremely dependent and depressed.

In the summer of 1836, Lee described to Carter the annoying complexity of health seeking. "I myself have more confidence in the continuous journey, diversifying the scene, amusing the mind and endeavouring to strengthen the body. Perhaps the waters of some of these springs may act as tonics upon her system and thereby produce much good," the doubting but loyal husband wrote. "Her nervous system is much shattered, she has almost a horror of crowded places, an indisposition to make the least effort, and yet a restless anxiety which renders her unhappy and dissatisfied." Both sympathy and exasperation characterized Lee's reactions to Mary's overall health. Also annoying was the regal entourage it took to reach the spas, including little children, two carriages, and four servants, a party "so large that it makes it unpleasant to visit any of our friends," who might otherwise cheer up Mary.[8]

In everyday life, Mary's habits also bothered Lee: She was untidy, while he was impeccable; she usually ran late, while he was always spot on time. It should not have surprised him that the fancy-free daughter of the large plantation at Arlington—who had had numerous slaves to serve her yet was now a relatively impoverished military wife surrounded by small tots—found managing a household with only one or two slaves a difficult experience. Still, he chafed against her mismanagement, despite his gentleman's code, which reminded him always to be forbearing. On rare occasions, he found himself apologizing to dear old friends for her bad habits. In April 1834, when he was expecting the Talcott family to visit, he wrote Andrew Talcott, "Tell the ladies that they are aware that Mrs. L is somewhat addicted to laziness and forgetfulness in her Housekeeping. But they may be certain she does her best, or in her mother's words, 'the Spirit is willing but the flesh is weak.' "[9]

Occasionally, Lee allowed himself to express mild annoyance toward his wife, not so deep as his actual negative feelings, one can suppose. One time, when the Lees were stationed together in Fort Monroe, Virginia, Mary, who was on holiday in Arlington, asked him to send on a favorite dress. He had trouble finding it in her crowded closet and wrote back that he could not figure out which dress to send and then, reacting to her anticipated criticism, added, "If you have any need of funds let me know it & get such frocks as will suit yourself, since my taste is so *difficult.*" The remainder of this letter was quite loving.[10]

Only once, while he was in Ohio mapping that northern border, did the young husband lose his self-control and explode at his wife. On this occasion, all the more significant for its rarity, Lee broke his code of self-restraint, even while insisting that Mary had to follow hers. When Mary was at a spa, slowly recovering from a bout of illness and doubtless lonely, she had pushed him to drop everything and come back to her. "But why do you urge my *immediate* return, & tempt one in the *strongest* manner," he replied, paraphrasing her letter. "I rather require to be strengthened & encouraged to the *full* performance of what I am called on to execute. . . . I must not consent to do aught that would lower me in your eyes, my own & that of others." After this initial outburst of masculine assertion, as if catching himself in midtantrum, Lee muted his message. "If she to whose precept and example I had fondly looked to assist & guide me cannot at all times sufficiently restrain her own feelings to bear [separation] with patience & composure, what must necessarily happen, & what she must prefer me to perform?" Calming down to remind her of her duty, he then urged not blind submission to his demands but cheerful consent. "You see therefore Molly every consideration induces you to cheer up . . . & to meet with a smiling face & cheerful heart the vicissitudes of life."[11]

In this revealing communication, Lee criticized his wife for making his life harder when it was her duty to soften his travails with support. And he reminded her of the shame, in her eyes, in his, and perhaps even more important, in those of the world, should they not both do their duties. But then he also promised her great happiness if, out of her innate womanly affirmativeness and good sense, she would just do her duty and allow him to do his. Here was the gentry husband leading and instructing his wife, the patriarchal code in practice.

Years later, in a letter to a female friend of long standing, Lee described an ideal wife of his acquaintance, rather unlike the actual spouse whose difficulties often frustrated him over the years. One Captain Elzy, Lee observed, had been ordered, a week after his marriage, to fight in Mexico, where he had remained three years, after which he had been sent to remote posts on the American frontier so often that for four years the couple had not been able to establish housekeeping. Now he was stationed in Baltimore, from where Lee wrote, "Capt. Elzy has just arrived from Charleston on a visit to his pretty wife. She is a true soldier's wife, never complains. Is resigned & cheerful under all circumstances."[12] Lee could dream of an ideal wife, whose self-control and insistent good cheer would perfectly match his own.

Almost always, Lee covered up his negative feelings and expressed concern for his wife's health and admiration for her fortitude, sometimes expressing a longing for reunion. Thus, in 1837, he wrote home to Virginia from Saint Louis, "I am very anxious to get back. And my desire to be again in the midst of you and [your] mother and the children and the rest is sometimes almost uncontrollable. . . . Kiss them all for me. Dear little woman, I am so glad she is hearty."[13] Affectionate attachment was the norm, resentment the exception.

While he struggled to serve his wife, Lee's eye roved. Even during his engagement, he told stories in which he projected his own desires onto others, while censoring them by writing in a jesting tone. For example, in January 1831, at his post on Cock-spur Island after the Christmastime social whirl of nearby Sa-vannah, Lee wrote Carter about the escapades of one of their mutual acquaintances. "You never saw a fellow take a thing more kindly than Sweet Charles does his marriage. . . . There is not a party of any kind afloat, but what he is prancing away in his black tights & white silks, dancing & flirting with all the girls, while the Madam is at home in care of her health."[14]

Other fantasies had more edge. In 1833, two years after his marriage, Lee wrote Jack Mackay—the friend of his youth with whom he remained more open than with any other man, until Jack died in 1848—"I have comforted myself by practicing what you so strongly recommend, Patience." He then described sev-eral units of his regiment that were polishing up in preparation for a military expedition that might take them far from the post for considerable time. "The poor young soldiers Jack require all your sympathy. [Their wives] are not all Niobes and will prove themselves Penelopes"—Niobe being sexually unfaithful and maternally vain, for which Apollo and Artemis killed her chil-dren and Zeus turned her to stone, while the faithful and ever-chaste Penelope put off all suitors when her husband Odysseus disappeared for decades, wandering the earth. "Among them are three brides, and one of them not more than a week old, besides some others that are quite as pretty and of as tender feelings, some others again are more advanced and their husbands on their return will be welcomed by one more than they take leave of. What a picture Mackay for a bachelor of your tender heart—I am to console them and am in the right disposition to sympa-thize with them, as Mrs. Lee and her little limbs are at Arlington. The Miss Masons are well and as sweet as ever." Bettie and Mat-tie Mason were two aristocratic young girls Lee often sought out at the spas over at least the next decade. He called them "angels" but also "gay & agreeable" girls with "numerous acquaintances & for all I know lovers."

It is problematic whether or not Lee allowed himself to console the tender or the advanced, Niobe or Penelope, or to know what was the nature of his long-term relationships with Bettie and Mattie Mason, although he believed that some married women and single young things would be tempted to step beyond marital conventionality.

Even if he considered the Mason girls to be essentially angels, Lee wrote racy letters to them. In one, he described two sets of Saint Louis newlyweds. One young bride of a "loafer from Natchez" was "very pretty, an heiress & just from the altar. She has not yet laid aside the manners she acquired in her belleship," Lee told the two teenage girls. She "sits during dinner expanding her large eyes & pouting her pretty lips & has all the appearance of one that has not found matrimony what it is cracked up to be." This frank flirt was sure to cuckold her husband, Lee implied. If Lee enjoyed this young woman's flirtatiousness, he also mocked the new marriage of an aging general, Edmund Pendleton Gaines, with a much younger widow. "She declares that the Genl. has more than fulfilled every promise he ever made her & that he could not have believed that they could have again experienced in all their freshness the joys of wedded life. I am afraid at seventy they will prove too exhausting to his veteran frame. He already appears to be sinking . . . & her prospects are very good of again becoming a happy widow."[15]

This was quite suggestive humor to share with tender young girls. Yet Lee often included his wife in such banter, as when he wrote her in August 1837, "Tell Miss Mattie I should *admire* to be of their traveling party this summer, though she may congratulate herself that I shall not have an opportunity of indulgence in either my *paternal affection* or *punishment* on her."[16]

Here, playful and somewhat erotic high jinks were wound in a kind of mock triangular fashion between husband, wife, and "lover."

During at least the first twenty years of his marriage, until his rather belated religious conversion in his mid-forties, Lee developed intense relationships with a variety of young women, to whom he often expressed emotions similar to those he shared with the Mason girls. Lee carried on a long correspondence with Martha Custis Williams—known as "Markie"—who was Mary's first cousin and his distant cousin. Shortly after it began, the thirty-seven-year-old Lee asked longingly in one letter written in 1844, when Markie was nineteen, "Oh Markie, Markie, when will you ripen?" A year later, he told her that her letter had given him "infinite pleasure" and that "I have thought upon it, slept upon it, dwelt on it (pretty long you will say) & have not done with it yet." Although the letters continued for most of the rest of his life, they lost most of this early intensity in exchange for formulaic and distant courtliness.[17]

Lee was far more bawdy with several other young women, including Tasy Beaumont, a Saint Louis teenager with whose family the Lees had boarded in the late 1830s. In one letter, written March 13, 1843, Lee passed on to Tasy a verse he claimed to have translated from Theocritus, the Greek poet.

> *Mild he may be, and innocent to view*
> *Yet who on earth can answer for him? You*
> *who touch the little god, mind what ye do.*
> *Although short be his arrow, slender his bow:*
> *The King Apollo's never wrought such woe.*

Two days earlier, Lee had written to "My Beautiful Tasy," "I wish you were here in person for I am all alone, my good dame [being away]." It was often when his wife was absent that Lee's feelings went astray. In this instance, he gave Beaumont news of his son, six-year-old Rooney (the nickname of William Henry Fitzhugh Lee), who was "growing apace in more ways than one & I am afraid is no better than he should be. He turned up one morning in a young ladies bed & seemed so pleased with his quarters that he could not be got out, till I sent him word if he had not 'get out of that' I would pull them both out by the heels. You must have taught him those tricks Tasy for he never learnt them from his father."[18] Tasy was knowing—"advanced"—and Lee was open with her.

Lee's bluntest correspondent was Eliza Mackay, John's younger sister, a young woman with whom he spent considerable time both before and after his marriage. "I have not had the heart to go to Savannah since you left it," he wrote to her in 1831, the year of his marriage, after she had returned home to nearby Beaufort, South Carolina. He had been pining for letters from her: "But you will send me some, sometimes, will you not Sweetheart?" And then that evening a letter from her arrived. Unfortunately, Lee was occupied with Captain Richard Delafield and others on the engineering staff. The discussion had just reached the issue of construction cranes when Lee glanced at his watch and saw that it was 11:00 P.M.; Delafield and the others not taking the hint to leave, he simply moved to the other side of the room and entered a "conversation" with Eliza. "But I can only stay with you while they are present. For there is a room to my left which has many charms for me & through the door which is partly open, I see a spot where it would rejoice me to place myself." That was, of course, his bedroom and his bed, where people of the Victorian era often took love letters for a private read.[19]

Later that year, Lee responded to the arrival of a letter from Eliza, "I am truly happy . . . that you are again downstairs," by which he meant her letter, not her person. He was becoming addicted to the pleasures her letters contained, he told her, quite explicitly: "See what a great temptation to sin you will give me. Do spare me the blame of its commission." "Commission of sin" was the most commonly used, lightly encoded Victorian-era expression for masturbation, one possible result of taking such a letter to bed.

The climax of this correspondence came in a letter of January 4, 1832, when Lee told "Miss Eliza (My Sweetheart)," just after her wedding, "I have been in tears . . . at the thought of losing you. Oh Me! Mr. Gilderoy you are a lucky fellow." And then he wrote that he had been "wondering upon all that was going on," the night after the wedding. "And how did you disport yourself My child? Did you go off well, like a torpedo cracker on Christmas morning?" Lee was asking Eliza Mackay Stiles if she had had an orgasm the first time she went to bed with her new husband.[20]

Especially in the context of the "temptation to sin" missives that preceded this letter, it is clear that Robert and Eliza had a bold and lighthearted erotic relationship. Of course, these were letters—by definition literary sublimations of sexual desire—and this was a form of "letter sex," as it were. But they were written, sent, and read following a relationship that earlier had proceeded in the flesh in Savannah.

How far did this or any of these relationships go? Perhaps they were just literary fantasies. Yet gentlemen such as Lee could not always achieve the purity of behavior for which they strove. Their sexual codes, untrue to their desires, often produced hypocrisy and covering up. Lee's erotic life may or may not have included dalliances that would have sullied his reputation if they became known, which they did not. Yet Lee's literary candor was absolutely astonishing, given the conventions of Victorian-era romantic correspondence, which licensed hints about actual sex but not ones nearly this broad, even with lovers in the full sense of the word.

Lee was never this direct and expressive about any other intimate subject: Everywhere else he guarded his feelings by cloaking them in conventional, ritualized literary formulas. There was more "personality" here—more individuation of expression—and less impersonal ritual than in any other part of his correspondence, and almost certainly in his life as well, whether or not these "other women" were his lovers. Given his almost obsessive clean living, his increasing Christian piety, and his growing formality with other men, this sector of his life was the largest impediment on his road to self-control.

Occasionally, Lee painted himself in the passive role to the aggressive woman. Sometimes he commented this way on the behavior of women and men in general, as he did when observing a group of snowbound Christmas revelers in 1851: "The young people have been quite assiduous in their attention to each other, as their amusements have necessarily been indoors, but the beaux have successfully maintained their reserve so far, notwithstanding the captivating advances of the belles." A few years earlier, Lee had remarked to his confidant Andrew Talcott about the behavior of one young woman with whom he had danced away an evening, "Sally is as blythe as a larke & admitted me (an innocent man) into her bed chamber a few days after the frolick."[21]

This was a most dangerous orchard for a gentleman to enter; even if he tasted its fruits, Lee could not allow himself to move there. Repressing but never entirely eliminating the considerable emotional audacity these letters suggest, Lee consciously strove to conquer sexual desire outside of his marriage: He quite systematically enlarged his personal reserve until martial ardor would be the only strong emotion he would be able to express to the hilt.

Chapter 3

FATHERHOOD AND SALVATION

*J*ust before Lee was to go into battle in Mexico in 1847, when his thoughts quite naturally turned to mortality, he learned that Harry Delafield, the son of his longtime Engineering Corps comrade, Major Richard Delafield, had died of the measles. After expressing sympathy for his distraught comrade, he wrote Mary about the impact of that death on him. "Oh how I pray that my dear boys may be preserved to me. I shudder with horror as the thought sometimes comes over me that I may never see them again. But I will hope & trust in Him who gave them to me & has preserved them till now."

While Lee was steeling himself for his own potential death, little Harry's demise had reshaped his fears into an even worse scenario. He instructed Mary about preparing his children for the ever-possible imminence of death, "Guard & control them I pray you. Teach them so to live as to be always ready to die & never to forget their absent father." He then was swept with nostalgia and loneliness. "My sweet little daughters are ever present to me & I daily long for their sweet little mouths to kiss. I try to make friends with all the little girls I meet for their sakes, but I can see none to fill the longings of my heart." Then his thoughts turned again to his sons, especially the littlest, four-year-old

Robert, Jr. A little Mexican boy he observed had reminded the father of his son. In a "velvet cap & coat & a nice little whip," the lad had been riding a goat, which had been saddled and bridled, with an older brother about the size of Rob's ten-year-old brother, Rooney, walking by his side. "The little fellow was as happy as a bird," Lee remarked. Recently, Lee also had seen a lovely little black pony with a silver-studded saddle and bridle, which he tried to buy for his children for the considerable sum of one hundred dollars, without success.[1]

This moment of unusual introspection led Lee into his innermost thoughts concerning his children. In his childrearing even more than in censoring his wilder impulses toward women, he revealed the urgent necessity he felt to impose systematic repression on himself. And while Lee turned away from the joys and terrors of life through self-denial and stern child rearing, he also thirsted for religious conviction, in order to reach the highest level of self-control, where temptation to sin might be pushed away forever.

As a young officer in antebellum America, where genteel officers did not carry their families to hardship posts, Lee was bound to be away from his family most of the time. This freed him to carry on an enjoyable independent social life, but absence also made him miss his children terribly. To Jack Mackay, to whom he wrote many of those letters about the ladies and whose bachelorhood he sometimes envied, Lee wrote from Saint Louis in 1837 about how bad he felt when he had been compelled to leave his two-week-old son, Rooney, on two days' notice. "Mackay I am the father of three children, and you are but a leafless bough! They are whole children Mackay, and so entwined around my heart, that I feel them at every pulsation. You say right, life is too short for them and their mother to be in one place and I in another. I am hurrying back with all dispatch."[2]

Guilty that he could not be with his children in their forma-
tive years, Lee found it difficult to square his career with his fatherhood. He wrote to his mother-in-law in 1838 about his
frequent and prolonged absences, protesting that he would "always be anxious to return to you," and then continued, "I think it
is my duty to make a sacrifice . . . to try and advance myself in
my profession, and be thereby enabled to give our dear children
such an education and standing in life as we could wish." The
bitterest memory he might have "would be that I had given
them reason to think I have preferred my own ease and comfort
to their welfare and interest and have not improved such opportunities I might possess for their advantage."[3]

This argument about serving the greater good by being absent demonstrated both resolve and underlying doubt. Lee felt
his absence from his large and growing young family and well
understood how his children would miss him. After all, his own
father had gone away forever before he could know him.

It is also possible that Lee used duty as an excuse to free
himself from the burdens of wife and children. He loved them,
to be sure, but he may have preferred to be off with other men
and engaged in his profession, about which he could be obsessive. At the same time, it was his duty to express tender regard
for his family, and he would have been especially apt to voice
his concern to his mother-in-law, who could thereby serve as a
witness to his affection rather than his absence.

Nervousness and the desire to control from a distance characterized the frequent directives the absent Lee sent home. For
example, when his eldest son, Custis, was only ten months old,
Lee wrote to his mother-in-law with fears about what well might
prove to be her daughter's parental shortcomings. Mary "will
have every *wish* to make him [become] all that you desire, but
between you & I, I fear that her discipline will be too lax, too in-
constant & too yielding to effect much more than her excellent

example will perform." Mary was at risk of allowing Custis to develop bad habits that "may go far to spoil him." When Lee had
last been home, he had seen enough of his son to reassure himself that "he is as beautiful as love himself," but that in itself was
a cause for worry, because "he is *too sweet* & that his moral and
mental improvement may keep pace with his personal is my
daily prayer."[4] Lee had seen too many spoiled Virginia gentry
children, even among his siblings, who had come to bad ends.
He also wanted his boys to be tough and manly men, which
often brought young bloods to bad ends, although he did not
seem to fear that potentially bad result as much.

Because of his certainty about the natural propensity to
sin—the Calvinist remnant in the core of Romantic Evangelical-
ism—Lee was certain he had to discipline his children into re-
nouncing their wickedness. But this could not be accomplished
by paternal dictation, which would not lead children to internalize morality but only teach them to act according to form when
in danger of being found out. Lee insisted that correct parenting
would "not only make the child obey externally but internally to
make the obedience sincere and hearty."

Alternate acts of kindness and hard discipline were the hall-
marks of paternalism—of the sort Southern men impressed on
their slaves as well as their children, and military officers on
their men—and in this sense Lee was expressing a cultural as
well as a personal sentiment. He would not have expected that a
mother, a member of what he considered the softer sex, would
understand these twin demands as well as a father did. Because
he was so often absent, family duties—both feminine and masculine—fell on Mary, whom Lee could advise from a distance
and also blame. And these were idealized rules, far easier to suggest from afar than to practice in the flesh.[5]

Yet even as the masculine Lee admonished his wife to make
their son less sweet and more disciplined, he also could be

swept by feelings of warmth and affection. Such emotions conformed with the kinder side of paternalism—after all this was
what made men *gentle*men, with hardness always available
when needed. But many of his contemporaries thought Lee had
an extra dose of sentimentality. For example, when his firstborn
son was just over a year old, Lee wrote to Mary, "My sweet little
boy, what would I give to see him! The house is a perfect desert
without him & his mother. [If] I could only feel his little arms
around my neck & his dear little heart fluttering against my
breast, I should be too happy." Even in this letter, Lee admonished his wife: "Don't let him be spoiled, direct him in everything & leave nothing to the guidance of his nurse." If he feared
his wife might provide insufficient guidance, he feared even
more for the results should she turn his son over to a slave
woman as a baby-sitter.[6]

Each new child produced a surge of affection within Lee's
bosom. In at least one instance—the birth of Rob in 1843—Lee
was away from Arlington on duty in the army. The abstractness
of the birth dissipated for him when he heard the news—he
connected to his new baby immediately by awakening old sentiments roused by prior births. "It is strange how my heart
yearned towards him as soon as I heard of his *existence*," he
wrote to his mother-in-law four days after the event. Although
he had been thinking only of Mary's safety during the pregnancy and labor, "no sooner was I conscious of his birth than all
my affections were awakened."[7]

As his children grew, so did Lee's gnawing anxieties about
his capacities as a father in the face of the ability of human nature and of the world to bring down his children. The snares of
temptation multiplied for adolescents and even adults, Lee believed. Therefore, assiduous supervision might well prove insufficient, which led to heightened demands for discipline, in an
endless cycle of fear and suppression.

When he was on the Texas frontier in 1856, Lee described his fears about Fitzhugh, by then a nineteen-year-old junior officer in the army. "He gives me many anxious days & sleepless nights, & adds more than years to the gray hair in my head," he wrote to Mary. Fitzhugh seemed to him always affectionate and disposed to do right, yet he could also be "thoughtless—impulsive, & . . . guided more by his feelings than by his reason." All Lee had to do was to look at all those promising but careless gentry lads who went astray to make his anxiety soar. "So many young men threw themselves away before they were aware how tightly they were bound in the chains of idleness & vice." Lee was very concerned about Fitzhugh—one of those children-as-containers into whom he poured his concerns about the ever-ominous human capacity for plunging into the abyss: "It is . . . so important for the young to acquire habits of self-control and self-denial [until] reason is able to exert her power, truth becomes apparent & passion and self love controlled."[8] Here was the crux of the Calvinist matter: Self-control had to be not merely imposed but internalized early in life in order to guarantee correct reasoning and decision making later on. Would Fitzhugh, or any of his children, ever develop enough inner discipline to reach sufficient self-mastery?

At times, it must be said, Lee could take real pleasure in the wildness of his children, particularly his sons when they were very young. When Custis—known as "Boo"—and Rooney were little, Lee wrote at the end of a letter to his brother Carter, "Boo & Rooney with four of their little playmates have been keeping such a laughing, bawling, jumping rumpus and a rioting around me that I hardly know what I have written, and Mr Rooney is at this moment jerking the cover of my table with one hand and cracking me over the head with the broom with the other." In this mode, six years later, he reported to an old chum that "Rooney is a big double fisted fellow with an appetite that does honour to his big mouth & all the others are growing in mischief as well as size."[9]

Such celebrations of animal energy were the exception to the long-term rule, which was discipline. In this department, Lee was a Virginian Lord Chesterfield. Daughters got their share of advice, but with sons it was all the more firm. As the eldest son, Custis got the first full round of advice; as the more impulsive one, Fitzhugh got the most pointed and angry round; as the baby, Rob got off rather lightly.

More broadly, Lee had restated the full aristocratic code in an earlier ritual incantation to the teenage Custis, then at West Point.

> You must study to be frank with the world; frankness is the child of honesty and courage. Say what you mean to do on every occasion, and take it for granted you mean to do right. If a friend asks a favor you should grant it if it is reasonable; if not, tell him plainly why you cannot; you will wrong him and yourself by equivocation of any kind. Never do a wrong thing to make a friend or keep one; the man who requires you to do so is purchased at a sacrifice. Deal kindly but firmly with all your classmates. You will find it the policy which wears best. Above all, do not appear to others what you are not. If you have any fault to find with anyone, tell him, not others, of what you complain. There is no more dangerous experiment than that of undertaking to be one thing before a man's face and another behind his back.[10]

And so on and so forth.

From the moment Custis reached the military academy in 1850, Lee kept close tabs on his performance and peppered him with advice. Whenever Custis failed to measure up to his father's old record, he got a warning as well as support. Thus, when Custis received eight demerits for misconduct, after liquor was discovered in his room, his father, who never had received a single demerit, was mortified. "I hope your demerit . . . will not be sufficient to injure your standing, but it may require a greater exertion on your part to gain an offset in your class mark." Really, Lee believed, Custis was not trying as hard as he might. "I do not think you lack either energy or ambition. Hitherto you have not felt the incentive to call it forth."[11]

Lee never let up on Custis's performance. Just before Custis's midyear exams in his second year, his father wrote him, "I shall be very anxious about you. Give me the earliest intelligence of your standing, and stand up before [the examiners] boldly, manfully; do your best, and I shall be satisfied." The anxiety about the performance was more sincere than the boilerplate about doing his best—winning was the goal. When the subsequent class standings showed Custis second to the future Union general O. O. Howard, his father admonished him, in anticipation of the final exams to come in a few months, "you must press forward in your studies. You must crowd that boy Howard. You must be No. 1. It is a fine number. Easily found and remembered. Simple and unique. Jump to it fellow."[12] Custis must have seen through the falsely bantering tone of this demand.

Even when Custis was doing fine, his father's compliments were clouded with anxiety. After a visit to West Point, during which Lee had received "the commendations of your officers, which gave me the greatest pleasure I have ever experienced," he confessed to his eldest son his "anxious thoughts all the way home" that Custis might do "nothing to forfeit" such praise, that he should "neglect no branch & no point" of his work, and continually exercise "*strength, fortitude & capacity.*" Nothing was enough, as something always could be lost. In this letter, one can sense the way in which the fatherless and relentlessly perfectionist Lee had driven himself when he had been at the Point. When he wrote his firstborn son, he lacked a model for giving appropriate encouragement.[13]

Not entirely surprisingly, given this paternal compounding of the normal rigors of West Point, as Custis's exams neared at the end of his second year, he began to express depression about his education and his whole life. In response, his father wrote him a jaunty and cheerful letter, stressing the power of positive thinking. How could such a fine "young soldier tall & straight, capable & willing (I hope) to do his work be cast down," he began, not quite sensing how sharing that parenthetical moment of fear might affect his son. Lee continued that Custis should never feel isolated and down when all the home folks were cheering for him. "Think of *all* at home. Think how they *think* of you. Think how they *talk* of you. Think how they *feel* for you. But let that *gladden* your heart." Then Lee added the Panglossian argument: "All is bright if you will think it so. All is happy if you will make it so." And then, the realist sally: "Do not dream. . . . Look upon things as they are. Make the best of them . . . strive hard to make them so." And then the bad-medicine approach: "Sad thoughts . . . are necessary & good for us. They cause us to reflect. . . . Do not yield to them. But use them as a medium through which to view life correctly." Lee then went on to describe a big wedding the family had just attended, as if to show Custis the continuity of life, the bigger and happier picture. And he signed off, "good bye my dear son. Love always your devoted father."[14] The son was once more reminded by this guilt-inducing valediction that he was either to perform perfectly or disappoint his father.

Custis pulled out of this depression and finished at the top of his West Point class, but later he had longer and deeper bouts of depression, including one that lasted most of the last decade of his life. It would be incorrect to blame the father for his son's depressiveness, but his father added to his burdens when he sent Custis so much instruction about moral perfection, striving for perfect performance, and, in the guise of empathy, qualified approbation even when the chips were down.

Toward his second son, Fitzhugh (Rooney), Lee was even more judgmental, as was Mary. She was certain that he had to remain "under [his father's] eye," and he believed that Rooney "thinks entirely of his pleasures & not what is proper to be done." Although Lee also wrote supportive letters when Rooney was down in the dumps as a student at Harvard,* they read rather like those he sent to Custis under similar circumstances.[15]

Rooney had always been the reckless son. When he was eight, ignoring his father's earlier warnings, he climbed by himself into a hayloft and accidentally cut off the ends of two fingers with a chopping knife. Lee, who had a special abhorrence of physical dismemberment, which he may have associated with the sort of disfigurement common among poor white men and battered slaves, became very angry at the son he also nursed gently. He expressed his concern and his anger most directly in an admonitory letter he wrote to Custis soon after the event.

---

* While at Harvard, Rooney roomed with Henry Adams, who, decades later, in his celebrated *Education,* offered this recollection:

> Lee, known through life as Roony [*sic*], was a Virginian of the eighteenth century much as Henry Adams was a Bostonian of the same age. Roony Lee had changed little from the type of his grandfather, Light Horse Harry. Tall, largely built, handsome, genial, with liberal Virginian openness towards all he liked, he also had the Virginian habit of command and took leadership as his natural habit. No one cared to contest it. None of the New Englanders wanted command. For a year, at least, Lee was the most popular and prominent young man in his class, but then seemed slowly to drop into the background. The habit of command was not enough, and the Virginian had little else. He was simple beyond analysis; so simple that even the simple New England student could not realize him. No one knew enough to know how ignorant he was; how childlike; how helpless before the relative complexity of a school. As an animal the Southerner seemed to have every advantage, but even as an animal he steadily lost ground. (Ernest Samuels, ed., *The Education of Henry Adams* [Boston: Houghton Mifflin, 1973], 57)

"My only consolation is that this severe lesson will never be forgotten by himself or his brothers & sisters," the lesson being that he had been "punished for . . . inattention and disobedience" with his self-amputation. Custis, Rooney, and all the other children ought now to have learned their lesson and to be strengthened in the path of rectitude. The worst of it, according to the father, was the grief Rooney's act had caused his parents, especially him. "If children could know the misery, the devastating sorrow, with which their acts sometimes overwhelm their parents they could not have the heart thus cruelly to afflict them. May you never know the misery I now suffer & may you always be preserved to me pure & happy."[16]

Lee's declaration of wounded self-absorption took paternalism a *very* long way in the direction of arguing that children existed for their parents, of whom they were extensions, rather than as persons in their own right. Such child rearing played on shame about physical disfigurement as well as on guilt: The underlying fear was of the capacity of the child to fail his father and the family reputation. Lee may have felt empathy for his wounded son, but he expressed only anger because he thought his main task was to guarantee his son's soundness—what he termed his purity—for purposes of family continuity and honor. The father was the guardian who sought to ward off all possible stains to the family of which he was the head and commander. Lee was determined not to permit any evocation of recent Lee family history while he was the man in charge.

Three months after Rooney had disfigured himself, his father recounted a moral tale to him about an exemplary son. He had heard the story, Lee wrote Rooney, during his subsequent travels up north. A New Hampshire farm lad named Harry, who was about thirteen, "the age of Custis," had been assisting his father in the woodlot that winter. The boy drove the wood sled home to stack the firewood they had already cut while his father stayed on to cut another load. When he returned, the boy saw his father lying cold and stiff on the ground under a tree limb he had felled. Alone in the woods with the first corpse he had ever seen—his father no less—Harry did not panic but loaded the body onto the sled and returned home, where "his mother was greatly distressed at the loss of her husband, but . . . thanked God who had given her such a good son." Then Lee delivered the moral of this homily to his self-damaging, truant son, as if he could possibly have missed the point. "You and Custis must take great care of your kind mother and dear sisters when your father is dead. To do that you must learn to be good [and] to 'keep his commandments, and walk in the same all the days of your life.' "[17] Sons would one day be fathers, which meant that they carried the burdens of inherited patriarchal obligation and had to learn, at great peril, to walk that walk.

Provoked by such terrible moments as that of Rooney's self-maiming, Lee often reached great depths of negativity. The realities of punishment loomed large and dark—in fact, the story of little Harry and his dead father was a representation of hell, should Rooney continue to fail his father. The worst crime was disobedience to the will of the father, earthly steward of God the Father. In his lecture about fatherhood, Lee assumed the role of the Protestant preacher, quoting Scripture to force Rooney to consider the evil of his ways. He was, of course, acting from his sense of duty, writing from love and not just anger, but such words must have burned themselves into his sons' souls.

Very occasionally, Lee caught himself in sanctimonious sermonizing and made light of himself. Once, when he was dilating yet again on the theme of the properly distant gentleman to Rooney in a letter in 1858—"I hope you will make friends . . . with many who deserve this feeling, but indiscriminate intimacies . . . can always be avoided by politeness & civility"—he suddenly caught himself and added, "you see I am following my old habit of giving advice which I dare say you neither need nor require."[18]

Lee seemed to have relaxed a bit when it came to rearing his youngest son and namesake, Robert E. Lee, Jr. In memoirs published many decades after his father's death, Rob recalled that his father romped with the older children but was physically affectionate only with him and his younger sister, Mildred, the last Lee offspring. "The two youngest children he petted a great deal, and our greatest treat was to get into his bed in the morning and lie close to him, listening while he talked to us in his bright entertaining way." He especially liked Rob and Mildred to tickle his hands and feet, telling them stories in return. Yet even the more indulged youngest son vividly remembered his father's harder side. For example, Lee's obsessive punctuality made a deep impression on Rob, especially as his mother chronically ran late, which often led to sharp words from the head of the family. In sum, though Rob recalled that his father was often "joyous and familiar" with him, he was also "very firm on all proper occasions, never indulged us in anything that was not good for us, and exacted the most implicit obedience." Rob believed he had internalized the habit of obedience. "I always knew that it was impossible to disobey my father. I felt it in me, I never thought why, but was perfectly sure when he gave an order it had to be obeyed." The undoubted warmth of Rob's memories contained substantial if only partly acknowledged fear of a father who had to be obeyed, not through fear of physical punishment but with unquestioning submission nevertheless. With his youngest son, however, Lee achieved a better balance between discipline and affection than he had with his older boys. Rob was the son who would be most comfortable in the world and with himself in later life, yet even he felt his father's distance and austerity.[19]

Lee was aware of his penchant for ex cathedra preaching. However, he gave no sign that he understood the negative impact he had on his sons with his harsh and constant strictures, which he continued to offer for the rest of his life, so unquestioning was his sense of higher paternal duty.

For his daughters, the moral stakes were primarily domestic rather than public perfection, but Lee could be just as demanding of them. Even when his daughter Agnes was just turning seven, the charming little stories he told her often contained explicit morals. Thus, during a respite in the war in Mexico, his thoughts turned to her and her sisters while he was in the process of befriending a little girl named Charlottita (much as his thoughts in Mexico had turned to his sons when he had heard of Harry Delafield's death): He described his new surrogate daughter in a manner equally affectionate and instructive. "She said she wanted to go to her *Mamasita* . . . so I carried her out of the palace & she gave me some very sweet kisses & bade me adieu. She is always dressed very nicely . . . and keeps her clothes very clean. I hope my little girls keep theirs just as nice, for you know I cannot bear dirty children. You must therefore study hard & be very nice girls & do not forget your Papa."[20]

When she was sixteen years old, Agnes asked her father, posted in Texas, "what a young & feeble girl can do" with her life. This was the query of a dutiful young daughter to her much admired father rather than a challenge from a rebel in the making. She was asking what fulfillment would be available to her within her prescribed role. "She can do a great deal if she has properly trained her faculties," her father replied. "I would not expect her to excel in manual or laborious labour," as did young women of the lower classes, a loss of standing Lee would never suggest. "But if she had attended to her moral, mental & physical culture, & acquired the habit of practicing politeness, gentleness, courtesy & a regard for the rights & feelings of others, she will be able to exercise much influence & accomplish much good. It is by persuasion & not force that she can operate. . . . Cultivate the powers of pleasing."[21] This was conventional advice about fitting into genteel femininity, into a role supportive to men; such a role, although subordinate, also demanded strenuous, lifelong effort.

Softer didacticism characterized Lee's instructional letters to his daughters. One morning in 1853, Lee took up his pen to write to thirteen-year-old Annie: "At dawn when I arise, and all day my thoughts revert to you. . . . I hope you will always appear to me as you are now painted in my heart, and that you will endeavor to improve and so conduct yourself as to make you happy and me joyful all our lives. Diligent and earnest attention to all your duties can only accomplish this." Then Lee broadened the purpose of his advice to encompass the public impact any member of the Lee family might make. Lee was superintendent at West Point at this time, and not only was he fully aware that the cadets looked to him as a "Marble Model" but he also assumed they would minutely examine the conduct of his children, to see if he was as firm with them as he was with the cadets, toward whom he was consciously acting in loco parentis. Telling her to cultivate good posture, he wrote Annie that "the cadets will . . . naturally say that he had better attend to his own before he corrects other people's children, and as he permits his to stoop, it is hard he will not allow them."[22] According to her anxious father, Annie had to both cultivate the powers of feminine pleasing and maintain a ramrod military bearing.

In Lee's mind, there was one major moral difference between his boys and his girls, having to do less with their divergent social roles than with their inward piety. In common with most nineteenth-century Americans, Lee assumed that women were by nature more open to God. At times, particularly in the early 1850s, when he was undergoing wrenching religious expe-

riences of his own, that sensibility led him to drive his daughters all the more forcefully, as he believed their souls had such
great spiritual potential for evil and for good. Moreover, their
spiritual fates were intertwined with his: In the eyes of the
world, their transgressions could bring not just themselves but
their father and the entire Lee family down in scandal. Especially given the relatively recent family record, albeit of the
men, Lee's daughters' salvation was especially urgent for him.

Early in 1852, Lee wrote a tortured letter to his mother-in-
law concerning the education of his daughters, in which, reflecting the Calvinist elements of his view of human nature, he was
even more punitive and less benevolent than usual. "Make them
regular, orderly & energetic in the performance of all their duties," he instructed. "This must not be *optional* [but] made habitual. We are so weak, shortsighted & ignorant . . . that we must be
made to do what is *right.*" Lee then made it clear that he was projecting his inward spiritual agony onto his girls. When he
searched his soul this way, it was with them and not with his
sons that he identified primarily; it was their souls and behavior
he needed to push toward salvation. After demanding fearfully
that their educations be made sufficient to their deepest needs,
he then vividly outlined the precipice over which they and he
might plunge. "God punishes us for our sins here as well as hereafter. He is now punishing me for mine through my children. It
is there I am most vulnerable; most sensitive, as I feel I deserve
it. I must bear it without complaint. But I pray he may spare
them! If they knew how I love them, how I feel through them, I
know they would spare me much I now suffer & all I apprehend."[23] Lee blamed his daughters for hurting him through
their spiritual unconsciousness, for failing to ease his moral
burden. Their spiritual peril tortured him almost as if they intended it, and he was angry with them. If they were saved, he
would be relieved of at least that fear. Like the little boy who

found his father dead in the snow, Lee's little girls might find his soul frozen to death, too late to save him and perhaps themselves. Morbidity characterized Lee's deepest anxieties for the welfare of his daughters, connected as it was to his own ultimate and everlasting spiritual end, about which he felt deeply frightened, especially at this stage in his life.

Lee's tormented inward state led him through a dark season of the soul, which may have lasted for several years prior to his religious conversion in 1853. He was a proud and independent man, very much used to thinking of himself not only as self-controlled but as a commander of other men as well as of his children. Only rarely did he write of his struggle or display this much soul-searching and religious introspection. Indeed, his Virginia Episcopalian brethren did not encourage flashy displays of religious fervor, although his faction within that church demanded the transformative experience of conversion and insisted that every saved person must live a fully committed holy life.[24]

One hot day in July 1849 in Baltimore, as he was going down this painful path, Lee reported to Mary, long since a reborn Christian, about the effect produced by a powerful sermon by Bishop John Johns, one of the leading lights of Evangelical Episcopalianism. We all should be driven to obey God's commands in order to "escape every evil & calamity," he wrote. "No one can be made more sensible of these [sins] than I am. But it is so difficult to regulate your conduct" by pursuing the good. "Man's nature is so selfish, so weak, every feeling & every passion urging him to folly, excess & sin [so] that I am disgusted with myself & sometimes with all the world. . . . Even in my progress I fail, & my only hope is in my confidence, my trust in the mercy of God which is deep and unbounded."[25] Lee had expressed his genuine disgust with the world most explicitly in his letter to his mother-in-law about his daughters. As that letter and this anguished passage make clear, he feared for them in the same breath that he feared for himself.

Not coincidentally, it was the death of his mother-in-law in April 1853 that pushed Lee even further along his spiritual path. She long had been more of a mother to him than had his natural mother, who had died in 1829, when he was just finishing West Point. In many ways, he had admired and trusted her intelligence and heart more than his wife's. Hearing from Mary about the death of "our dear mother," Lee replied to her that "the utter absence of every feeling of selfishness, so conspicuous in her own whole life, distinguished her last moments & her only care & regret was for others." Mother's death was a clear lesson to those who remained, which Lee discussed in this letter of mourning not in terms of his own sinful self but that of one "Miss B.": "I hope this great affliction will unlock her heart & open her eyes to her faults & weaknesses & cause her to throw off the cares for self that have hitherto afflicted her." That Lee was at least in part projecting here he made clear in another letter in which he wrote to Mary that the blow of his mother-in-law's death was so "sudden and crushing" that it caused him to "shudder at the shock." He believed her death had brought her the joys of heaven but that "I feel the anguish it has left to me." Temporarily feeling "arrested in the course of life," he soon pushed on with greater intensity, in part to be true to his mother-in-law's spiritual legacy, and three months later, on July 17, 1853, having finally attained the conviction that he had been saved in Christ, he bent his knee, bowed his head, and was confirmed in the church by Bishop Johns in Alexandria.[26] At last, in his forty-seventh year, he had found inward assurance.

A few years later, when both Anne and Agnes underwent conversion experiences, their father could relax somewhat about his daughters' new spiritual state. He wrote to Mary, "I have great comfort in my reflections about Anne & Agnes. I hope they will continue in their present blessed resolutions & acquire strength from heaven to enable them to carry them to Perfection."[27] Lee took this deepening piety into the Civil War, in which it would be endlessly tested.

Fatherhood meant guiding all his children toward both worldly competence and submission to the father above. Even conversion did not preclude further testing in the world: They could always backslide, and they would always have to evidence their faith in practice. After conversion, the believer had to do even more to get right with God, to purify worldly life, which felt even more temporary in the face of the certain knowledge of everlasting judgment—the prospect of that permanent home in heaven or hell.

Lee wanted a great deal for his children—they were undergoing a monumental test, as was he, and they needed to be well armed for their fearsome passage through the world of people and events as they reached toward heaven. He loved them, directed them, sought to protect and control them beyond his reach, beyond that of any father. His goal was to crush the sinner in order to save the spirit, but in the process—if fear predominated in what he conveyed and how his children received his instruction—affirmation of life also could be destroyed. At times, he cast his children out as loathsome sinners—even while he was doing the same to himself—by sending them messages of their worthlessness. At times, he clung to them, to their detriment, as a means of attempting to achieve through them a worldly happiness that was by religious definition and by temperament impossible for him to sustain; he then let them know that, despite his praise, they disappointed his deepest hopes for them.

One can see the yawning absence of his father in the modes through which Lee tried to compensate through his children for what he had missed. He was anxious to do right by them, using both affection and punishment. Acting on his inner conflicts, he bore down hard on them, giving them, almost certainly, more of a sense of the terrifying void than of ordinary contentment. As he went through the twin processes of spiritual conversion and fathering, he also killed the ebullience of his younger self or buried it so deeply that he became extraordinarily defended against the world, nearly impossible to reach within his guarded soul. More than ever, he spoke obsessively of duty and repression of self.

Chapter 4

RACE AND SLAVERY

Often a keen observer of the belles and beaux of his social class, Lee paid relatively little attention to those outside his charmed circle. In this he was typical for his time, place, and social station. Occasionally, Lee would remark on the shenanigans of poor whites, notice the strange peoples who were beginning to immigrate into Southern cities, and, when he went to subdue them, discuss Mexicans and Indians at somewhat greater length. Again in keeping with others of his milieu, he had relatively little to say about slaves, preferring the euphemisms *servants* or *people* when he did notice them. But he was more comfortable with blacks, in a paternalistic fashion, than he was with other, more threatening out-groups. At times, Lee did ponder slavery, particularly as political divisiveness spun out of control in the sectional crisis of the late 1850s.

Lee did not think within a consciously political framework and instead accepted social obligations as a matter of birth and rank. Having no quarrel with the status quo, he resented the machinations of both Northern and Southern political agitators who called the nation as it was into question. In 1861, when choosing sides became inevitable, he backed into his secessionist position as passively as possible, again accepting rather than

actively choosing his social and political role. In this almost apolitical passivity, he resembled stereotypical Southern women
more than politically hot-blooded Southern men. Yet secession,
the war, and its aftermath finally politicized Lee—a major and
very late change in his thinking.

As an army officer, Lee worked where he was sent, which
most often meant leaving the confines of old Virginia, to which
he was deeply attached. When out on the southern and western
frontiers, where the army established its main bases during the
vigorously expansionist antebellum period, Lee was compelled
to confront a much rawer economic and social scene. For example, the Saint Louis of the late 1830s, when the Lees lived there,
was a particularly disorderly and filthy boomtown on the far
western frontier. Leading one of the first major civic projects of
the Engineering Corps, Lee contributed mightily to the growth
of the city by designing a series of massive dikes that would
keep the port clear of silt. He also led teams that cleared out
rapids further up the Mississippi.[1] He was an excellent engineer—indeed, such problem-solving was a key to his intellectual
style, which almost precluded politics, that messy sort of problem muddling that gave him headaches.

Lee felt banished to the backwoods by his assignment to
Missouri. Making the best of it, he sometimes could not resist
commenting on the amiable barbarism of frontier types. In a
letter to his mother-in-law late in 1839, when he was at the brink
of receiving a leave of absence to visit home, he made a more
pointed than usual social commentary. "The lower class are a
swaggering, noisy set, careless of getting work except occasionally, for which they get high wages and which goes at the the-
atre, etc., but [they are] a well disposed people in the main too,
and somewhat amusing." Even those members of what passed
for the local elite struck him as a bit grasping and grubby and
lacking in gentility of pursuits and manners. "Those of the

higher order . . . are very kind and friendly, engrossed in business in which too it seems their pleasures all consist." Even the landscape reflected the crudeness of its developers. "The country in the neighborhood is rich and fertile but little improved, and having been originally prairie is *growing* up in *shrubby trees.* The inhabitants seem to give but little attention to agriculture or perhaps everything is new." Really, there was little here fit for well-bred people. "I cannot find any children here in whom I can take any pleasure, they are demanding and dirty and uninteresting." For Lee, such observations about déclassé, ill-bred elite children were harsh social commentary indeed.

Duty demanded Missouri, but the heart yearned for Virginia: "I am very anxious to get back to see those dear little ones again." During the long voyage back to Arlington, he wrote to his cousin Hill Carter,

> I suppose you have heard of my escape from the West. You must not understand that I am displeased with the state of things in that country; on the contrary I think it is a great country and will one day be a grand one, all is life, animation and prosperity, but that it is far more pleasant for *me* to be here than there. I felt so elated when I again found myself in the confines of the Ancient Dominion that I nodded to all the old trees as I passed, chatted with the drivers and stable-boys, shook hands with the landlords, and in the fullness of my heart—don't tell Cousin Mary— wanted to kiss all the pretty girls I met.[2]

Everything about Virginia was better: It was settled, cultivated, beautiful. The social ranks were arranged properly, and Lee could be comfortable greeting each one in its established and conventional manner. Sociable plantation masters and not grasping businessmen dominated the social scene, and their daughters were bred to be appropriately kissable. In sum, the West might be the future, but Virginia was tradition and home.

If Westerners were a class apart, so were the waves of immigrants from places such as Ireland and Germany. In his early years, Lee would have met almost no Jews, for example, as few of them lived in the antebellum South. In August 1840, however, when he was vacationing at White Sulphur Springs, in the Virginia mountains, he wrote his wife about the Hoffman family of Baltimore. "My room unfortunately is very near & looks into their establishment, the only objection I have to it. Seeing them from a distance I have always felt a repugnance to approach them, & now that I am compelled to witness their ridiculous pride, superciliousness & shallowness it amounts to an annoyance."[3] Stereotypical along the same lines from which he formed his responses to poor whites and white entrepreneurs out west, this comment contains considerable disdain. Perhaps the repugnance amounted only to an annoyance, not the sort of obsession with which others in antebellum America greeted the appearance of Germans and German Jews, but Lee was drawing the social line quite clearly: He would not befriend the Hoffmans in the light and casual way he would fellow well-born white Anglo-Saxon Protestants at the springs.

When it came to the Mexicans, whom he confronted during the American war of conquest, Lee, in common with his fellow officers, felt considerable contempt. He admitted that the United States had "bullied" Mexico, of which he felt "ashamed," but Mexico had been "drubbed" and the annexation of her territory ought to proceed apace. Anyone could see that the Mexicans were inferior: Their skin color, their lazy habits, and their Roman Catholicism gave them away. "It is a miserable populace," he wrote to John Mackay. "Always feared & truckled to by their own government, idle worthless & vicious. . . . Without a government, without an army, without money & revenue, these people are unable to prosecute war & have not power to make peace. They will oblige us in spite of ourselves to overrun the country & drive them into the sea." Once in the hands of proper people, Lee wrote in his white American expansionist mode, "this would be a magnificent country."

For Lee, who had a keen eye in such matters, one measure of the Mexicans was the inferiority of their women. "I can't say much for the beauty of the Senoras that I have seen yet," he wrote Mary in 1846. "They have dark eyes & beautiful teeth. I have been told that there were some handsome ones but have not seen them yet." In a later comment to Mary, he generalized once more: "The Mexicans are an amiable but weak people. Primitive in their habits and tastes." Such a backward race ought by natural law to be displaced by more civilized folk: They did not deserve their land, much of which was too lovely for such as they. Lee wrote to an old army comrade during a respite in the war, "In fact I was charmed by Tampico & if it depends upon my vote it will never fall back to Mexico. It would not be characteristic of the Anglo-Saxon race to permit it."[4]

Such beliefs in Anglo-Saxon racial superiority and the inherent right of conquest had long characterized American attitudes toward the native peoples they were in the process of conquering and shoving aside. Lee articulated such values when he met Indians on the western frontier in the 1830s and when he fought Comanches as commander of the Department of Texas in the 1850s. Even when he was writing about peaceful contacts with Indians in a rather sympathetic manner, he found them primitive objects of his civilized gaze; when he was fighting them, as was true of Mexicans during the war against them, curiosity diminished and contempt surfaced.

While surveying a beach along the south end of Lake Michigan in 1835, he later wrote to Mary, Lee noticed "a handsome bark canoe, guided by one squaw sitting in the stern, & *towed* by two others on the beach, at the end of a long line & attached to their shoulders by a long leather strap, somewhat resembling an ox yoke." Although this scene was primitive, with women serving as beasts of burden, Lee seemed fascinated: There was something ladylike about these women despite their crude appearance.

> In the canoe were three small children, the whole party was very neatly dressed, the women in short petticoats coming no lower than the knee, with a kind of short gown or jacket above them, their hair in one long plait at their backs & a large silver plate suspended at their breast—When opposite to me the one in the boat in a more melodious tone than I expected would have come from so rough an exterior said something to the others, who very abruptly waded out to the canoe, in water above their knees, & with more modesty than I have seen practiced by some of our ladies in a waltz, got in & shoved off in deep water.

Lee then momentarily reversed the status of the savage and the civilized, as if he were looking at himself through their eyes. "They must have been either alarmed by my *rough exterior,* or the [surveying] instrument; for a little distance higher up [the beach], they resumed their former mode of travel."[5] For Lee, there was something essentially good about women, even those of such a lowly race, while even the most civilized of men, which is to say white officers and gentlemen like himself, could have a savage side. Describing the women of strange peoples, Lee could be at his most generous.

Lee was often harsher in reporting life among the primitives, even about Indian women during peacetime. For example, while clearing the rapids where the Des Moines flows into the upper Mississippi, Lee wrote back to Mary to be sure to tell Boo "I see plenty of Indians pulling their canoes along the river, dressed in all their finery and blankets and some not dressed at all! We had a visit from *Black Wolf,* a Sac, the other night with two or three others, who as usual wanted *eat.* His papoose was lying asleep in the bottom of the canoe entirely uncovered and a prey to the mosquitoes; his squaw *Mouma* . . . was steersman, and Mouma's *Mauma* naked to the waist was sick with 'much whiskey.' "[6]

In 1836, when Lee prepared to fight the Seminoles, he wrote his dear friend Eliza Mackay Stiles that the army was intending "to keep in subjugation the Indians and the Negroes in that quarter."[7] That, of course, was the ultimate purpose of military contact with the Indians, by whatever means necessary, with force the customary method. Cultural relativism never applied to Indian *men,* especially warriors.

Lee's most protracted period of Indian fighting took place in the late 1850s, when his cavalry regiment struggled to subdue the stubborn Comanches. Nothing unexpectedly feminine characterized this tough and elusive warrior people in Lee's eyes. As he reported with ironic anger to Eliza Stiles in 1856, "We are on the best of terms with our neighbors the Comanches & I am happy to believe that there is no love lost between us. I see more of them than I desire, & when I can be of no service take little interest in them." At best these were pitiable losers, and at worst ogres in the guise of humans whom it was his job to kill. On April 12, 1856, he wrote to Mary, "Their paint and ornaments make them more hideous than nature made them & the whole race is extremely uninteresting," and added in August of that year, "These people give a world of trouble to man and horse, and poor creatures, they are not worth it."[8] Without sustained personal reflection, Lee accepted the attitude of cultural dehumanization normal for antebellum white Americans, particularly those on the frontier, when they considered the Indian enemy.

Sometimes Lee interpreted his military task as a rather regrettable necessity, but more often he welcomed the destruction of the savages. About the protracted war against the Comanches, Lee wrote his wife in 1857, "I hear that my young Lts. have been active in their scouts during my absence. [They] have each . . . intercepted marauding parties of Indians, chastised them severely. Upwards of a dozen . . . were killed, more wounded, all their horses, animals, camp equipage captured. It is a distressing state of things that requires the applications of such harsh treatment, but it is the only corrective they understand & the only way in which they can be taught to keep within their own limits." In a more celebratory manner, in 1860, Lee wrote to his fellow army officer Major Earl Van Dorn that some civilians had overtaken three small bands of Indians, killing ten and recovering forty-three stolen horses. "I am glad of it, & only wish it had been accomplished by the Cavalry—I hope Lt. Cunningham, who is after [another] band may come up with it & punish it severely."[9] The sooner the contemptible enemy was eliminated the better, with whatever amount of killing necessary. These were not fellow humans, not even to the degree Mexicans were—they were below the social horizon, a race not really worth thinking about.

Because black slaves were permanent property, intrinsic not only to the wealth and social standing of the Virginia gentry class but to their very definitions of selfhood and personal liberty as well, they had to be dealt with—and sometimes, particularly when pushed by shifting Northern opinion, thought about—even though they were considered a deeply inferior race. Yet given their importance and their everyday presence, it is remarkable how little Lee, or the vast majority of his class, actually wrote about slavery, except for those few who made a profession of analyzing slave management or creating ideological and religious defenses of the peculiar institution. Of course, one cannot reconstruct conversations, in which slaves were apparently discussed rather a lot, but if someone else were doing the day-to-day management of slaves—an overseer often drawn from the poorer white classes—slaveholders did not necessarily descend to much thought about those people who drew their water and planted their crops.

Lee's father and his older half brother had lost almost all their slaves with their lands, and in his military postings Lee himself probably took along only a slave valet and a cook/laundress, although such body servants may have been hired from other slaveholders rather than owned by Lee. Mary Custis, on the other hand, had lived on a plantation that had about one hundred slaves, a few of whom took care of her daily needs, and some of whom she apparently owned personally, through bequests from various relatives. Only when her father, George Washington Custis, died in 1857 did Mary and Robert E. Lee come into legal ownership of hundreds of slaves at Arlington and other plantations.

Prior to the late 1850s, Lee's identity was less directly wrapped up in the productivity and submission of slaves than were those of most other gentry Virginians. His army career had allowed him to escape day-to-day awareness of blacks. He did note in passing in an 1832 letter to his brother Carter, when discussing a cholera epidemic in Norfolk, Virginia, "it has been confined almost entirely so far to the poor blacks and intemperate whites. Some families have lost *all* their servants."[10] This was a suggestive if inconclusive combining of slaves and poor white trash in Lee's mind, as if the lowest of the whites were in the same category as blacks. By 1832—in consideration of the feelings and beliefs of poorer whites as well as their increased political power—the democratized class and racial protocol was to group all whites versus all blacks. Here, Lee's negative view of the white lower classes remained more pronounced than Southern gentlemen could allow themselves to express in public. Free from managing blacks on his own plantation, he shared no compelling personal or political need to define himself in brotherhood with all whites, no matter how impoverished and crude.

After his mother had died in 1829, Lee long remained in a quandary about how to dispose of her house servants. "I do not know what to do [with them]," he wrote Mary from his military post two years later. "Perhaps if I was up there I might do something with Nancy. She once lived with the Fraziers & they might take her again," on hire. "I cannot *recommend* her as a good cook and washer to Captain [Andrew Talcott], nor would I be willing to take her myself." He did not know what to do with Catty or Jane, and "Letitia will have to be your femme de chambre & in the meantime you may do with them as you please if opportunity offers," almost certainly to hire them out rather than to sell them. "But do not trouble yourself about them as they are not worth it."[11] The youthful Lee did not want to be bothered with this group of what to him were no-account slaves, whom he saw both in a humane master's manner and as lazy family retainers to be taken care of, rather than as valuable workers or potential assets to be sold. Of course, one reason for this level of detachment was that Lee himself had not invested the initial capital in buying or raising these slaves.

Through the years, Lee occasionally exchanged slaves with other slaveholders and employed slave traders to hire out his slaves, sometimes granting them power of attorney. And in 1849, Lee expressed anxiety about losing the slaves he had brought to his posting in Baltimore, both because of a Maryland law that stipulated that any person bringing slaves into the state had to register them and pay a tax on each one and because, as he wrote Mary, "the abolitionists are very active here & opportunities great [for flight]. That is the experience of all that have brought their servants here."[12] The port of Baltimore provided an escape route for many fugitive slaves—that was the path chosen by Frederick Douglass, for one. And beyond that, slavery was rapidly decaying in Maryland, as it was in most of the northern tier of slave states: In 1850, of a total population of 212,418 in Baltimore, there were 25,680 free blacks and only 2,946 slaves. Most of the slaves were domestic servants, like those of Lee, many of whom mingled with free blacks, deepening the anxiety of the remaining slaveholders.[13]

No historian has established how many slaves Lee actually owned before 1857 or how much income he derived from this source. The more general point is that to some extent he was personally involved in slave owning his whole adult life, as was the norm for better-off Southerners, even those who did not own plantations. Unlike many other slaveholders in Baltimore, for example, he did not manumit his personal slaves while he lived in that city and, indeed, recoiled at the thought of losing them. He carried them back with him when he returned to Virginia.

When his father-in-law died, late in 1857, Lee was left with the jobs of supervising Arlington and the various other Custis estates, perhaps as many as three others. Moreover, the Custis will specified that these slaves be freed by January 1, 1863; therefore, Lee had the dual tasks of managing these slaves in the interim and then freeing them, immersing him in the contradictions of owning, protecting, and exploiting people of a different and despised race. It was very likely that the Custis slaves knew that they were to be freed, which could have only made Lee's efforts to succor, discipline, and extract labor from them in the meantime considerably more difficult.

Faced with this set of problems, Lee attempted to hire an overseer. He wrote his cousin Edward C. Turner, "I am no farmer myself & do not expect to be always here. I wish to get an energetic honest farmer, who while he will be considerate & kind to the negroes, will be firm & make them do their duty."[14] Such help was difficult to find or to retain, and despite himself Lee had to take a leave of absence from the army for two years to become a slave manager himself, one who doubtless tried to combine kindness with firmness but whose experience was altogether unhappy. Any illusions he may have had about becoming a great planter, which apparently were at least intermittent, dissipated dramatically as he wrestled with workers who were far less submissive to his authority than were enlisted men in the army. The coordination and discipline central to Lee's role in the army proved less compatible with his role as manager of slaves than he must have expected.

Sometimes, the carrot and the stick both worked ineffectively. On May 30, 1858, Lee wrote his son Rooney, "I have had some trouble with some of the people. Reuben, Parks & Edward, in the beginning of the previous week, rebelled against my authority—refused to obey my orders, & said they were as free as I was, etc., etc.—I succeeded in capturing them & lodged them in jail. They resisted till overpowered & called upon the other people to rescue them." Enlightened masters in the upper South often sent their rebellious slaves to jail, where the sheriff would whip them, presumably dispassionately, rather than apply whippings themselves. Whatever happened in the Alexandria jail after this event, less than two months later Lee sent these three men down under lock and key to the Richmond slave trader William Overton Winston, with instructions to keep them in jail until Winston could hire them out to "good & responsible" men in Virginia, for a term lasting until December 31, 1862, by which time the Custis will stipulated that they be freed. Lee also noted to Winston, in a rather unusual fashion, "I do not wish these men returned here during the usual holy days, but to be retained until called for." He hoped to quarantine his remaining slaves against these three men, to whom the deprivation of the customary Christmas visits would be a rather cruel exile, though well short, of course, of being sold to the cotton fields of the Deep South. At the same time, Lee sent along three women house slaves to Winston, adding, "I cannot recommend them for honesty." Lee was packing off the worst malcontents. More generally, as he wrote in exasperation to Rooney, who was managing one of the other Custis estates at the time, so few of the Custis slaves had been broken to hard work in their youth that "it would be accidental to fall in with a good one."[15]

This sort of snide commentary about inherent slave dishonesty and laziness was the language with which Lee expressed his racism; anything more vituperative and crudely expressed would have diminished his gentlemanliness. Well-bred men expressed caste superiority with detached irony, not with brutal oaths about "niggers."

The following summer, Lee conducted another housecleaning of recalcitrant slaves, hiring out six more to lower Virginia. Two, George Wesley and Mary Norris, had absconded that spring but had been recaptured in Maryland as they tried to reach freedom in Pennsylvania.[16]

As if this were not problem enough, on June 24, 1859, the New York *Tribune* published two letters that accused Lee—while calling him heir to the "Father of this free country"—of cruelty to Wesley and Norris. "They had not proceeded far [north] before their progress was intercepted by some brute in human form, who suspected them to be fugitives." They were "transported back, taken in a barn, stripped, and the men [*sic*] received thirty and nine lashes each [*sic*], from the hands of the slave-whipper . . . when he refused to whip the girl . . . Mr. Lee himself administered the thirty and nine lashes to her. They were then sent to the Richmond jail." Lee did not deign to respond to this public calumny. All he said at that time was to Rooney: "The *N. Y. Tribune* has attacked me for the treatment of your grandfather's slaves, but I shall not reply. He has left me an unpleasant legacy." Remaining in dignified silence then, Lee continued to be agonized by this accusation the rest of his life. Indeed, in 1866, when the Baltimore *American* reprinted this old story, Lee replied in a letter that might have been intended for publication, "the statement is not true; but I have not thought proper to publish a contradiction, being unwilling to be drawn into a newspaper discussion, believing that those who know me would not credit it; and those who do not, would care nothing about it." With somewhat less aristocratic detachment, Lee wrote privately to E. S. Quirk of San Francisco about "this slander. . . . There is not a word of truth in it. . . . No servant, soldier, or citizen that was ever employed by me can with truth charge me with bad treatment."[17]

That Lee personally beat Mary Norris seems extremely unlikely, and yet slavery was so violent that it cast all masters in the roles of potential brutes. Stories such as this had been popularized earlier in the 1850s by Harriet Beecher Stowe in *Uncle Tom's Cabin,* and they stung even the most restrained of masters, who understood that kindness alone would have been too indulgent, and corporal punishment (for which Lee substituted the euphemism "firmness") was an intrinsic and necessary part of slave discipline. Although it was supposed to be applied only in a calm and rational manner, overtly physical domination of slaves, unchecked by law, was always brutal and potentially savage.

Lee's views on slavery were considerably influenced by the opinions and activities of his wife and his mother-in-law, both of whom were deeply involved in the American Colonization Society, an early form of ambiguous antislavery activism, which sought to free the slaves by sending them back to Africa. As a young married woman, this project was a commitment of Mary's heart and not just her head. She wished to nurture, educate, and catechize the family slaves right away, in preparation for eventual manumission and export. She wrote her mother in 1834, "I hope that we may be able to do something in time for the spiritual benefit of those neglected slaves" and for their eventual freedom.[18] Because on these terms liberty meant expulsion of the entire inferior black race with whom whites could never imagine cohabiting on an equal footing, such colonizationism was racist antislavery doctrine.

In her diary for the 1850s, Mary frequently discussed this project. She joined her mother, she wrote, in the hope that one day all their slaves would be able to emigrate to Africa, so that they could "carry light & Christianity to that dark heathen country." Nevertheless, admitting to a "presentiment" that she would not live long enough to carry out this grand scheme, she proposed to try it gradually. She picked her slave William and his family to "act as pioneers," a kind of pilot project. And then she stated the larger purpose of the heart that lay behind her social project: "What is life worth unless you can accomplish in it something for the benefit of others, especially of those so entirely dependent upon one's will and pleasure."

Mary's body servant, Eliza, was another pet project. "I have always promised Eliza her freedom to emigrate to Africa in a few years. . . . If she will go to Africa she can have her freedom," Mary Lee wrote in her diary in 1853. She feared, however, that Eliza might "marry here and be unwilling to go, especially if she should marry a free man." In the event, Mary Lee noted in 1860 that Eliza had her freedom and that she now lived in Newport with her husband.[19] Somehow, Eliza had secured her freedom while avoiding being shipped back to Africa. Such was the outcome favored by the vast majority of manumitted slaves, whatever the desires of their former masters.

As an interim measure on her slaves' path to freedom and repatriation, Mary Lee, with the help of her daughters, set up a school for slaves, almost certainly a Sunday school, on the Arlington plantation. This was an unusual move, because the overwhelming majority of slave owners feared rightly that literacy would give slaves access to seditious abolitionist materials, which would lead them to demand or seize their freedom. In 1819, this concern had led the Virginia legislature to outlaw education for blacks, but several of Virginia's clergymen continued to encourage Sunday schools, arguing that the gentry class would answer to God, not to the legislature. It is not clear how many slaveholders in addition to the Lees followed this path of circumspect lawbreaking.

At least occasionally, Agnes Lee taught in this school for slaves in the mid-1850s. In her journal, she expressed her attitude and that of her father toward her students. "I must put down my pen . . . & go to teach my little scholars. We have a considerable number of 'ebony mites' as Papa calls them & as no one knows as much as another it makes their instruction very tedious." Off to school she went, only to find an empty room. "Well! I have gone down, I insist upon teaching them in classes & yet only one of my class ever arrived [in] time so I have employed this odd moment in writing."[20]

Agnes's pen dripped racial condescension even as she earnestly broke the law. Her view on her pupils' tardiness reflected the Southern white contempt for slaves' perceived lack of punctuality (although it must be noted that Northern factory managers had the same complaints about their workers, who also thus resisted discipline and set their own work schedules). The amused phrase "ebony mites" also demonstrated her father's doubts about a project in which he disbelieved, although he did nothing to stop it, probably regarding it as harmless. While influenced by Mary's colonizationist project, he was generally rather skeptical of its value, and sometimes he doubted whether Mary's do-goodism was a very wise course. In one rather complex case in 1841, Robert attempted to dissuade Mary's project of buying a slave off an unkind master in order to free him. "In judging of results you must endeavour to lay aside your feelings & prejudices & examine the question as thus exposed. In this matter is everything to be yielded to the servant & nothing allowed to the master? What will the effect of the precedent be on the rest [of the slaves and on] your father and his authority?" Lee promised that he would comply with her wishes, but he urged her to "consider well upon the matter & act for yourself."[21]

After her father's slaves became hers and Robert's, Mary hardened her attitude toward them. On February 10, 1858, when Robert was trying to sort out the chaos on the other Custis plantations, Mary wrote an old friend about his efforts "in trying to reduce these very complicated affairs into some order": "It is very unsatisfactory work for the servants here have been so long accustomed to do little or nothing that they cannot be convinced of the necessity now of exerting themselves," in order to speed up the accomplishment of the promise of freedom in the will. Actually, Mary was being illogical, as the promise had been given unconditionally, albeit for five years down the line. Then Mary continued, "unless there is a mighty change wrought in them I do not know" what good they will do themselves, "but at any rate we shall be relieved from the care of them which will be an immense burden taken from our shoulders."[22] Actual experience in manumission was hardly proving to be the fulfillment of the colonizationist dreams of years past.

Over the next week, Mary continued to brood. On February

17, she wrote to W. G. Webster that two white men had been "constantly lurking about with the servants & telling them that they had a *right* to their freedom *immediately* & that if they would unite & *demand* it they would obtain it." Only "the merciful hand of a kind Providence . . . prevented an outbreak. Their freedom is a very questionable advantage to any but ourselves who will be relieved from a host of idle & their useless dependents." Of course, colonization had always promised masters relief from their slaves, but here Mary Lee dropped the charitable aspect of the project—the rationalization that it was intended for the good of blacks—and treated manumission as a racial safety valve for white masters.

Not colonization but her father's will had freed these slaves, and Mary was retrospectively exasperated with him. "My dear father in his usual entire ignorance of the state of his affairs has left provision in his will which it will be almost impossible to fulfill even in double 5 years." Just sending them out of the state, which Virginians freeing their slaves were required to do, would be prohibitively expensive, she believed. She then drew the sarcastic conclusion that "we should be most deeply indebted to their *kind friends* the abolitionists if they would come forward [and purchase their] freedom *at once.*"[23]

It even gave Mary Lee a certain perverse satisfaction to note the virulent racism in Canada, that land of freedom to which thousands of slaves had fled, when she visited some hot springs there in 1860. "There are a great number of runaways here, but I have not met with any acquaintances," Mary Lee wrote her daughter Annie. "The white people say that before long they will be obliged to make laws to send them all out of Canada, so I see no place for them but Africa. I am told they suffer a great deal here in the long cold winters. After enticing them over here the white people will not let their children go to the same schools or treat them as equals in any way. Amalgamation"—interracial marriage—"is out of the question tho occasionally a very low white woman marries a black man."[24] Either blacks had to be dominated by kind masters within slavery, or else they had to be returned to Africa. They could never live in equality with whites anywhere in North America, and freedom would bring them only into a condition worse than slavery. The Canadian racism she observed confirmed Mary's beliefs in white supremacy and black degradation.

As the Civil War approached, given their experiences, both the Lees were disgusted with slavery. At the same time, they were prepared to defend it as the only viable safeguard of white control over blacks until that distant day when the South might be whitened through complete African repatriation.

It is with these slaveholding experiences in mind that one must read Lee's well-known—and solitary—analysis of slavery as an evil, in a letter that he wrote to Mary on December 27, 1856, prior to his sorry involvement in actual slave management. Responding to Northern antislavery activism, which he considered utterly provocative and irresponsible, without conceding that slaveholding was a sin or expressing personal or collective guilt about the institution, Lee discussed the evils of slavery and its ultimate disappearance. The conservative Lee reflected an older argument among slaveholders, that the peculiar institution was a "necessary evil," which had to be continued because of a lack of a plausible alternative. Hotter-blooded proslavery activists had, at least since the 1830s, been arguing that far from a necessary evil, slavery was a "positive good" for both masters and slaves, that it was kinder to workers than wage slavery in the North or in Europe—where slavery had been abolished—and that, as had been the case in Athens, it was producing a glorious cultural flowering of white liberty on top of a black slave base.

"In this enlightened age, there are few . . . but will acknowledge, that slavery as an institution, is a moral & political evil in
any country," Lee argued. "It is useless to expatiate on its disad-
vantages." Lee continued, "I think [slavery] however a greater
evil to the white than to the black race, & while my feelings are
strongly enlisted in behalf of the latter, my sympathies are more
strong for the former." The corruptions and trials of slavery for
the master class, which Lee here acknowledged while not
spelling them out, made the institution bad for them. On the
other hand, he continued, "the blacks are immeasurably better
off here than in Africa, morally, socially & physically. The
painful discipline they are undergoing, is necessary for their instruction as a race, & I hope will prepare & lead them to better
things." The plantation was a suitable and necessary school for
the perpetually childlike slaves: When sufficiently drilled in letters, Christianity, and internalized work discipline, blacks ought
to be freed and sent back to convert heathen Africa. But not yet.

How and when would this freedom arrive? Here, Lee
dodged a precise date in a fashion customary to colonizationists,
Evangelical Christians, and other traditionalists who followed
the necessary evil argument. "How long their subjugation may
be necessary is known & ordered by a wise Merciful Providence," Lee wrote. "Their emancipation will sooner result from
the mild & melting influence of Christianity, than the storms &
tempests of fiery controversy. . . . While we see the course of the
final abolition of human slavery is onward, & we give it the aid
of our prayers & all justifiable means in our power, we must
leave the progress as well as the result in His hands who sees the
end; who chooses to work by slow influences; and with whom
two thousand years are but as a single day." The notion of emancipation, tied not to human activism but to Christian resignation, meant that it might be another two thousand years—just a
wink in the eye of Jesus—until slavery would end. In the in-

terim, God would concern himself not with earthly liberation
but with the souls of the slaves (and their masters). So be it:
God's will be praised.

This argument for potentially infinite postponement was
outside and in fact contrary to the current of events: England
had abolished slavery in her colonies in 1833, and Denmark and
France in 1848; indeed, the czar would end serfdom in Russia in
1860. Lee was certainly aware of the European march toward
emancipation, which isolated the American South. And within
the United States, the sectional dispute had grown intense, cli-
maxing in the nasty guerrilla war in "Bleeding Kansas," which
was taking place while Lee was writing this letter. In this historical context, Lee's passivism was not an antislavery but effectively a proslavery position. Such theoretical, eventualist regret
as he expressed did not by any means preclude active defense of
the peculiar institution.[25]

For only one remarkable moment in 1849 had Lee pierced,
even partially, this defense-by-avoidance argument that slavery
was a necessary "interim" measure. This moment occurred in
the letter Lee wrote on that Baltimore July Sunday in 1849 when
the hellfire sermon of Bishop John Johns compelled him to introspection at the "folly, excess & sin" that had led him to be "disgusted with myself & sometimes with all the world." In the
midst of this self-scourging, Lee suddenly noted, as if he had
paid real attention in his heart to all the blacks he had doubtless
seen dressed up and on the way to their churches that hot Sunday, "The poor blacks have a multitude of miseries. I hope that
death that must come sooner or later will end them all."[26]

Perhaps there would be freedom for blacks sooner in heaven
than on this vile earth, but in the here and now, for at least a
morning, Lee felt their suffering in the context of his own sense
of enslavement to sin. This insight was at least in part a mo-

mentary, guilty identification with the slaves—even they were possessors of human souls to which the savior could come.

And yet such empathy ranked lower than Lee's identification with white slaveholders. Despite the coldness and arrogance central to their efforts to dominate what they were certain was the wholly inferior black race, Southern white gentlefolk such as Lee also felt at least glimmers of real human bonds with their slaves. The irony and the tragedy was that they subordinated such genuine feelings while, sometimes with regret, reinforcing both slavery and white supremacy. One of the socially conditioned reasons Lee built his boundaries and shut down his feelings was to avoid confronting more empathetically the evils slavery and slave masters did blacks. Yet turning a blind eye to the dehumanization and the corruption stemming from naked domination itself did damage to the master class.

Chapter 5

POLITICS AND SECESSION

*I*n a profound way, Lee believed in God's time, not man's, and God's disposition, not human politics. So when it came to grappling with the issue of slavery, he could not comprehend why men could not leave well enough alone until Christ made clear the path. Not that Lee was otherworldly—in his professional life he was an excellent engineer, a punctual and practical problem solver. But on major public conflicts, Lee had no active position. He was profoundly conservative in that he wanted to maintain what was with as much kindness and fellow feeling as possible, but he had no sense of how to adapt if conditions altered. Here his stoicism served as a protection against change, a means to help him persevere in his duty no matter what occurred; such passivity meant he drifted in the wake of events rather than participated actively in them or even sought to understand what was unfolding.

Antebellum American democracy was terrifically messy, and Lee, in common with far more of his fellow citizens than most historians suggest, really did not like it. He was of the old Virginia school, where, in theory, gentlemen did what was best for the public weal while the lesser sort deferred to them. Yet with the explosive westward expansion, coupled to dogmatically antielitist Jacksonian politics, in unquestioned ascendancy since 1828, aristocracy and deference had nearly evaporated.

Men of Lee's background and bearing were becoming social anachronisms. Therefore, some of them attempted to graft scientific expertise to their gentry origins and values as a justification for claiming leadership, but without much success. To take one example, in 1843 Lee watched with both amusement and a certain disdain for the democratic political process when his Engineering Corps comrade Henry Kayser ran for city engineer in Saint Louis. Lee hoped "that in your attending to your duties . . . in all professional matters your opinions & acts should be grounded by your judgment & not with a benefit of this or that party. . . . To become a political partizan would be derogatory to your office & profession, which I hope you will never descend to. . . . It would not be proper for you to make use of your office to influence the vote of any man, or to support or advance any party." In an earlier and very sarcastic letter, Lee had written Kayser that no "sensible man" would make the office of city engineer elective. "Still if they do & we good democrats do strange things some times, you must lay aside your foreign aristocracy & throw up your hat with the highest & hurrah with the loudest."[1] Lee found such democracy—which rejected leadership claims based on expertise or high birth—a most distasteful and alienating development. Lee criticized his friend for adjusting to the slovenly new order. And Kayser was thumped in the election, despite compromising himself.

Lee's antidemocratic tendencies were heightened by his membership in that self-consciously aristocratic clique, West Point graduates, especially those who remained in the peacetime army as professional officers. Separated by their intense training and their caste consciousness, often isolated geographically, as was Lee in frontier Saint Louis, aware that they were despised by the public and by a parsimonious Congress, they returned disdain for disdain. In 1838, Lee wrote from Saint Louis to John Mackay, "the manner in which the army is considered & treated by the country and those whose business it is to nourish & take care of it, is enough to disquiet everyone within the service, & has the effect of driving every good soldier from it, & rendering those who remain discontented, careless & negligent." Half aware that he was in effect accepting much of the criticism leveled at the officer corps by an ungrateful nation, Lee lashed out in considerable elitist anger about the "rights sacrificed at the shrine of popularity," about the popular attention paid "to the miserable slander of dirty tergiversators," those journalists and politicians who were all too prone to act against the army after smearing it with "filthy ex-parte evidence."[2]

Unsurprisingly, given his aristocratic values and his experience as a Virginian of the gentry class serving the unappreciated army on the crude frontier, Lee watched with a certain detached horror while the nation turned toward what he considered to be an alarmingly low democracy. In early 1852, for example, Lee rejected the expansionist craze that many Americans expressed during the tour of the Hungarian patriot and revolutionary Louis Kossuth. After the European revolutions of 1848 failed—political upheavals in which middle-class men fought aristocracies in order to create nations that Americans liked to believe would emulate the United States—Kossuth came across the Atlantic to gather funds and support, which led to considerable American boasting about building an empire for liberty in the continental United States and providing the powder and principles with which men such as Kossuth could blow apart the old European order. As the United States had recently and dramatically expanded through the Mexican War and treaties with the British in the Pacific Northwest, renewed expansionist enthusiasm proved highly contagious. In common with many conservative Southerners, Lee mistrusted the celebration of democratic imperialism Kossuth aroused, which Lee considered so much "falsehood and flattery" of the low electorate by leading politicians, whose cause might further abolitionist efforts when brought back home. American intervention in European power politics, which Kossuth's backers promoted, would not "advance republican institutions or the principle of self-government," Lee believed, and stirring emotions this way could only lead to support for a democracy that would grow more dangerous as it became more fervent.[3]

In general, Lee despised and feared politicians, who represented and exacerbated the wildly emotional nature of American civic life. Writing in his journal, probably during the Civil War, Lee held that "politicians are more or less so warped by party feeling, by selfishness, or prejudices, that their minds are not altogether balanced. They are the most difficult to cure of all insane people, politics having so much excitement in them."[4] This was really a blanket critique of democracy itself, even a kind of escapism from the public sphere. If gentlemen and experts did not rule in the spirit of the august and disinterested George Washington, others would, and Lee, one of the last high federalists, did not approve of the shameless vote grabbing and twisted propaganda such grubby politicians used. From Mexico, in 1846, Lee wrote Carter about the motives of power seekers: "There are many that cry 'Hurra for Clay' & 'Hurra for Polk,' & how few that raise their voice for their Country."[5] Whether ordinary voters were victims or causes of the jaded democratic process, Lee did not venture to discuss.

The best that Lee might anticipate from national politicians was pacification of disturbing issues, which especially after 1850 meant slavery. Thus, in the same 1856 letter in which he issued his slavery-as-a-necessary-evil-till-Christ-might-end-it-someday argument, Lee praised the antiantislavery efforts of outgoing President Franklin Pierce, who had had "facts to go on," with

which he had tried to "restrain supposition & conjecture, con-
firm faith & bring contentment." Pierce and James Buchanan
after him were "doughfaced" presidents—Northern Democrats
with Southern principles—who actually increased national divisions by arguing a pro-Southern line. But to Lee and others like
him, aggressive pressure for change stemmed from the "systematic . . . efforts of certain people of the North, to interfere with &
change the domestic institutions of the South." Their object, the
abolition of slavery, was "unlawful . . . irresponsible & unac-
countable & can only be accomplished by them through the
agency of a civil & servile war." The natural outcome of this
Northern, abolitionist, democratic thrust would be a race war,
that deepest fear of Southern slaveholders; a huge set of Nat
Turner– or John Brown–style murderous revolts. (Indeed, later
it was Lee who led the federal forces who put down Brown's violent insurrection.) In truth, Lee argued, after conceding the theoretical evil of slavery, if the abolitionist "means well to the
slave, he must not create angry feelings in the master" by pushing the end of slavery faster than the pace that a supervening
deity would ordain for some long-term, apolitical means of collective, voluntary enlightenment. And he concluded that he
found it "strange that the descendants of those pilgrim fathers
who crossed the Atlantic to preserve their own freedom of opinion, have always proved themselves intolerant of the spiritual
liberty of others."[6]

Abolitionists made moral and religious claims about the necessity to destroy slavery, thus threatening to destroy the nation
as a whole, Lee believed, without much consideration of those
Southerners who also made such assertions of spiritual superiority when they threatened secession. To them, the North was a
decadent land, where the virtue of the revolutionary fathers had
been essentially corrupted. Southern nationalists insisted that it
was they who defended the legacy of the Founding Fathers,

looked after labor properly, maintained appropriate social hierarchies, and refused to worship materialism. Only independence could purify the blessed southern portion of the nation and rescue the legitimate heirs of the Revolution, the true servants of God, from the decadent North. Lee agreed with most of this mentality, but he balked at accepting the logical political consequences.

Though Lee mainly criticized Northern antislavery agitators and politicians for upsetting the fragile national consensus, at times he also blamed the more radical proslavery agitators of the Deep South. As late as December 14, 1860, he wrote Custis of the slim hope he still held out that men of goodwill might steer the Union through the agitated political seas. Though he basically shared Southern resentments—"feeling the aggressions of the North, resenting their denial of the equal rights of our citizens to the common territory, etc."—Lee then attacked rabid secessionists. "I am not pleased with the course of the 'Cotton States' as they term themselves. In addition to their selfish, dictatorial bearing, the threats they throw out against the 'Border States,' as they call them, if they will not join them, argues little for the benefit or the peace of Va. should she determine to coalesce with them." In common with many of the Virginia gentry class, Lee resented the parvenu cotton planters of the Deep South, rude both in their large-scale, brand-new wealth and in their political opinions. He feared that these proven Southern radicals would trap him—and others like him—in their designs, which of course proved to be the case. "While I wish to do what is right, I am unwilling to do what is wrong, either at the bidding of the South or the North," Lee commented, in fear of fire-eater demagoguery. "One of their plans seems to be the renewal of the slave trade. That I am opposed to on every ground." Lee added to Custis, as if to distance himself from such rapacious men, "I am glad you had the people's houses repaired. I wish to make them as comfortable as I can."[7] As a proper, old-fashioned, paternalistic master, he would bear with slavery as a "necessary evil" while secessionists called it a "positive good," which ought to be expanded. It was also true, and less idealistic, that Virginia's economy, like that of much of the upper South, was based to a considerable degree on the sale of surplus slaves to the cotton states; reopening the slave trade would have undercut the monopoly in this traffic.

Vexed though he was by Southern hotheads, Lee sided with them as the sectional conflict divided the nation. Republicans were anathema to him, and, when considering the far more conservative Democrats, Lee identified with their Southern wing, which, by late 1859, had become essentially secessionist. In April 1860, Southern Democrats insisted that the party adopt a slave code to guarantee permanent legal protection for their "property" in the territories, a proposal that would mean that all future states would in effect become slave states. As these Southerners knew it would, this demand split their party because Northern Democrats, under the leadership of Stephen A. Douglas, though willing to defend slavery as it stood, could not make themselves champions of its expansion—in which they did not believe—and retain any hope of winning the North the 1860 election. After Douglas prevailed in the party convention, the Southern Democrats bolted the party, reformed themselves, and nominated Vice President John C. Breckinridge, the proslavery Kentuckian, as their candidate for the presidency. In response to these events, Lee wrote Major Earl Van Dorn, a Mississippian, "If Judge Douglas would now withdraw & join himself & party to aid in the election of Breckinridge, he might retrieve himself before the country & Lincoln be defeated. Politicians are too selfish I fear to be martyrs."[8] Here, in the name of peace, Lee was calling for Northern Democratic capitulation to a proslavery, Southern-nationalist rump Democratic Party, a naive and wildly implausible proposition at best. And Lee was also continuing to take the rather facile route of blaming politicians rather than looking more deeply into political issues.

As were many conservative Southerners, the old-fashioned Lee was a reluctant Confederate; he resented being forced into secession by base leaders and democracy run amok. This Olympian stance was a relic from an earlier age of political discourse, when gentlemen were disinterested and above partisan divisions.

Although he had not often trumpeted his rather unformulated nationalism, as a self-created heir of George Washington and as a professional officer who had spent his entire adult life taking the nation's bread, Lee was a Unionist as well as a proud Virginian until secession forced him to choose between these two loyalties. At one level, this was an agonizing decision, but at another it proved to be a natural extension of his class, sectional, and racial identity.

As late as 1857, despite the terribly divisive events that were shredding the nation, Lee wrote his brother-in-law Edward V. Childe, praising Childe's unequivocal defense of the Union. "I was . . . much pleased to find by your article for the [Boston] 'Courier' that you [could] rightly . . . & forcibly expose the threatened evils to your Country. That your Country was the *whole* Country. That its limits contained no North, no South, no East, no West, in all its might & strength, present & future. On that subject my resolution is taken, & my mind fixed. I know no other Country, no other Government, than the *United States* & their *Constitution*."[9] Even in his nationalism, however, Lee described the nation as a voluntary confederation of states, using the plural *their*. This was shorthand for a belief in the primacy of the rights of states—the increasingly anachronistic position to which Southerners clung.

Not until the election of Abraham Lincoln and his antislavery and entirely Northern Republican Party did Lee reconsider his Unionism in any fundamental way, and even then, hoping against hope for a peaceful national resolution, he equivocated. A month after that election, in his letter criticizing Southern as well as Northern "dictatorial bearing," Lee wrote to Custis that he had at least some faith that the lame-duck Congress and President Buchanan might be able to cobble together another sectional truce—which they tried with the so-called Crittenden Compromise—though the Republicans would reject such proposals: These "propositions . . . are eminently just, are in accordance with the Constitution, and ought to be cheerfully assented to by all the States. But I do not think the Northern and Western States will agree to them. It is, however, my only hope for the preservation of the Union, and I will cling to it to the last."[10]

And yet, even before this letter, and before December 20, 1860, when South Carolina seceded from the Union, and well before the firing on Fort Sumter the following April 12, which led to the secession of Virginia five days later, Lee was preparing himself, albeit in considerable frustration and anger, to follow the South out of the Union. In a December 3 letter to his son Rooney, Lee first explained his shifting loyalty, using what was soon to become to him a self-evident truism, which he would reiterate in the months to follow. "Things look very alarming. . . . I prize the Union very highly, & know of no personal sacrifice that I would not make to preserve it, *save that of honour.* I must trust in the wisdom & patriotism of the Nation to maintain it."[11]

With what political unit, then, would honor rest? Lee made the second half of his position quite clear by January 16, 1861, when he wrote his cousin Annette Carter. After repeating the formula of denying no sacrifice save honor, he wrote, "If the Union is dissolved, I shall return to Virginia & share the fortune of my people." The next week he wrote his cousin Markie

Williams, who lived in the North, "If a disruption takes place, I shall go back in sorrow to my people & share in the misery of my native state, & save in her defense there will be one soldier less in the world than now." He then hinted at taking up farming and staying out of any civil war but dropped such potential neutralism almost immediately. Over the next week, the latter part of his formula evolved slightly until it was framed in a famous metaphor, articulated first in his January 29 letter to Rooney: "If the Union is dissolved & the government disrupted, I shall return to my native state & share the miseries of my people. Save in her defense, I will draw my sword no more." In his resignation from the army on April 20, Lee only slightly rephrased this incantation, "Save in defense of my native State, I never desire again to draw my sword."[12]

And who were these "people"? What was the core meaning of "my native State," of "Virginia," upon which Lee's deepest loyalty was settling? Here Lee was clearest on the day of his resignation from the United States Army, whose command he had been offered, when he wrote to his Unionist sister, Ann Marshall: "With all my devotion to the Union and the feeling of loyalty and duty of an American citizen, I have not been able to make up my mind to raise my hand against *my relatives, my children, my home.*"[13] When the crisis came, Lee chose to defend his family, his cousinage, his class, his home, his Virginia (slavery included)—all that was most concrete—against the far more abstract Union.

Mary Custis Lee's choice followed the same path. If anything, she had been a stauncher Unionist than her husband prior to the secession winter. As late as February 9, 1861, she wrote Eliza Mackay Stiles that she wished that the rest of the South "had left Carolina *alone*" in secession. Despite the "villainous attacks" on her husband in the New York *Tribune,* despite the skulking abolitionists who had nearly caused a slave revolt

at Arlington, despite the decades of "meddling by northern fa-
natics" and by Northern politicians, who ought "to be hung as
high as Haman, . . . yet after all these wrongs I would lay down
my life, could I save our *Union*. What is the use of a government
combined such as ours, if any one part has the right, for any
wrong real or imaginary, of withdrawing . . . and throwing the
whole into confusion." This "Revolution" instigated by South
Carolina, would be accorded only the "reprobation of the World"
and punishment from the Almighty. To her daughter Mildred
she wrote on February 19 that "both parties are in the wrong in
this fratricidal war. . . . I see no right in the matter." On February
24, in another letter to Mildred, writing with the same faint religious hope her husband was expressing, she added, "I pray that
the Almighty may listen [to patriots] & that the designs of ambitious & selfish politicians who would dismember our glorious
Country may be frustrated—especially that our own state may
act right [and become] the *peacemakers.*"[14]

Yet when her husband had made his choice, Mary not
merely went along with him but agreed with him from conviction. She wrote to a clergyman acquaintance that the Union was
now but "an *empty name,* its flag dishonored by those who furl
it." Washington, the national capital, had become a "military
despotism," and it was her husband's "office *now . . . to defend*
his state" at whatever personal cost.[15]

Although he had backed into a commitment to the emerging Confederacy, Lee continued to protest against the dissolu-
tion of the Union and to hope and pray that somehow matters
would cool down and war would be averted. He blamed extrem-
ists, grieved over the country he had lost, and resigned himself
as a Stoic and a Christian to whatever the fates might bring.

"As far as I can judge from the papers we are between a state
of anarchy & Civil War," Lee wrote Mary on February 23, 1861.

"May God spare us from both. It has been evident for years that the Country was doomed to run through the full length of democracy. To what fearful pass it has brought us." Lee then repeated his despairing formulation, "I fear mankind for years will not be sufficiently christianized to bear the absence of restraint and force." And, stoically realizing the inevitability of the oncoming tragedy, he continued, "I must try & be patient & await the end for I can do nothing to hasten or retard it." Or as he put it to Markie Williams, "I can only see that a fearful calamity is upon us, and fear the country will have to pass through for its sins a fiery ordeal." Perhaps war would purify the corrupted American people through a massive remission of sin through blood. The apocalypse appeared to be at hand.[16]

At least Lee insisted on calling events by their real name: "Secession is nothing but revolution," he wrote Rooney on January 29. "It is idle to talk of secession. Anarchy would have been established & not a government" by the patriots of the American Revolution and the fathers of the Constitution had they included the right to secession in their construction of the Union. Why employ this prattle about "secession as it is termed politely," he added the next day to Custis, when in fact it was "revolutionizing."[17]

But while disbelieving in the legality of secession, Lee went along with it. Right after equating secession to anarchy, Lee added to Rooney, "Still, a Union that can only be maintained by swords and bayonets, and civil war that are to take the place of brotherly love and kindness, has no charm for me."[18] As was true of many reluctant Confederates—the so-called conditional Unionists—secession was a default position. If the Union acted to preserve the Union by forceful and illegal means, such as firing on Southern men or calling for a military force to put down secession, they would go out and join their fellow Southerners.

Southern men who preferred the nation as it had been would never accept this Northern redefinition of nationalism made through force.

Even as war approached, Lee wished for some magical deliverance. Perhaps, he wrote Agnes, his native state might discover some redemptive formula—"as she was chiefly instrumental in the formation & inauguration of the Constitution, so I would wish that she might be able to maintain it and to save the nation."[19] As late as April 25, three days after he had accepted command of the Virginia Confederate military forces, Lee wrote to his cousin Cassius Lee about the possibility of a peaceful settlement. Cassius Lee had forwarded a letter written by the Reverend James May of the Virginia Theological Seminary, requesting that Robert E. Lee try to act as an arbitrator, a great sectional peacemaker in the tradition of George Washington. "No earthly act would give me greater pleasure as to restore peace to my country," Robert wrote Cassius to tell May. But he did not act on this impulse.

> I fear it is out of the power of man & in God alone must be our trust. I think our policy should be purely on the defensive. To resist aggression & allow time to allay the passions and allow reason to resume her sway. Virginia has . . . joined the Confederate States. Her policy will doubtless therefore be shaped by united councils. I cannot say what it will be. But trust that a merciful Providence will not turn his face entirely from us & thrust us from the height to which his smiles have raised us.[20]

Perhaps, God willing, the attack might not come.

Lee submitted his honor and that of the South to a providence he hoped was merciful. His unquestioning and in-

escapable sense of belonging had led him backward into a conflict he barely understood. In his self-conception, he remained
the passive servant of the fates.

The process might have been reluctant and only partially
conscious, but Lee had followed the South into secession as a
matter of second nature. He would not sit on the sidelines but
would do his duty to his "homeland" as he always had. Once he
had made his decision, he never looked back, never expressed
the slightest remorse. He was always more Southern, as well as
Virginian, than he had wanted to acknowledge, even to himself;
this political commitment was to grow and harden during the
war until he became the chief incarnation of the Confederate rebellion.

Chapter 6

THE TRIALS OF WAR

*N*o soldier brought a more sterling reputation into the Civil War. In breeding and bearing, in experience and social skill, and in that magic ingredient, charisma, Lee was without peer in the professional army. As he first had appeared at West Point, so he remained: something of a living legend. General Winfield Scott, who pleaded with Lee to take charge of the Union army at the onset of the war, praised him as "the greatest military genius in America." For Southerners, Lee's grandeur transcended the military. As one Texan said of him in 1860, "He is a 'Preux chevalier, sans peur and sans reproche' "— a perfect knight, fearless and stainless. And shortly after Lee had taken charge of Virginia's mobilization, the *Richmond Dispatch* editorialized that "a more heroic Christian, noble soldier and gentleman could not be found," adding in a subsequent issue that "no man is superior in all that constitutes the soldier and the gentleman—no man more worthy to head our forces and lead our army. There is no one who would command more of the confidence of the people of Virginia. . . . His reputation, his acknowledged ability, his chivalric character, his probity, honor, and—may we add to his eternal praise—his Christian life and conduct make his very name a 'tower of strength.' "[1]

In general, as they seceded and prepared to fight, Southerners believed that their superior honor and Christian virtue, of the sort they projected onto Lee, would lead them to an inevitable and quick victory. Then reality set in. The Civil War was no jousting contest, and all that inflation of Lee's name—which he did not invite but could not deflect—almost inevitably crumbled under the grind of a prolonged, inglorious, and brutal conflict. When Confederate dreams of easy victory collapsed, Lee's reputation was one casualty. A long, hard war challenged Lee's personality as much as his skills. Austere and self-critical, he lacked the flexibility to negotiate relationships with the Southern people or their leaders with comfort and confidence. Lee's stoic reserve restrained him from the heroic gestures expected of him, and, more generally, his antidemocratic and antipolitical values, frequently out of step with Confederate expectations, led him to gloom as the Confederacy experienced seemingly endless internal conflicts.

Lee's war can be divided into three parts. For the first thirteen months, from April 1861 until May 31, 1862, Lee did quite badly and was shunted into secondary military commands. The second phase began precisely on June 1, 1862. On that day, after Joseph E. Johnston was severely wounded during the peninsula campaign of George McClellan, which badly threatened Richmond, Lee was thrust into field command of the Army of Northern Virginia by President Jefferson Davis. Repelling McClellan, Lee began his most ebullient period of command. Albeit at great cost in men and material, Lee and his lieutenants and his men achieved a series of major victories over the Union. This triumphant period was ended by the terrible defeat at Gettysburg on July 4, 1863. During the final twenty-one-month period, which ended in surrender at Appomattox on April 9, 1865, Lee tenaciously but grimly held on to command, with decreasing expectation of victory.

During the spring of 1861, Lee was occupied with trying to mobilize an eastern Confederate army from scratch. On July 21, when the Confederates defeated the Union army at Manassas (Bull Run), the first sizable battle of the war, Lee was stuck back in Richmond in a bureaucratic role. On July 28, he was given his first field command, trying to defend what was to become West Virginia. Not entirely due to his own shortcomings, Lee failed to coordinate his efforts with other commanders and on September 10–15 lost the battle of Cheat Mountain and with it West Virginia. This first major Confederate defeat, particularly disillusioning after the relatively easy victory at Manassas, shocked and angered the Confederate public. Because so much had been expected of Lee, his fall from popularity was especially steep. On November 6, in considerable disgrace, Lee was sent to the coast of South Carolina and Georgia to try to organize a defense against amphibious Union operations without the benefit of an effective Confederate navy. This was an extremely difficult if relatively minor post, and although he limited the Union army to outer coastal conquests, Lee believed he failed in this task, too, an opinion quite widely shared in the Confederacy. On March 4, 1862, Jefferson Davis called Lee back to Richmond to act as his military adviser, believing he would make a loyal and useful subaltern. Davis, a West Point graduate, Mexican War veteran, and former secretary of war, was chock-full of his own military ideas, and Lee served him with considerable deference. There he squirmed until Johnston's injury created an opening for him. Thereafter, his role, reputation, and self-image grew dramatically with military success.

Despite his great powers of self-control, inside Lee remained a self-doubting human being rather than a paragon of certitude, and his experiences in the first thirteen months of the war seemed to bear out his fears. Lee was quite articulate about the trials war offered him and the Southern people. In his letters during this period, he offered an extended negative commentary on the peerless general others expected him to be, a role which he strove to fulfill even as he doubted both his own capacities and the will and discipline of the people.

Reversal in battle and a free press can turn the reputation of even the most golden cavalier into dross in a hurry, as Lee experienced after his defeat at Cheat Mountain. Lee was well aware that his reputation was sliding away. As he wrote Mary on October 7, "the movements of our army cannot keep pace with the expectations of the editors of papers. I know they can arrange things satisfactorily to themselves on paper. I wish they could do so in the field." Beyond criticizing Lee's military capabilities, the Richmond papers also began to insinuate that the Lees' marriage was dissolving. "I am content to take no notice of the slanders you speak of but to let them die out," Lee wrote his very wounded wife with both resolve and considerable contempt for the popular press. "Everybody is slandered, even the good. How should I escape?"[2]

By the time he had returned to Richmond on October 31, 1861, Lee was being called "Granny Lee" and the "King of Spades" by many of his soldiers for his supposed fretfulness and timidity, derisive terms soon picked up in the newspapers. Unable to escape these labels because he lacked a field command, Lee was an unpopular choice to replace Joseph Johnston. At that time, the Richmond *Enquirer* reported in obvious reference to Lee that "you only have to go into the army, amongst the men in the ranks, to hear curses heaped upon West Point and the spade."[3] The Confederate enlisted men and the press had the normal antielitist quotient of contempt for the brass. Lee's aristocratic origins and demeanor as well as his professional training, subjects of praise in good times, were easily turned against him when he was perceived to have failed.

Even if he sought to rise above criticism from disreputable

newspapermen, Lee felt the insults more than he could admit to Mary or even to himself. The war literally had come home to the Lees less than a month after it began, when the Union army seized Arlington plantation, which occupied strategic high ground overlooking Washington. An outraged Mary Lee wrote to the Union colonel who had commandeered her house, protesting both "enormities" perpetrated by the occupying soldiers "upon every *defenseless* person they meet" and the sight of "men, women & children flying in terror." Further, she had not been permitted to move her personal belongings to safety. "It never occurred to me . . . that *I* should be forced to sue for permission to enter *my own house* and that such an outrage as its military occupation to the exclusion of me and my children could ever have been perpetuated by anyone in the whole extent of this country." If Mary Lee retained a vestige of her Unionist sensibility (to which her phrase *this country* still referred), this incident turned her almost instantaneously into a Yankee-hating Southern nationalist. For the rest of the war—indeed, the rest of her life—she continued to fume about the pollution of "my beautiful home . . . *so used,*" which the Union officially confiscated in 1864 and turned into a military cemetery.[4]

Robert E. Lee's reaction to this loss was at times equally angry. He wrote one of his daughters on December 25, 1861, that Arlington, if not destroyed, "has been so desecrated that I cannot bear to think of it. I should have preferred it to be wiped from the face of the earth . . . rather than to have it been degraded by . . . those who revel in the ill they do." Lee then caught himself in his unchristian anger: "You see what a poor sinner I am, and how unworthy to possess what was given me; for that reason it was taken away." If he could calm himself and mute his fury, perhaps God's grace might shine on the Lee family once more. "I pray for a better spirit, and that the hearts of our enemies may be changed." More often, especially to assuage his in-

furiated wife, Lee refrained from railing at the Union and tried
hard to accept this loss as both inevitable and as a test of Christian character. "You had better complete your arrangements &
retire further from the scene of war," he urged Mary immediately after she had left home. "It is sad to think of the devastation, if not ruin it may bring upon a spot so endeared to us. But
God's will be done. We must be resigned." To Lee, resignation
meant self-abnegation, as true duty was based on pure self-
sacrifice, and in this sense loss was a test of virtue.

On January 19, 1862, in a letter to Custis from the Carolina
coast, Lee toted up the personal losses the war was bringing the
family, even should the Confederacy win. "I expect to be a pau-
per if I get through the war. . . . The bonds that I hold of the
Northern railroads & cities will all be confiscated & those of the
Southern states will be much depreciated & cannot pay interest
so my revenue will be much reduced if not cut off. Everything at
Arlington will I fear be lost." Then he calmed himself with the
Stoic's firm conclusion: "But if honour & independence is dealt
us I will be content."[5]

Bottling up his feelings with the defenses of honor, under
the calm surface Lee's anger against the Union mounted. In this
same letter, he noted the suffering of the South Carolina civilians whose fine homes were being polluted as Arlington had
been and wrote, "No civilized nation within my knowledge has
ever carried on war as the United States government has against
us." He defined this desecration more clearly as "hateful" Union
forces razing the countryside in compensation for their "despair
of ever capturing a city they deign to ruin," by which he meant
Charleston, Savannah, or Richmond for that matter.

On September 8, 1861, prior to Cheat Mountain, Lee had issued special orders to his troops: "The eyes of the Country are
upon you. The safety of your homes, the lives of all you hold
dear, depend upon your courage and exertions. Let each man be

victorious, & that the right of self government, liberty & peace, shall in him find a defender." This was the modest political program of a moderate Confederate, one which did not even mention independence as a war aim; the statement is notable for its lack of the furious grandiloquence that was quite common Confederate fare elsewhere. There was something curiously unwarlike about the pronouncement, as if war might still be a temporary aberration rather than an escalating and deepening chaos.[6] More generally, Lee remained notable for his lack of ritual insults directed against the enemy, although he had his moments.

While Lee was becoming somewhat more political in his analysis of events—and the Civil War was nothing if not intensely political—this hesitant development was not central to his interpretation of war, which, not surprisingly, was religious. In the late summer of 1861, while trying to rally the civilians in western Virginia and to deal with the measles epidemic among his troops, Lee paused to relate to Mary his impressions of one road, which he had last ridden in 1840, "on my return to St. Louis, after bringing you home. If anyone had told me then that the next time I traveled that road would have been on my present errand, I should have supposed him insane. I enjoyed the mountains as I rode. The views were magnificent. The valleys so beautiful, the scenery so peaceful. What a glorious world Almighty God has given us. How thankless & ungrateful we are, & how we labour to mar His gifts. May He have mercy on us!"[7] It was as if Lee were almost refusing to internalize the warrior's role, the nationalist's self-righteousness. He had to steel his nerve and that of others, of course, but he resisted internal hardening through emotional disengagement or deadening. As he wrote in the summer of 1862 to Mary, "In the prospect before me I cannot see any ray of pleasure during the war; but as long as I can perform my service to the country, I will be content."[8]

And he remained possessed of his sense of general human sinfulness; of the limits of humanity's knowledge and of the efficacy of human action. In his mind, war would always remain a divine punishment for himself and for his people. That he had lost during his first prolonged experience of civil war only intensified his concerns.

Lee's Stoicism and Christian resignation, always important, deepened profoundly during the war, until they became incantations of faith, rays of hope amid the destruction and loss. It was as if he believed that did he not focus himself that way, rage and destructiveness might overtake him.

Right after the Union army seized Arlington, Lee took a day away from mobilizing Virginia troops to attend the opening of the annual convention of the Protestant Episcopal Church in the diocese of Virginia in Richmond. There he heard Bishop William Meade, leader of the evangelical branch of his church, whom the Lees revered, preach a sermon on the occasion of the fiftieth anniversary of his ordination, taking as his text, "And Pharaoh said unto Jacob, How old *art* thou?" Jacob had answered Pharaoh that though he had been on pilgrimage for 130 years, compared to the untold years and the attainments of his fathers, "few and evil have the days of the years of my life been." As Lee was entering a struggle whose duration, harshness, and conclusion he could not even imagine, he must have compared himself to Jacob and to George Washington and found himself unlikely to succeed. "It was most impressive & more than once I felt the tears coming down my cheek," Lee wrote his wife. "It was full of humility and self-reproach."9*

---

* On March 14, 1862, Lee, in Richmond, wrote Mary that "our good & noble Bishop Meade died last night. [Yesterday evening] he sent for me [and] said he wished to bid me good bye. . . . Called me Robert & reverted to the time I used to say the catechism to him. He invoked the blessing of God upon me and the country. He spoke with difficulty & pain, but perfectly calm and clear. His hand was calm & pulseless, yet he shook mine warmly. I ne'er shall look on his like again." This was the perfect death, inwardly calm, for a great man, the sort of man after whom Robert E. Lee modeled himself (D&M, 128).

Such were the means by which Lee tried to abate Mary's fury over the seizure of Arlington and her fright over hunting for a safe home. "I must now leave the matter to you & pray that God may guard you. I have no time for more. I know & feel the discomfort of your position but it cannot be helped." Lee was too occupied to dwell on his personal losses; were he to do so, he was telling himself as well as Mary, whom he was nearly scolding, anger might distract him. Resignation could defend against such strong feelings, which were sins in themselves, whatever provoked them.

Lee ritualized this admonition, reiterating it time after time to Mary when she expressed her fears and considerable anger about the war, as well as when he expressed his own strong feelings. "In this time of great suffering to the state & country, our private distresses we must bear with resignation like Christians & not aggravate them by repining, trusting to a kind & Merciful God to over-rule them for our good," a typical message went. And when he was about to take to the field for the first time and was worried about his own life, he projected his fears for himself onto his family: "I may go at any moment, & to any point where it may be necessary. I shall feel anxious about you & the girls, & but for my firm reliance upon our Heavenly Father would be miserable."[10] As the crisis deepened, so did a compensatory faith that was at once defensive, distancing, and reaffirmative.

Yet a palpable bleakness of spirit occupied him most of the time. Writing his Christmas letter to Mary in 1861 from his remote and frustrating post in South Carolina, all was loss. Arlington, on which he dwelled despite telling Mary that she should not, was occupied and no doubt ruined, and with it the "relics of Mount Vernon"—Lee's sacred ties to the legacy of George Washington. So what was left? "They cannot take away the remembrances of the spot . . . that to us rendered it sacred." Accepting that the Custis estate had been physically pulverized and had effectively disappeared—"foully polluted," as he termed it in a later letter—Lee expressed the wish to purchase Stratford Hall, the Lee ancestral home, lost by his father and by Black Horse Harry: "That is the only [remaining] place . . . that would inspire me with feelings of pleasure & local love." Stratford Hall was an even more forlorn hope, Lee was fully aware. The Civil War was destroying this Virginian's deepest sense of place, the site of the core values of home and family for which he was fighting. Fundamentally, all was separation and abandonment.

Lee then connected the most local to the most international. During the Trent Affair—the American seizure of two Confederate diplomats off a British ship—over which the Union and the English were making noises of war, Lee, unlike many Confederates who hoped the English would enter the war on their side, believed that because Union leaders were "not entirely mad" they would settle rather than risk British intervention. No, Lee wrote, "we must make up our minds to fight our battles & win our independence alone. No one will help us. We require no extraneous aid, if true to ourselves [and] patient."

Lee linked his most personal sense of the costs of war with the Confederate national struggle by way of a spiritual analogy. Remembrance of good Christmases past filled him with pleasure, he reassured Mary.

> For those on which we have been separated we must not repine. If it will make us more resigned & better prepared for what is in store for us, we should rejoice. . . . If we can only become sensible of our transgressions, so as to be fully penitent & forgiven, that this heavy punishment under which we labour may with

justice be removed from us and the whole nation, what a gracious consummation of all that we have endured it will be![11]

Lee was one in spirit with those Southern theologians who were seeking to turn the wartime Confederacy into an avowedly Christian republic.[12] For such believers, war was an enormous purification ritual, in a very immediate sense. He—or that nation—who purged himself of sin surely would be rewarded. Such a position might explain defeat at least as well as victory, given the innate human propensity to sin, but there also was an activist admonition wrapped within this creed of resignation. For a godly people could *choose* to be up and about the Lord's work with all their might—perhaps then the reward of victory would come at God's merciful hand. Of course it was finally up to Him, but the path to His service was nevertheless discernible. Duty and discipline followed.

This was not a sudden discovery by the newly minted Confederate general but an extension of his peacetime beliefs. For example, in 1854 he had written to Markie Williams concerning her feelings on the death of a dear friend:

> The conflict you feel between the infirmity of human nature, & the aspiration for the high & holy spirit to accomplish all that is right, is not unnatural; & must be constantly experienced. . . . Nor is it possible for us always to do "the good we would" and omit "the evil we would not." Still we need not be discouraged either in our efforts or hopes, or be depressed by the failure or futile attempts of others. Toil & trust, must be our aim, as it is our lot.[13]

This true advocate of discipline must have known that he had sometimes lapsed himself: Only through an awareness of his own shortcomings would true discipline emerge. Lee admonished Williams to become, as he strove to be, another Christian stoic and moral athlete, for men and women did the running and God furnished the finish line.

The armed forces provided a perfect profession for duty-minded men such as Lee. For them, the fixed command structure imitated the heavenly hierarchy, and military rewards and punishments from on high resembled the route of each person's final dispensation. Duty, Honor, Country was the code at West Point, a sort of militarized civil religion, which Lee reaffirmed frequently throughout his life, even after leaving one country for the next.

In 1848, while serving on a court-martial panel during a lull in the Mexican War, Lee wrote to Carter, "Military discipline requires subordination of one's feelings as well as conduct, & those whose duty it is to preserve it, cannot be too cautious how they encourage the exhibition of it in subordinates against their superiors. It is sapping the foundations of all military organization."[14] There was nothing ambiguous about Lee's disciplinarian bent, in Mexico or in the Civil War; indeed, the military at war provided a clear course for religiosity enacted—discipline, discipline, discipline—even if ultimate victory were unclear. "In times like these . . . the practice of self-denial & self sacrifice was never more greatly demanded," Lee insisted, if one were ever to achieve "the advancement of some praiseworthy object."[15]

Basic training in martial discipline was best accomplished when unformed recruits were isolated from the civilian population, the better to be drilled. As the war started, Lee admonished the commanders of Virginia regiments to take their troops to exclusively military spaces. "It will be necessary to remove them from the towns . . . & establish them in camps, where their constant instruction & discipline can be attended to," he wrote one colonel. "They will the sooner become familiar with the necessi-

ties of service, & be better prepared for its hardships." So infan-
tile were these raw sons of Southern plain folk, that even with
the best of officers to indoctrinate them many would collapse at
training camps. "Our poor sick, I know, suffer much," Lee wrote
his wife on September 17, 1861. And then he blamed them
rather than their lack of previous exposure to diseases such as
smallpox and measles for their illnesses and deaths. "They bring
it on themselves by not doing what they are told. They are worse
than children, for the latter can be forced." Such unmilitary recruits were subject to easygoing moral depravity as well as to
illness. In a letter to a brigade commander already in the field,
Lee observed, "I need not call the attention of one as experienced as yourself to the necessity of preventing the troops from
all interference with the rights and property of the citizens of
the State & of enforcing rigid discipline & obedience to orders."[16]

Self-abnegation was the first rule of discipline. In a culture
in which elite men bristled with honor and found slights everywhere, asking them to ignore the demands of the ego was difficult. Lee tried. For example, when he reorganized several
regiments early in the war, Lee had to demote Philip St. George
Cocke from brigadier general to colonel, which he hastened to
reassure Cocke was "dictated by necessity & not by choice." Lee
was careful in how he framed the letter accompanying this
order. "Recognizing as fully as I do your merit, patriotism & devotion to the state, I do not consider that either rank or position
were necessary to bestow upon your honour, but believe that
you will confer honour on the position." However tactfully he
put it, Lee was aware that he was demanding that Cocke subordinate his personal honor to institutional necessity, and so he
appealed to Cocke's sense of the higher good, which might miti-
gate what this honor-bound gentleman doubtlessly would take

as an insult.[17] Cocke acceded to the order, whether or not Lee had mollified him.*

If, however, an officer were stubborn in placing personal honor and rank over cooperation and subordination, Lee could come down on him very hard. When one Captain Payton protested too frequently and vigorously after being placed under the command of Captain Henderson of the Confederate navy, Lee made the order perfectly clear and then added, with rare bluntness, "In a war such as this, unanimity and hearty cooperation should be the rule. Petty jealousies about slight shades of relative command and bickering about trivial matters are entirely out of place and highly improper, and, when carried so far as to interfere with the effectiveness of a command, become criminal and contemptible."[18]

Lee sought to reinforce discipline over his family as well as his army. Even his young daughters were to subordinate individual desire to the common good as war demanded. Thus, through Mary, he scolded "little Agnes," a normally fun-loving twenty-year-old, for the contents of a gay letter she had sent him. Agnes "is full of projected visits about the State, Brandon, Cedar Grove &c, & of having 'pleasant times,' as if enjoyment was the order of the day. I hope no other times may befall her, but in my opinion these are serious times & our chief pleasure must be what is necessary & proper for the occasion." In his

---

* Lee's military application of his class sensibilities cut both ways. On the one hand, in his meritocratic mode, he wrote Jefferson Davis, "If you can . . . fill these positions with proper officers, not the relatives & social friends of the commanders, who, however agreeable their company, are not the most useful, you might hope to have the finest army in the world." On the aristocratic side of the ledger was Lee's remark to Mary about the son of Edward Turner of "Kinloch," a Carter relative who, in September 1861, had hand-delivered Mary's letter to him: "Beverly Turner . . . is a nice young soldier. I am pained to see fine young men like him, of education and standing, from all the old and respectable families in the State, serving in the ranks. I hope in time they will receive their reward." In this context, it must be noted that Lee's sons rose very quickly in the ranks during the war, to the resentment of others around Lee, who believed their commander was practicing nepotism (Lee to Davis, Fredericksburg, March 21, 1863, quoted in Douglas Southall Freeman, *Lee's Dispatches* [1915] [Baton Rouge: Louisiana State University Press, 1957], 82–83; Lee to Mary Custis Lee, Valley Mountain, September 17, 1861, in D&M, 73).

sweet-sixteen letter to little Mildred, written from Savannah early in 1862, Lee admonished his youngest daughter as well in the direction of sacrifice and discipline. "We [Southerners] were getting careless & confident & required correction. You must do all you can for our dear country."[19]

What was true of those rampant, self-serving egos in the army—what even tinged his judgments of his daughters—was all too characteristic of Southern people as a whole, Lee feared. They were failing to remake themselves, arm themselves morally, truly give up self and materialism through commitment to the war effort. "The people here are very kind & polite," he wrote Mary from South Carolina late in 1861, but they "are much exercised about their property & people, [and] do not seem to realize the necessity of exertion on their part to avoid the evil or defend themselves, but are willing to leave that to others." Perhaps punishment at the hands of the enemy might finally serve to discipline them to the demands of war and its god. "We have all at the South had so easy and comfortable a time, that it is difficult for us to practice the self denial & labour necessary for our present position. . . . It will require misfortune & suffering I fear to induce us to do what we ought to do."[20]

Lee and Southern people got a great deal of what he half wished for. In the fall of 1861 and the spring of 1862, when the Union made stunning advances, some of them in Lee's area of command, Southern morale plummeted, Lee's included. Although he did not precisely blame himself, Lee often expressed what can only be called defeatism, both personal and collective.

When he had still been in the mountains of western Virginia, Lee wrote Custis about the "disaster at Cape Hatteras" on August 27, when Benjamin Butler had seized key posts in the outer North Carolina islands. This "was a hard blow to us," Lee wrote, but "we must expect them, struggle against them, prepare for them. We cannot be always successful and reverses must come. May God give us courage, endurance and faith to strive to the end."[21] But this was only the first of a string of reverses. Soon, the Union navy occupied Ship Island, off Biloxi, Mississippi. And then, just as Lee was arriving in South Carolina, on November 7, the enemy won a smashing victory at Port Royal and then built major fortifications on the South Carolina Sea Islands, which threatened the entire South Carolina and Georgia coast—Lee's command. During the next few months, the Union army made further incursions in North Carolina and occupied all of Kentucky. Then, under U. S. Grant, the Union won major victories at Forts Henry and Donelson in northern Tennessee on February 6 and 16, 1862, and went on without opposition to occupy the state capital, Nashville, the following week.

Lee's poise slipped under all these reverses (which only made him human). Arriving in South Carolina, Lee confessed to his daughter Mildred that he believed he had been sent off on "another forlorn hope expedition. Worse than western Virginia."[22] Lee's heart sank further over the next four months, as the enemy gained more of the sacred Southern soil, in his area of command and elsewhere.

His strategic situation was nightmarish. Along the complicated Carolina coastline, with its myriad islands and waterways, the presence and power of the Union navy increased daily, and Union skill in amphibious landings improved, while the Confederacy lacked opposing vessels. Thus, while the Union advanced according to its schedule and struck where it willed, Lee could only try to amass sufficient firepower at static land bases to limit the incursions along the partly indefensible coast. After three months of such necessarily incomplete defense of his sector, Lee wrote his wife with a certain desperation, "There are so many points of attack & so little means to meet them on water, that there is but little rest."[23]

Lee developed a strategy to cope with the situation, but it

was a defensive strategy requiring Fabian patience rather than vigorous, heart-stirring advance. While setting up his batteries around Charleston and Savannah, Lee described his overall strategy to General Samuel Cooper, inspector general of the Confederate army, on January 8, 1862. He wished to convey "the hope rather than the confident assurance, that when completed, armed & manned, if properly fought, the enemy's approach ought to be successfully resisted." To this tentative hypothesis Lee added a caveat, "I am aware that we must fight against great odds, & always trust that the spirit of our soldiers will be an overmatch to the numbers of our opponents." This was the first articulation of a sensible fear Lee held until the end of the war. Then Lee offered a rather detached assessment of Union strength. "The forces of the enemy are accumulating, & apparently increase faster than ours. . . . With his means of transportation & concentration, it would be impossible to gather troops, necessarily posted over a long line, in sufficient strength to oppose sudden movements. Wherever his fleet can be brought no opposition can be made to his landing, except within range of our fixed batteries." But Lee had only limited manpower, heavy weaponry, and funding with which to build the necessary fortifications.

Therefore, the only obvious form of defense was to pull the enemy inland, away from the protection of its naval guns. "The farther he can be withdrawn from his floating batteries the weaker will he become, & lines of defense, covering objects of attack, have been selected with this view." Lee wanted to concentrate his limited resources, which meant strategic retreat. "I am in favor of abandoning all exposed points as far as possible, within reach of the enemy's fleet . . . & of taking interior positions, where we can meet on more equal terms," Lee wrote on February 19 to the commander at Charleston, adding a few days

later to Mary that it was "prudent & proper" to abandon all islands that might be cut off by the enemy navy.[24]

Although quite effective in limiting the Union advance, this
strategy was unpopular. Lee knew that Southern honor demanded the aggressive defense of every inch of Confederate
soil, although even this stance was less esteemed than going on
the attack. In fact, he shared these values, even when they con-
tradicted his cooler professional judgment. Such military passivity must have deeply depressed Lee.

The clearest evidence of Lee's emotional ebb came in a letter
that he wrote from Savannah on March 2 to his "Precious
Annie," which was intended for her sisters as well. He complained of "small means & slow workmen" and civilians who
"have been content with themselves & their dimes." As if to tell
her how he distracted himself from his travails, he wrote, "I
think of you all, separately & collectively, in the busy hours of
the day & the silent hours of the night, & the recollection of each
& every one whiles away the long nights, in which my anxious
thoughts drive away sleep." Lee had never mentioned insomnia
before—an almost invariable symptom of depression—and
here he explicitly linked sleepless anxiety with his military problems. Yet even when he was this far down, Lee was able to separate his current terrible dilemma from his more general sense of
life, which remained affirmative: "I always feel that you & Agnes
at those times are sound & happy & that it is immaterial to either
where the blockaders are or what their progress is in the river.
[Events] in these perilous times to our country . . . look dark at
present. . . . But they will brighten after awhile, & I trust that a
merciful God will arouse us to a sense of our danger, bless our
honest efforts & drive back our enemies to their homes."[25] Wishful thinking was important, even if Lee had to write it out to his
daughters in an effort to reaffirm it for himself.

As if his current military posture were not trouble enough, Lee was also terribly apprehensive about future manpower requirements in his part of the Confederacy. "I tremble to think of the consequences that may befall us next spring when all our twelve months' men may claim their discharge," he wrote a Charleston confidant. "At the opening of the [summer's] campaign our enemies will be fresh & vigorous, after a year's preparation [and] we shall be in all the anxiety, excitement, & organization of new armies."[26]

Far from admiring his troops, Lee believed that they lacked discipline and probably were incapable of it. Veterans of the old army on both sides of the conflict had difficulty concealing their disdain for the altogether too independent and democratic troops in the new mass armies, and Lee was no exception. The new troops were so negligent that they often created their own problems, Lee believed. Commenting on February 23, 1862, on the terrible news from Tennessee, Lee wrote to Custis that although "the victories of our enemies increase & consequently the necessity of increased energy & activity on my part, our men do not seem to realize this, & the same selfishness & carelessness of their duties continue." His men were failing him, which meant he feared he might fail. "We have nothing floating which can contend with [the] enemy. [Perhaps] we shall be overrun for a time, & must make up our minds to great suffering," he wrote in considerable distress to his eldest son.

On the same day, he wrote Mary that "our soldiers have not realized the necessity of endurance & labour . . . & that it is better to sacrifice themselves than our cause." He then repeated his real fear that his command would be the next to be crushed. "I hope [we] will keep them out," he said in obvious doubt. "They can bring such overwhelming force in all their movements that it has the effect to demoralize our new troops." He longed for some "veteran troops . . . they would soon rally," he told Custis.

While the enemy was "threatening every avenue . . . pillaging, burning & robbing . . . with impunity," his own troops seemed fully unprepared. "I am dreadfully disappointed at the spirit here."[27]

Not merely were Southern soldiers failing, in Lee's eyes so were Southern civilians. They carried on their shallow everyday lives and let others do the work; they pursued their "trivial amusements" rather than sacrificing all to the war effort; they worried about every dime of their own rather than engaging their fortunes and their hearts in the struggle. They wallowed in the most corrupting elements of the capitalist marketplace, buying and selling to their personal advantage rather than proceeding fairly, just like a bunch of degenerate Yankees. They refused to realize their mortal danger. They were failing to create a truly Christian Confederacy.[28]

"I hope our enemy will be polite enough to wait for us," Lee wrote his girls shortly after arriving in Savannah. "We must make up our minds to meet with reverses & overcome them." Such anxiety continued during his whole period of command along the coast. He wrote Mary in February 1862, continuing to fear, as he had for three months, that Savannah might fall. "I hope God will at last crown our efforts with success. But the contest must be long & severe, & the whole country has to go through much suffering. It is necessary we should be humbled & taught to be less boastful, less selfish, & more devoted to right & justice."[29] God had to be harsh to teach the lessons of justice and duty to such a sinful people.

When he was calm, Lee understood quite realistically that the South was bound to suffer some reverses. Dealt a weak military hand in South Carolina, as he had been in western Virginia, Lee managed about as well as any mortal might have; yet, ever the perfectionist, he was thoroughly demoralized because, whatever the objective military weakness of his troops, he had failed to measure up to his own high expectations. The Union had won engagements and gained ground on his watch. He never concluded that he was a failure as a leader, although his gloomy prognostications can be seen as projections of a looming sense of defeat. To a considerable extent, in implicit violation of his code of honor, he did blame others, although not specific persons, as did many other generals (and as he did later in the war). It was the soldiers as a body, the people as a whole, who were not sufficiently dedicated to attain victory. It was they who needed to taste defeat (a humiliation he was tasting every day) in order to gain the moral right to a final victory, should that be the will of merciful providence.

In the early spring of 1862, the Union was on the march, seemingly everywhere, and Lee was not the only Confederate to apprehend impending disaster. But Lee also responded deeply to the widely shared opinion that he had been performing poorly, an evaluation he found hard to externalize or to deny completely. The language of Stoicism and Christian resignation might explain defeat up to a point, but it could only exacerbate his sense of moral responsibility for defeat, even as he criticized Confederate soldiers and civilians. Hence the gloom.

When Lee was recalled to Richmond on March 4, 1862, he took this, perhaps correctly, as punishment from Jefferson Davis for a bad performance along the Carolina coast. Shortly after he arrived back in the Confederate capital, Lee spelled out this sentiment in an outburst of self-deprecation. "No one has a right to look for any happiness these days except such as he might derive from his efforts to do his duty," Lee wrote Carter on March 14. He then continued in a manner remarkable for a man normally characterized by great self-control, "I am willing to do anything I can to help the noble cause we are engaged in, & to take any position; but *the lower & more humble the position the more agreeable to me & the better qualified I should feel to fill it.* I fear I shall be able to do little in the position assigned me & cannot hope to satisfy the feverish & excited expectation of our good people."[30] Expressing himself through the language of Christian humility, Lee revealed that his self-confidence had nearly disappeared along with his reputation and his faith in the Southern people.

Lee had been removed from his second-rate place in the field and relegated to an even lesser advisory staff job as Davis's factotum. He could do nothing to redeem his besmirched honor in such a position, and he knew it. Still, this was just another trial, and he determined to soldier on as well as he could, however limited the role or the potential rewards. Lee had not thought through what it might mean should he win the confidence of Jefferson Davis, which he proceeded to do over the next three months by pitching in without complaint and without demanding another chance in the field.

Though her husband did not complain to anyone, Mary Lee did, at least to old friends. On March 8, she wrote to Eliza Mackay Stiles about Lee's new position, his lack of public standing, and his silent resignation. "Now they have got into trouble they send for him to help them out, & yet he never gets any credit for what he has done. . . . He never complains or seems to desire anything more than to perform his duty, but I may be excused for wishing him to reap the reward of his labors."[31] This letter was almost certainly an accurate documentation of how Lee was handling himself when his career had hit rock bottom. While he put a brave face to his grave anxiety and prepared for whatever might come, his equanimity was strained almost to the breaking point.

If Robert E. Lee had died on May 31, 1862, he would have received only a footnote in the history books as an intelligent and dutiful, passive and punctilious officer who had failed in his two commands. But then luck interceded.

Chapter 7

AUDACITY

With the Union army on the outskirts of Richmond, Confederate commander Joseph E. Johnston gravely wounded, and Johnston's second in command too ill to serve, Jefferson Davis turned to his military aide, Robert E. Lee, as the least implausible alternative.

Lee's appointment aroused a flurry of attacks in the Richmond papers, which characterized him as a timid, ineffective, and out-of-touch West Pointer. Many of the military men in the field did not know their new commander firsthand and naturally feared that his negative reputation might be accurate. One afternoon shortly after Lee's appointment, Colonel Edward Porter Alexander, an artillery officer, happened to meet Colonel Joseph Christmas Ives, who, like Lee, was attached to Jefferson Davis's staff. As the two rode along together, Alexander lamented the military status quo, which featured a combination of inadequate resources and a passive defensive posture on the lines in front of Richmond. "Our only hope is to bounce [the enemy] & whip him somewhere before he is ready for us, and that demands audacity in our commander. Has General Lee that audacity?" Alexander asked. Ives heard Alexander's fears out and then, Alexander later wrote, "stopped his horse in the road to make his answer more impressive. . . . 'Alexander, if there is one man in either army, Federal or Confederate, who is, head & shoulders, far above every other one in either army in audacity that man is General Lee, and you will very soon have lived to see it. Lee is audacity personified. His name is audacity, and you need not be afraid of not seeing all of it that you will want to see.'"

Lee's everlasting sobriquet thus was born out of Alexander's anxious question, although it is not clear how Ives had gained his impression of Lee. Audacity was to become a "prophecy . . . literally fulfilled," Alexander later recalled, and forever after historians have argued over how to evaluate the outcomes of that audacity, not whether or not it existed.[1] In fact, audacity was uncharacteristic of Lee before he took this command, as well as for much of the time after he lost at Gettysburg; but for the year in which he dominated the war in the eastern theater, audacity was no overstatement.

Yet what appeared in later light to have been prophecy could have been just Ives's wishful thinking had not Lee stepped up and delivered decisive and successful leadership, which he did almost immediately. Within weeks, he reorganized his staff, renamed his command the Army of Northern Virginia, and, in the decisive and aggressively offensive Seven Days Battle, from June 25 until July 1, 1862, drove George McClellan away from Richmond and back to his bridgehead on the York River, from which he reembarked for the North, badly beaten. For the next year, with the exception of the bloody strategic defeat at Sharpsburg, Maryland (which the Union called Antietam), Lee won a series of smashing victories against McClellan and against John Pope, Ambrose Burnside, and Joseph Hooker, his successors in the Union command, at the Second Battle of

Manassas, August 28–30, Fredericksburg, December 11–15, and Chancellorsville, May 1–6, 1863, following which Lee marched northward, apparently invincible, into Pennsylvania.

Victories such as these resurrected Lee's reputation and with it his self-esteem. He found and expressed capacities within himself that he must have come to doubt. Now, with fortunes reversed, it was as if he had suddenly come into focus and found his true vocation as a victorious commander on the biggest stage of the war.

Of course, it did not hurt his efforts that the generals on the other side were incompetent blunderers. Without refighting old battles and reassessing military reputations, it does seem clear that battles can be evaluated from the point of view of who lost more than who won, and Lee had great good fortune in his opposite numbers. Battle being in this sense a relative struggle, Lee, however talented he may or may not have been, bested his weak Union counterparts, demoralizing them as he thumped them time after time during his annus mirabilis.

From the start of that year, with his back to Richmond, Lee knew he had no choice but aggression if he was to save the Confederate capital and, perhaps, the whole war. Out of necessity came engagement, and Lee immediately experienced an explosion of energy—that "audacity" of which the men around him became so aware. From a stance of dutiful resignation, he suddenly moved into violent action—controlled violence to be sure, but violent action nevertheless. He became an extremely offensive-minded general, for better and for worse. This might not have been what he anticipated of himself, given his prior experiences. At the moment when it was most needed, aggressiveness thrust up through his passivity and deep reserve. In a sense, the most approximate emotional precedent for such an outburst was the considerable erotic energy that had periodically forced its way up through the carefully controlled exterior the young Lee had normally shown the world in his relationships with young women. And now, when all the chips were down for him and his new army, Lee found a parallel and even greater release in making war as a conscious act. Given the choice, he would attack, not wait—as he said at one point, demonstrating his nervy predilection, "we must decide between the positive loss of inactivity and the risk of action."[2]

Lee's officers and, perhaps more unusual, his men were deeply impressed with him from the Seven Days battle through Gettysburg and to a considerable extent until Appomattox and afterward. Much of their admiration came, of course, from the fact that under him they won their battles, but more generally there was something ineffable in his masculinity, his calm and reserved but powerful charisma, his manner of wearing the habit of command, which doubtless inspired them. Edward Porter Alexander put it as well as any when he wrote that "like the rest of the army generally, nothing gave me much concern so long as I knew that General Lee was in command. I am sure there can never have been an army with more supreme confidence in its commander than the army had in General Lee. We looked forward to victories under him as confidently as to successive sunrises."

Of the many markers of this esteem, none was as powerful as the time Lee rode up to some Texas troops about to go on the attack in the summer of 1864. "The old man, with the light of battle in his eyes, & in the joy of seeing [the Texas brigade] arrive, rode up behind their line, following them in the charge," Alexander later recalled. Seeing that Lee was placing himself at great risk because of his bond with the men, "at once the men began to shout, 'Lee go back! Lee to the rear!' " and a major then took Lee's horse by the bridle and pulled him, with considerable force, back to safety from the line of attack.[3]

This powerful rapport was not based on familiarity; Lee was

most certainly not one of the boys. He neither drank nor participated in yarn telling by the campfire at the end of the day, preferring to retire to his tent, write letters, and read his Bible and
Marcus Aurelius. The few times he emerged from his privacy of
an evening were memorable events to his staff, from whom he
usually kept a considerable distance. He also guarded his own
counsel. He did solicit advice but made decisions with firmness
and often without disclosing his reasoning. Conversely, he
trusted his major corps commanders to execute battles, once he
had set out the parameters. Generally, he was kind and considerate but distant and proper, in a rather courtly and old-fashioned
highly formal manner, often to the point of offending those in
greatest proximity to him by what they felt was hauteur. In
many respects, his style echoed that of his great hero, George
Washington, whose subordinates had admired him greatly
while resenting him as well.

It also must be emphasized that intrinsic to Lee's awesome
presence was his generally buried but nevertheless evident
anger. When Lee lost his temper—more often in a manner that
was cold rather than hot but always quite obvious—he made his
mostly youthful subalterns shrink in shame. Such displays were
not infrequent, as two young officers of Lee's inner military
family often noted. One was Walter Herron Taylor, who carefully and painfully illustrated this side of Lee in confidential letters he wrote during the war; the other was Edward Porter
Alexander, Lee's most talented and versatile artillerist, who,
after the war, discussed such displays of anger in his personal
reminiscences, though he expurgated them before publication.

One evening during a staff meeting, Lee heard a teamster,
about one hundred yards off, cursing and beating a mule. Such
maltreatment of animals infuriated Lee, and Alexander thus immediately observed that "peculiar little shake of his head" and
the "snapping at his ear" that signaled Lee's anger. The usually

soft-spoken Lee "then shouted out in a tone which I thought would scare anybody, 'What are you beating that mule for.' " Believing he was being kidded and not recognizing the source, the teamster answered in what Alexander called a "Georgia cracker whine, 'Is this any of you-r-r mule?' " This produced an "awful moment" for the staff, which found the unconscious insubordination hilarious: "Not one of us dared crack a smile," Alexander remembered. Lee reined in his anger and finished off the meeting. After that, however, "I have no doubt he . . . made good his claim to the mule . . . to the teamster's entire satisfaction," Alexander concluded dryly, "but I never heard any particulars."

Alexander recalled several more serious and sustained bouts of anger. Most notable was one incident in which Lee took after his entire staff. One evening, all of them distinctly heard Lee ask them to prepare to start down the road by 2:00 A.M. However, shortly after 1:00 A.M., the obsessively punctual general was dressed, breakfasted, mounted, and furious with them for not being ready at that hour. As it was for plantation owners, so it was for this military commander: All time was his time, nonnegotiable and absolute, and to be late was to affront his authority. At 1:30 A.M., Colonel Charles S. Venable, who had camped with Lee, hurriedly came after Alexander, who was smoking a leisurely postbreakfast cigarette at his tent, a short ride down the road. "Aleck, Come on! The Old Man is out here waiting for you & mad enough to bite nails. . . . Two o'clock was the hour he told us all last night, but now he swears he said one. And he scolded everybody & started off all alone . . . and the rest of the staff are coming along as fast as they can." When Alexander saddled up hurriedly and rode out into the road, Lee greeted him, "with the very utmost stiffness and formality, 'Good morning, General Alexander. I had hoped to find you waiting in the road for me on my arrival.' " When Alexander replied with all the good nature and blandness he could summon up that Lee had told him two o'clock was the appointed hour, Lee then replied with a "very severe emphasis . . . 'One o'clock was the hour, Sir, at which I said I would start!' "

Lee then castigated Alexander for not finding a local citizen to serve as a guide that morning. "I felt like telling him that all the citizens of the neighborhood, strong enough to carry a musket, had been conscripted, but I did not dare to," Alexander wrote sardonically, thus demonstrating that Lee's unreasoning and arbitrary temper was making him angry in return. Lee then called out to a lowly courier to serve as his guide, telling the "deeply mortified" Venable that his staff had disappointed him. Next, Lee insisted on rousting an old man out of his bed to serve as another guide, asking directions "in quite a stern voice," and the poor fellow, a French Canadian who could barely reply in English, failed to understand Lee's problem. Alexander could barely repress his amusement at Lee's condescending and botched attempt to show Alexander how one used locals as scouts. In the event, after taking the barefoot old man well down the road, Lee finally let him go back, and the party "had no trouble anywhere" in finding their way, Alexander recorded. Subsequently, Lee gave Venable the cold shoulder for two full weeks before gradually resuming his former kindness.[4]

Walter Herron Taylor, Lee's adjutant general throughout the war, the man with the greatest and most continuous proximity to him, offered the most sustained commentary on Lee's impressiveness, as well as his often frosty distance and considerable temper. Twenty-three years old when he first went to work for the fifty-four-year-old general in May 1861, Taylor was deeply impressed by the man he first met. Decades later, he could still recall the moment: "I was at once attracted and greatly impressed by his appearance. He was then at the zenith of his physical beauty. Admirably proportioned, of graceful and dignified carriage, with strikingly handsome features, bright and penetrating eyes . . . he appeared every inch the soldier and a man born to command." Taylor wrote about this first meeting to his closest friend, "Oh! Mr. Barrot he's a trump, a soldier, a gentleman & above all a Christian."[5]

Although Taylor's awe—the response meeting Lee had aroused in other men ever since his West Point days—always remained, familiarity bred considerable irritation with and resentment of other of his commander's qualities. In a stream of letters written during the final two years of the war to his fiancée, Bettie Saunders, Taylor analyzed this side of his intense relationship with Lee.

Taylor's Lee was quite demanding and often inconsiderate. Knowing his adjutant was a committed Christian, Lee rarely gave Taylor the time to go to the Sabbath services that he himself almost invariably attended, Taylor complained to Saunders in August 1863. And, "if anybody is to be waked at night, to receive the innumerable dispatches, to remain in camp when all are away," it was Taylor. He was glad to "feel that I am of such use. I never worked so hard to please anyone, [but] with so little effect as with General Lee. He is so *unappreciative*." Everyone else on the staff complimented Taylor on his endless efforts, "but I want to satisfy him." Taylor realized "how silly & sensitive" he must seem voicing such complaints, but he wanted *Lee* to praise him; "Then I'll be satisfied."

Several months later, Taylor noted that Colonel Venable was seeking another post (in the event, he stayed with Lee until the end of the war). "The truth is Genl. Lee doesn't make our *time pleasant here* & when promotion is offered his staff elsewhere, it is not to be wondered if they accept."

Even while resenting Lee's self-absorption and frequent crossness, Taylor continued to be impressed by his utter commitment to duty and his ever-deepening piety. One Sunday late in 1863, for example, Taylor was riding with Lee at a "pretty fair gait" when they came across a sizable group of the men engaged in the Sabbath service. Lee at once halted to listen to the singing. "He heard the whole sermon and then as the benediction was pronounced reverently raised his hat from his head [an]d received the blessing. . . . It was a striking scene and one well calculated to impress solemnly all who witnessed it." Even if there was something self-conscious about Lee's piety, Taylor still thought he impressed religiosity on the men, reminding them of their sanctified service to the Confederacy. Lee cut a magnificent figure, if not a spontaneous one.

Occasionally, Lee made the effort to be more thoughtful toward his young subordinate, though he often laced consideration with sarcasm. For example, one day in January 1864, Taylor wrote Bettie, "the General just looked in upon me and kindly inquired if I had a sore throat (my neck tie was carelessly cast aside), remarking at the same time that I should take some exercise & must ride out every day. It is kind of him thus to think of me, but the Chief forgets that if I were to run off daily, I alone would suffer because of the necessary accumulation of work during my pleasure taking." Balancing resentfulness and pleasure in Lee's attention, Taylor implied that his boss had wrapped kindness in a rebuke, solicitousness in an empty promise.

When Lee was absent, Taylor was always filled with apprehension that he might make mistakes when left in charge. On March 4, 1864, he told Bettie, "when the General arrived I was all anxiety," for if there had been disorder in his responses to enemy moves, "I alone would receive the blame." In this instance, Taylor reported, "to my infinite gratification and comfort, he had no fault to find," unlike other times. Yet Taylor was also relieved whenever Lee departed, as then he could temporarily enjoy being out from under the chief's thumb. Such release could even overcome Taylor's desire to visit his fiancée in Richmond. On August 7, 1864, from the trenches in Petersburg, a half-day ride away, Taylor wrote, "No doubt you have heard of the visit of my Chief to Richmond. I need hardly tell you that I declined to accompany him, which declination on my part was however perfectly unnecessary as he hadn't the faintest idea of taking me with him." On another such occasion, Taylor begged off accompanying Lee, only to be attached to Jefferson Davis as the president rode back to the capital, an event Taylor found excruciating, as he considered Davis an even more unpleasant bird than his Old Man.

When Taylor went off on an excursion of his own, he was always anxious about his reception when he returned. On August 15, 1864, for example, he wrote Bettie, "I cannot even go out to dinner without being aroused from the table to return to camp as 'General Lee wishes to see Col. Taylor.' " On this occasion, Taylor returned with his nose obviously out of joint, and then "the General and I lost temper with each other." Taylor blamed himself—"I am so distressingly fiery, so lacking in humility"—and he indicated that, as usual, he had been the one to blow up, while the boss remained steely and cold, thus making Taylor appear to have been the one at fault. "I couldn't help it however; he is so unreasonable and provoking at times. I might serve him for ten years to come and couldn't *love* him at the end." The next morning, apparently without saying anything, Lee "presented me with a peach, so I have been somewhat appeased. You know that is my favorite fruit," a preference that Lee certainly knew as well. "Ah! but he is a queer old genius. I suppose it is so with all great men." Lee doubtlessly intended this gesture just as Taylor took it, as an act of reconciliation, although a few words approaching apology might have diminished the distance Lee maintained by refusing to say anything overtly kind to his subaltern, which might have muted his hard mastery.

Taylor realized that Lee practiced self-denial at least as much

as denial to others. On November 7, 1864, Taylor had taken possession of a fine house for the Lee staff and "had his room nicely
cleaned out and arranged, with a cheerful fire, &c, &c," to which
the general barely responded. "It was entirely *too* pleasant for
him," Taylor concluded, "for he is never so uncomfortable as
when comfortable." Demanding an almost inhuman level of service from others, Lee was the first to don the hair shirt, as Taylor
understood, if with a certain ironic annoyance.

After years of admiration, resentment, fear, and feelings of
inadequacy, Taylor began to assert himself a bit more, to risk an-
gering the chief without quite such paralyzing anxiety. To take
one wonderful story, in late November 1864 the proprietor of
the splendid Edge Hill plantation offered his house to Taylor for
Lee and his staff. "After fixing the General" in the best front bedroom, "I concluded I would have to occupy one of the miserable
little back rooms," Taylor wrote, "but the gentleman of the house
hinted that I might take the parlour and this decided me . . . and
here I am finely fixed . . . with piano, sofas, pictures, rocking
chair, &c, &c." Probably wondering what Lee would say about
his choice of rooms, Taylor was not to be disappointed. "I believe
the General was pleased with his room and on entering mine remarked 'Ah! You are finely fixed; couldn't you find *any other
room*'—No—said I, but *this will do*. I can make myself tolerably
comfortable here." He was struck dumb with amazement at my
impudence & soon vanished."

Taylor had learned to cope with the general's wrath, simply
not letting it get to him so deeply. Thus, on December 18, 1864,
he went off to dinner, anticipating and accepting the response
this would arouse in Lee. "Returned home to be snubbed by the
General for having dared to absent myself from my office, completed more work than I care to do on a Sunday, smoked the
pipe of peace, concluded that I was on friendly terms with all
the world, including the General, and settled into a state of ab-

solute . . . contentment." Two could play the game of sarcasm and withdrawal; as Lee's vexation and his cold responses rarely varied, Taylor finally learned how to endure and even manage his chief.

His bluff finally called, Lee could then approach Taylor with a bit of solicitude. Indeed, during the last Christmas of the war Lee proposed that Taylor spend the holidays with his mother and sweetheart in Richmond, and while he was absent actually took note of how much work he expected from Taylor. "And since my return," wrote Taylor, "has insisted on dividing the labour. . . . He told me he had often thought I had too much to do and he did not wish me to do all the work" and therefore gave Taylor an aide.

Lee certainly knew the end of the war was approaching, and he seemed to have tried to make amends. As a matter of the heart, however, it was too late—Taylor could not warm up to him, if that is what Lee wanted. In fact, Taylor had come to have his doubts about Lee, thinking of him as too conventional and unimaginative to strike out in some daring new manner of warfare as the times required. On February 20, 1865, he wrote Bettie, "Oh for a man of iron nerve and will to lead us! . . . There can be no trifling, no hesitation now without ruin. Our old Chief is too law abiding, too slow, too retiring for these times." Catching himself in nearly treasonous sentiments, Taylor backtracked. "Nevertheless he is the best we have, certainly the greatest captain and in his own safe & sure way will yet, I trust, carry us through the greatest trial yet."

By this time, Taylor did not seek to deny his resentment of Lee's haughty ways even when he was trying to think generously about him. Searching for a means to obtain a furlough for Bettie's cousin John, he figured that the only way would be to work through Lee's son Fitzhugh, whose approval, Taylor wrote, "may possibly accomplish what I desire, as he, you know, is one of the *royal family* & of course his action should be sustained."[6] Taylor never felt accepted within a circle Lee reserved only for his kin, nor did he believe that Lee was open enough to share a bond of genuine trust and affection.

With his excellent ear for his chief's language, Taylor, even more than Alexander, gave a close reading of Lee's character when he was under continual wartime pressure. Clearly, Lee was demanding, aloof, and irritable, and yet he also kept his temper under close guard, almost always using sarcasm and the cold shoulder rather than shouting and other forms of manifest rage. Anger was sinful, growing from pride, and Lee dampened himself down so fully that few could penetrate his reserve deeply enough to see what lay beneath the placid surface.

When Lee went into battle, it was another matter. Here, those closest to him recognized the unmistakable symptoms of "rage militaire" in Lee, for whom release began only when combat was approaching. Beyond the twitch of the head and the snatch at the ear that he exhibited at such times, several commentators remarked on an aura that overcame and suffused Lee's face. Francis Lawley, an English journalist, noted of Lee going into one battle, "No man who, at the terrible moment, saw his flashing eyes and sternly-set lips, is ever likely to forget them . . . the light of battle . . . flaming in his eyes."[7] Several others commented on the unverbalized rage in Lee's eyes. Some profound passion overcame the warrior Lee at such moments— both as a response to enormous danger and as a spur to action.

And if the enemy was on the ropes, Lee insisted that his subordinates go in ruthlessly for the kill. When, for example, one of his young commanders allowed part of a Union army to escape after a victory over them, Lee turned on him, shouting, "that is the way you young man always do. You allow these people to get away. . . . Go after them and damage them all you can."[8]

Battle allowed Lee to unleash his deepest passions for perhaps the only times in his life. Here was the place where raw emotion emerged from that bastion of self-control in a manner he could consider legitimate. Not that he failed to direct the flow of battle as best he could, but he positively relished destruction in this one great theater of risk and death while in mortal combat with the enemy. Perhaps this was the central cause of Lee's undoubted audacity; he courted and enjoyed such elemental confrontations.

As is true of many warriors, Lee could even discover in battle a sensibility of the sublime lying on the far side of anger, an almost loving passion for destructiveness. To give a stunning example, as he watched the Union army march in serried ranks into a veritable slaughterhouse at Fredericksburg on December 13, 1862—a battle in which Lee's army inflicted approximately 12,600 casualties at a cost of only 5,000, one of the most one-sided battles in the war—Lee was reputed on fairly good authority to have made his famous remark, "It is well that war is so terrible—we should grow too fond of it!" This was to relish the prospect of the killing of thousands of the enemy, to enter fully into the spirit of war, where destructiveness took on its own unspeakable beauty.[9]

To reach the goal of such satisfying victory, organization, subordination, and control were necessary, and whatever may have been Lee's reputation as a kind man, even greater was it as a disciplinarian. He was unapologetic about his consistent demands for hard work and duty, something he felt was lacking in the Southern mentality, which he often saw as jury-rigged out of romantic and slapdash flights of fancy. In response, he could be the sternest Roman general of them all, as he was right after he took command when he wrote Jefferson Davis,

> Our people are opposed to work. Our troops, officers, community & press. All ridicule & resist it. It is the

very means by which McClellan has & is advancing. Why should we leave to him the whole advantage of labour? Combined with valour, fortitude & boldness, of which we have our fair proportion, it should lead us to success. What carried the Roman soldiers into all countries, but this happy combination. The evidences of their labour last to this day. There is nothing so military as labour, & nothing so important to an army as to save the lives of its soldiers.[10]

Lee was in part doubtless responding to attacks on him in the press for insufficient dash, but even after his own valor, fortitude, and boldness became clear, he continued to insist on an unending regime of discipline.

The Army of Northern Virginia never achieved enough order to please its commander, who throughout the war was obsessed with desertion, malingering, and straggling—all characteristics of amateur mass armies. "I fear . . . estrays . . . is one of the evils resulting from the laxity of discipline of the army," Lee wrote to General Lafayette McLaws on July 25, 1862, as he requested suggestions from McLaws about how to strengthen the power of regimental and brigade commanders. "It will require the united efforts of all to remedy. . . . Should any particular cases of misconduct be reported, examples will be made of the offenders."[11] He wrote dozens of such messages to his subordinates over the next three years.

Both singly and in groups, the men seemed to Lee quite inventive in their shirking. Commenting on one South Carolina regiment to General James Longstreet on August 1, 1862, Lee wrote that when it came to preventing nighttime desertions, at least in certain regiments, pickets were "useless . . . and it can only be accomplished by employing a guard around the encampment. I desire that you will take every necessary step to enforce discipline." This armed camp had guards pointing their rifles inward toward potential deserters rather than outward against the enemy, and presumably "every necessary step" in this case would include using those rifles, as well as courts-martial and firing squads, to prevent flight.

Men in this regiment as in others also used wily legalistic arguments to try to escape back home, Lee was well aware. Some junior officers were simply writing their own discharge papers, obtained by "fraudulent and false representations," thus exercising a power reserved to Lee, he wrote Longstreet. If a man claimed to be over thirty-five and thus eligible for discharge, the officer writing the papers had to be able to certify that age legally. As for the eighty men who alleged they had been enlisted only for service in western Virginia and thus merited furloughs and transportation back home, this could only have been the "assertion of the men themselves" and should have been dismissed out of hand by the regimental commander. Evidently, these men had gotten their way, and their absence was not reported until the day after they decamped, indicating to Lee a habitual and "exceedingly lax state of things in that command, inviting the serious attention of their superiors."[12]

After the triumph at the Second Battle of Manassas, as his army marched northward into Maryland in September 1862, Lee's greatest concerns were straggling, looting of Unionist civilians, feigning illness, and outright deserting by that considerable number of men who composed the "cowards of the army." Lee wrote President Davis on September 7, "The discipline of the army, which from the manner of its organization, its constant occupation and hard duty was naturally defective, has not been improved by the forced marches and hard service. . . . The material of which it is composed is the best in the world, and if properly disciplined and instructed" would defeat any enemy. "Nothing can surpass the gallantry and intelligence of the main body, but there are individuals, from their back-wardness in duty, tardiness of movement, and neglect of orders, who do it no credit."[13] Enough bad apples threatened to rot the barrel.

Following the strategic defeat at Sharpsburg, Lee went so far as to blame discreditable troops for the loss. "The usual casualties of battle have diminished [the army's] ranks, but its numbers have been greatly decreased by desertion and straggling. This was the main cause of its retiring from Maryland, as it was unable to cope with advantage with the numerous host of the enemy." Whatever other shortcomings might have contributed to this single major reversal during Lee's annus mirabilis, including defects in his own generalship, Lee subordinated to the problem of indiscipline among the men: "Straggling and . . . depredations . . . are so discreditable and prejudicial to the efficiency and discipline of the army." Lee was still complaining thus to Longstreet six weeks after the battle.[14] Like a latter-day Puritan, Lee tended to use human sin as the universal explanation of failure.

Systematic and institutional response—as opposed to merely complaining—was in order, Lee believed, although the remedies were not so clear. As would a tough plantation manager, Lee proposed treating malingering soldiers like recalcitrant slaves. Generally, Lee appeared to believe that "inefficient" officers lacking in mastery were to blame for allowing ordinary foot soldiers to get away with malingering in all its forms and that indiscipline "arises not from a spirit of disobedience, but from ignorance." Thus, several times, he urged upon the Confederate authorities a vast strengthening of the inspector general's office, with a much stronger and permanent presence in the field. This professional cadre, Lee hoped, would set the right tone and enforce the right rules, in tandem with a reformed adjutant general's office that could try and punish offenders more efficiently. This "corps of officers [will] teach others their duty, see to the observances of orders, & to the regularity & precision of all movements" and educate amateur officers who were by nature, Lee chose to believe, not disobedient but ignorant. Interestingly enough, Lee mentioned the French armed services as his model in this department. He and the gentlemen in Richmond—and in Washington for that matter—were aware that European military staff work was far more sophisticated than what was practiced in both the Union and Confederate armies. Whether such systematic discipline could be either invented whole cloth or effectively imposed on citizen armies during wartime was another matter. Nevertheless, Lee, a gentleman of the planter class and a professional soldier with an engineer's bent, explained not only Sharpsburg but the threat of a general defeat on a lack of control from the top of the Confederate army, which was insufficiently indoctrinated and trained to effectively discipline the inherently disorderly masses of enlisted men.[15]

Short of an unlikely systematization of command, Lee could only propose strengthening the control of whatever authority was at hand. Quite frequently, he urged his corps commanders to tighten their ships, and he promised to back them up even if at times they might err on the side of being arbitrary and authoritarian. In one not so unusual case, after Stonewall Jackson had arrested one of his officers on shaky cause, Lee wrote in Jackson's defense that he would not provide a judicial investigation of the case after the fact. "The exercise of this power may sometimes appear harsh, and in some cases may actually be so. But the power itself is one too important and essential to the maintenance of discipline to be denied because it may be abused."[16] In this case and in many others, Lee argued that examples of discipline be set whenever possible. It is impossible to reconstruct how many deserters were shot under these circumstances—although Jackson in particular was well known for trying and shooting many of them—nor how many other punishments were exacted for various forms of malingering, nor even whether Lee always knew when senior officers abused their powers. The predisposition was not for leniency but for toughness, even at the risk of arbitrariness and injustice.

The manner in which Lee could store up and finally express a grudge on the issue of indiscipline is evident in a special order he gave in October 1864 to disband an unnamed unit as a final response to years of what he considered unforgivable group behavior. "The —— battalion, for cowardly conduct on every battlefield from Gettysburg to the present time, is unworthy of a place in the Army of Northern Virginia. It will be marched to its Division Headquarters Wednesday afternoon at 4 o'clock and surrender its colors and be marched to the rear in disgrace." Lee could imagine no punishment more severe than this dishonoring and public shaming of an entire regiment. "The General commanding the Army of Northern Virginia regrets that there are some brave officers and men belonging to this organization who must share in its common disgrace, but the good of the service requires it, and they must bear it like brave soldiers." The weight of Lee's judgment went against the guilty, even if the innocent were swept up in the dragnet. Lee was rarely this overtly angry or judgmental, but that he held his army to high standards was clearly demonstrated in this significant case, in which he did not hold his negative emotions close to his chest.[17]

During his great string of victories, overwhelming pride and a certain egotism previously quite uncharacteristic of him began to appear in Lee's commentaries on the war. Describing in his official report the victory at Glendale on June 30, 1862, during the Seven Days Battle, Lee argued that "could the other commands have cooperated in this action the result would have proved most disastrous to the enemy." And, after McClellan had retreated toward the protection of his navy at Harrison's Landing following the battle at Malvern Hill during the night of July 2, "leaving the ground cluttered with his dead and wounded," Lee concluded that "under ordinary circumstances the Federal Army should have been destroyed. Its escape [owed primarily to] the want of correct and timely information."[18] In this report, written eight eventful months after the battle, with negative events reduced in his memory, Lee ignored the fact that Malvern Hill had been a poorly organized and bloody Confederate defeat, after which McClellan's lieutenants had unsuccessfully urged him to counterattack. Indeed, the notion of a total victory that would vaporize the enemy army in one battle remained Lee's unrealistic goal right through Gettysburg. Other generals on both sides also harbored what can only be considered a Napoleonic grand illusion of total victory, but Lee was remarkable in the tenacity with which he held this belief, which both grew out of his "audacity" and reinforced it.

In his general orders thanking his troops for their conduct at the smashing triumph of Fredericksburg, Lee approached immodest boasting, at least by his standards, barely remembering to thank the Almighty for the victory:

> The immense army of the enemy . . . gave battle in its own time, and on ground of its own selection. It was encountered by less than 20,000 of this brave army, and its columns crushed and broken, hurled back at every point with such fearful slaughter, that escape from entire destruction became the boast of those who had advanced in full confidence of victory. That this great result was achieved with a [small] loss . . . only augments the admiration with which the com-

manding general regards the prowess of his troops, and increases the gratitude to Him who has given us this victory.

By this point, Lee had internalized a belief that his army was unstoppable, although the war still had to be fought to its conclusion. The Army of Northern Virginia had come to embody the best of the Confederate nation, in the opinion of its commander. "The war has not yet ended. The enemy is still numerous and strong, and her country demands of the army a renewal of its heroic efforts in her behalf. Nobly has it responded to her call in the past, and she will never appeal in vain to its courage and patriotism." Lee sensed that 1863 ought to bring about that great and final victory—Fredericksburg writ large. "The signal manifestations of Divine mercy that have distinguished the eventful and glorious campaign of the year just closing give assurance of hope that, under the guidance of the same Almighty hand, the coming year will insure the safety, peace, and happiness of our beloved country, and add new lustre to the already imperishable name of the Army of Northern Virginia."[19]

Chancellorsville, Lee's most daring victory, dramatically heightened his sense that his army was destined for imminent triumph: "The dangers and difficulties . . . under God's blessing, were surmounted by the fortitude and valor of our army. The conduct of the troops cannot be too highly praised. Attacking largely superior numbers in strongly entrenched positions, their heroic courage overcame every obstacle of nature and art and achieved a triumph most honorable to our arms."[20] Lee seemed to overlook the fact that the battle really was won when, by almost miraculous accident, a local farmer disclosed a road through the woods that allowed Stonewall Jackson to pounce on the enemy army and roll up its flank. Additionally, Joseph Hooker had failed to commit a large portion of his army to the battle, retreating in great confusion instead. Rather than drawing realistically modest conclusions, Lee almost asserted that his army could win any battle against the Union enemy, no matter how numerous or well entrenched it might be. The power of superior will, not brilliant (and lucky) tactics against a weakly commanded opposition, was the lesson Lee chose to derive from Chancellorsville.

There was something in the rhythm of this string of postvictory pronouncements that, in an additive way, suggested invincibility. Many other historians have commented that Lee at war was "Virginia-centric," that he downplayed the importance of other theaters, particularly the western, where the Confederacy first began to lose the war. Lee himself argued to Jefferson Davis that by augmenting pressure in the east he would prevent the Union from siphoning off troops and supplies for their western campaigns, thus linking the two regions. Beyond that, it was clear at the time that the Richmond–Washington corridor was indeed in both political and dramaturgical terms the main theater of the Civil War and that total victory there would have meant winning the war. Indeed, as the last major act in the war, the Union finally took Richmond and caused Lee to surrender in April 1865. Lee and his men became fixated on this drama, as was natural given their elemental struggle, and they grew to believe that they could bring it off against all odds, predicating their faith on their almost uninterrupted experience of victory against extreme adversity after Lee had taken charge. Gone, at least in this context, was most of Lee's stoic fatalism and Christian resignation. His martial spirits had soared, and he was expressing a belief in himself and his army of an activist sort to which he had never been given. That he did so was, of course, under the circumstances, only human. He had formed a bond with his men and they with him, in a solidarity that amounted to a collective if never a democratic faith.

Also human in this context, if a great departure from his normal humility, was a striking and endemic contempt for the enemy that also entered Lee's vocabulary for the first time during his great year of victories. Undoubtedly reflecting and amplifying attitudes widespread in his army, Lee despised generals Pope, Burnside, and Hooker, whom he defeated in turn, after Lincoln had cashiered McClellan and searched for a general who could at long last best Lee.

In an only half-joking letter, Lee wrote Mildred that her brother Rob was "off with Jackson & I hope will catch Pope and [the Unionist Lee relative] Louis Marshall. I could forgive the latter for fighting against us, if he had not joined such a miscreant as Pope."[21] For Lee, who avoided ritual insult, that was strong language indeed, whatever its context.

After Ambrose Burnside took charge of the Union army, Lee awaited his attack from carefully chosen high ground on the south side of the Rappahannock River behind Fredericksburg. Burnside insulted and infuriated him, as he was preparing to offer battle, by demanding the surrender of the city according to his timetable, "[Burnside] said if it was not yielded by 5 p.m. they would shell the town at 9 a.m. today. . . . I was moving out the women & children all last night & today. It was a piteous sight." When Burnside's attack finally came, it was a badly organized charge of one regiment after another into the teeth of the impregnable Confederate position. Three days later, after Burnside withdrew his army back over the river under cover of nightfall, Lee wrote to Mary, expressing intense contempt of the enemy: "I had my suspicions that they might retire during the night, but could not believe they would relinquish their purpose after all their boasting & preparations, & when I say that the latter is equal to the former, you will have some idea of its magnitude. . . . They went as they came, in the night. They suffered heavily as far as the battle went, but it did not go far enough to satisfy me." After that fairly virulent declaration of destructiveness, Lee continued, generalizing toward what he hoped would be a successful conclusion to the war through total victory, "The contest will have now to be renewed, but on what field I cannot say. As regards the liberation of the people, I wish to progress in it as far as I can." Even four months later, when he wrote his final report of the Battle of Fredericksburg, Lee could not conceal his contempt for Burnside, and indeed for the Union Army of the Potomac as a whole. "The attack . . . had been so easily repulsed and by so small a part of our army, that it was not supposed the enemy would limit his efforts to an attempt which, in view of the magnitude of his preparations and the extent of his force, seemed to be comparatively insignificant." With a lighter flicker of disdain, Lee had written to Mildred on Christmas Day, "I am . . . happy in the knowledge that Genl Burnside & army will not eat their promised Xmas dinner in Richmond today. I trust they never will."[22]

During the five-month *sitzkrieg* after Fredericksburg and before Chancellorsville, Joseph Hooker, who took command of the Union army, boasted of his prowess while he raided Confederate territory in a manner Lee considered both foolishly ineffective and uncivilized, as it damaged only civilians rather than Lee's army. After several weeks of these raids, Lee wrote to Agnes that "Genl Hooker is obliged to do something. I do not know what it will be. He is playing the Chinese game. Trying what frightening will do. He runs out his guns, starts his wagons & troops up and down the river, & creates an excitement generally. Our men look on in wonder, give a cheer, & all again subsides 'in statu quo ante bellum.' " And after another month of Hooker's maneuvers, Lee wrote to his daughter-in-law, disparaging Union technological advances along with their generalship, "We are up to our eyes in mud now & have but little comfort. Mr. Hooker looms very large across the river. He has two balloons up in the day & one at night. I hope he is gratified at what he sees."

By late April, concluding that Hooker amounted only to a low parody of a general, Lee could barely contain his amused disdain for him. In this mood, he wrote to his wife. "The enemy is making various demonstrations either to amuse themselves or deceive us, but so far they have done us little harm. Last week they infested"—like vermin, as it were—"all the fords of the upper Rappahannock . . . Tuesday they abandoned them." They subsequently feinted down the river, "formed in line of battle, threw out skirmishers, advanced their artillery, brought up their wagons, built up large fires, & after dark commenced chopping, cutting & sawing as if working for life till midnight, when the noise ceased & at daylight had all disappeared." Peculiar wasting of energy characterized a buffoonish enemy. "I suppose they thought we were frightened out of all propriety & required refreshment." Then the next day "a party crossed at Port Royal in their pontoon boats, stole from our citizens all they could get and recrossed before we could get them. Their expeditions will serve as texts to the writers for the *Herald, Tribune* & *Times* for brilliant accounts of grand Union victories & great rejoicings of the saints of the [Republican] party." Lee anticipated that when actual battle came, he would fight the real fight and, against such a paper tiger of an enemy, certainly emerge victorious. "I hope God in His own time will give us more substantial cause for rejoicing & thankfulness."[23]

When Hooker finally launched his real attack in early May at Chancellorsville, Lee's army, although outnumbered two to one, won its most spectacular victory of the war. After this event, against such a contemptible enemy, with such a tested and superior force, Lee had come to believe that the final battle could not be long distant. Surely, coming after so many other victories, Chancellorsville must have been a divine signal.

Surely Armageddon was at hand, when the Army of Northern Virginia would battle for the Lord and win total victory.

Lee had in part become apocalyptic—nearly mystical—in this belief in one great and final blow, but he had also begun to advance, for the first time, a political understanding of the war, quite unlike his previous apolitical belief in duty. He augmented audacity with this political understanding.

Even before Chancellorsville, at least in private correspondence with his wife, Lee had started to develop a political analysis of what victory might require. Lee began his discussion with Stoic incantations familiar to him, though he asserted that victory was seemingly in his grasp, an un-Stoic, unresigned conclusion. "If our people are true to our cause & not so devoted to themselves & their own aggrandizement, I think our success will be certain. We will have to suffer & must suffer to the end. But it will come out all right." And then Lee moved into a far more modern political analysis. "If successful this year, next fall there will be a great change in public opinion at the North. The Republicans will be destroyed & I think the friends of peace will become so strong that the next administration will go in on that basis."[24] In what was to come, Lee acted on the basis of a clearly political grand strategy, quite appropriate to a civil war within a democracy, in which midwar elections in the Union could well decide the outcome of the whole struggle. An enormous enough victory would demoralize the Northern public, who, first in the midterm elections of 1862 and then in the 1864 presidential contest, would turn out their war party and elect the Democrats who would sue for peace on the basis of Southern independence, a plausible scenario. At times, Lee was even more impatient, anticipating a total destruction of the Union army in one decisive campaign. In this mode, Lee was prophetlike, standing at Armageddon for the Confederacy and the Lord.

To be sure, Lee was not naive about the odds. He fully real-

ized that he was winning his battles at a great cost in irreplaceable manpower, while the Northern army, with its larger
population base, could continue to grow. Again, before Chancellorsville, he wrote to James A. Seddon, the Confederate secretary
of war, "While the spirit of our soldiers is unabated, their ranks
have been greatly thinned by the casualties of battle and the diseases of the camp. . . . The great increase of the enemy's forces
will augment the disparity of numbers to such a degree that victory, if attained, can only be achieved by a terrible expenditure
of the most precious blood of the country." But then he placed
sacrifice in a political rather than a Christian framework. "The
lives of our soldiers are too precious to be sacrificed in the attainment of successes that inflict no loss upon the enemy beyond the actual loss in battle."[25]

Therefore, it was on to Gettysburg. The enormous pride and
contempt for the enemy born from a year of victories, with
Sharpsburg forgotten and Chancellorsville the final proof of superiority, coupled to his political imperatives, led Lee to enter
the maelstrom. He stripped Richmond of most of its defending
forces and proceeded northward, reputedly telling several of his
generals, "we shall probably meet the enemy and fight a great
battle, and if God gives us victory, the war will be over and we
shall achieve the recognition of our independence."[26] This was,
of course, a high-risk political and military strategy, an extension of one that had already proved very costly, but Lee was profoundly convinced that his army could pay the necessary price
and do the deed. In this belief he had the support of his soldiers
and of the Southern people, to whom there seemed to have been
an unfolding and unstoppable cumulative logic to victorious
events. This was an unusual emotional period for Lee, a kind of
prolonged rage militaire, during which he became convinced
that God rode with him and that the fates had been transcended.

As he invaded the North, whatever his ultimate goal, Lee subdued his language but not his implicit political message. To Jefferson Davis, he put the politics of conquest mildly, almost as if they were to be a natural outcome of the military campaign he was unleashing. Lee told Davis that it was time to face the growing disparity between the sizes of the two armies, with the Confederate forces weakening relative to the Union: Now was the time to go for broke, not later. "Under these circumstances we should neglect no honorable means of dividing and weakening our enemies that they may feel some of the difficulties experienced by ourselves. It seems to me that the most effectual mode of accomplishing this object, now within our reach, is to give all the encouragement we can, consistently with the truth, to the rising peace party of the north."[27] Lee was instructing Davis about the propaganda front, but for him the greatest propaganda would be the deed.

Despite his embrace of realpolitik, Lee also instructed his troops that they were a Christian army, unlike the Union barbarians who had assaulted Southern civilians and polluted Virginia. There should be no more instances of "straggling and looting" as there had been during the Sharpsburg campaign. He reminded his men

> that they have in keeping the yet unsullied reputation of the army, and that the duties exacted of us by civilization and Christianity are not less obligatory in the country of the enemy than in our own. . . . No greater disgrace could befall the army, and through it our whole people, than the perpetration of the barbarous outrages upon the unarmed [civilians] that have marked the course of the enemy in our own country [for which] we cannot take vengeance . . . without low-

ering ourselves . . . and offending against Him to whom vengeance belongeth, without whose favor and support our efforts must prove in vain.[28]

Such a Christian army, purified through noble action, could, after it was victorious, assure the Northern people that the Confederacy would be fully trustworthy as a neighboring country with which they could live in peace. Indeed, such a Christian army, representative of a superior version of American civilization, might enlighten the people of the North and lead them toward reformation of their own heathen land into a truly Christian commonwealth. Surely the time had come, *our* time had come, which was *His* time, too.*

---

* The prior September, before marching up into Maryland, there had been a greater disparity between what Lee had told Davis and what he had proclaimed in public as his war aims. To Davis he wrote that his army was "not properly equipped" for a full-scale invasion, but that "we cannot afford to be idle, and though weaker than our opponents . . . must endeavour to harass, if we cannot destroy them." But in a declaration to the people of Maryland, he trumpeted that he had come "to aid you in throwing off this foreign [yoke]," ending the "wrongs and outrages that have long been inflicted upon the citizens" of that naturally Southern, slave-holding state. Lee may have been of two minds, both the realist who wrote to Davis and the strident liberator of his proclamation. In either event, the Lee who marched into Pennsylvania the next year had far greater expectations (Lee to Davis, near Dranesville, September 3, 1862, in D&M, 292–93; Lee to "The People of Maryland," Near Fredricktown, September 8, 1862, in D&M, 299–300).

Chapter 8

DEFEAT AT GETTYSBURG

*A*ll the military élan that the Army of Northern Virginia had accumulated during its year of great victories could not carry it across the powerfully entrenched high ground the Union held at Gettysburg nor make the uncoordinated Confederate attacks any more viable. Gettysburg rather resembled Fredericksburg in reverse. The frontal-charge offensive, particularly when conducted piecemeal, always lost in Civil War battles, as Gettysburg demonstrated once again. Nor was Lee's hand or any other form of overall guidance clearly apparent during the vacillating events of the final two days of the battle, except when Lee sent General Pickett's men on their disastrous charge. In addition, Lee squandered the opportunity to move to another field, where the Union would have been compelled to attack, as the Confederate army was so deep in Union territory. James Longstreet was right in offering this line of reasoning to Lee before the battle, which he did with great clarity. But Lee may have been transfixed by the triumphant precedent of Chancellorsville, where he had been so badly outnumbered, while at Gettysburg his army about equaled that of the Union Army of the Potomac, for one of the few times during the war. Although no one has been able to reconstruct Lee's thinking during this battle, it seems clear enough that his mis-reading of the lessons of Chancellorsville, his sense of destiny, his pride, his contempt for the enemy, and his aggressiveness carried him into one battle too many.

Lee's complex, contradictory, and evolving reactions after the defeat merit close analysis. It was not so simple a matter as taking the blame for the defeat upon himself, as the legend and a legion of ex-Confederate admirers—including Douglas South-all Freeman in the 1930s and many later writers and filmmak-ers—would have it. When one subjects the sequence of Lee's ex post facto statements about the battle to dense scrutiny, they de-pict not a perfect saint of self-abnegation but a troubled man trying to come to terms with a major defeat by positing a variety of exculpatory explanations. As events receded, memory and need rapidly reshaped the searing reality.

The report of Lee at Gettysburg that most closely ap-proaches the authenticity of a reliable eyewitness account was written by Lieutenant Colonel Arthur J. L. Fremantle of the Coldstream Guards. Attached to Lee as an observer at the time, Fremantle published his journal in England a few months later. After Pickett's survivors retreated to the Confederate lines, Lee rode among them with a "placid and cheerful" face, as was ha-bitual to him, Fremantle reported, and encouraged the returning soldiers with such words as "all this will come right in the end: we'll talk it over afterwards; but in the mean time all good men must rally. We want all good and true men just now to bind up [their] wounds and take up a musket." Many of the men took off their hats and cheered Lee, Fremantle wrote. Apparently com-posed with his men, Lee shared his sorrow with the English-man: "This has been a sad day for us, Colonel—a sad day; but we can't expect always to gain victories." When General Cadmus Marcellus Wilcox rode up to Lee, "almost crying [due] to the state of his brigade," Fremantle recounted, Lee shook his hand

and told him cheerfully, "Never mind, General, *all this has been MY fault*—it is I that have lost this fight, and you must help me out of it in the best way you can." It was unclear whether Lee was referring to the carnage of the whole battle or just to Wilcox's portion of it. But taken altogether, Fremantle felt a profound admiration for Lee's expressions of self-control on such a dark occasion and for absorbing, as it were, the "whole weight of the repulse."[1]

There is no evidence to corroborate the legend that Lee rode among the common soldiers and confessed his failings—that grief he shared with one general officer only. It would not have been in his aristocratic character, nor would it have made good sense in terms of discipline to have made such a confession to all and sundry, an act Lee would have found unacceptably humiliating. Nor was this taking of the blame anything but Lee's immediate response to the worst afternoon of the battle and to the necessity of rallying his discouraged general, a process he never repeated. What followed in the ensuing days and months was an agonized compound of regret, deflection, denial, self-reproach, blaming others, and an underlying sense of irretrievable loss.

Lee's first reports to Jefferson Davis were written out of numbness and anxiety for the immediate safety of his army—a phase that lasted until his army had completed its withdrawal into Virginia on July 14. The day after the final assault up Cemetery Ridge, he told the president that on July 2, the second day of the battle, "we attempted to dislodge the enemy, and though we gained some ground, we were unable to get possession of his position." On July 3, during a "more extensive attack . . . the works on the enemy's extreme right & left were taken, but his numbers were so great and his position so commanding, that our troops were compelled to relinquish their advantage and retire. . . . The enemy suffered severely in these operations, but our own loss

has not been light." Defeat no longer appeared here in bold relief, as it had immediately after the battle, but was softened in
rather distancing and abstract prose.[2]

Three days later, Lee wrote Davis stressing his successful
tactical withdrawal from the battlefield, using a euphemism to
describe the results of the battle itself. Lee explained that his
July 4 letter had "informed you of the unsuccessful issue of our
final attack on the enemy in the rear of Gettysburg. Finding the
position too strong to be carried, and being much hindered in
collecting necessary supplies for the army by the numerous bodies of local and other troops which watched the passes, I determined to withdraw to the west side of the mountains. This has
been safely accomplished with great labour." This literary rendering of recent events suggested that a sort of equivalent to a
victory had been accomplished following that earlier "unsuccessful issue." The same day, despite hearing that his son
Fitzhugh had been captured by the enemy, Lee wrote to his wife,
"We are all well & bear our labours & hardships manfully. Our
noble men are cheerful and confident."[3]

By July 8, within this renewed and ritualized effort to regain
unblemished self-control, while asking for all possible reinforce-
ments from the president, Lee wrote Davis that "though reduced
in numbers by the hardships & battles through which it has
passed [this army's] condition is good and its confidence unimpaired." Deeply concerned that the Union would attack his
weakened army, which was backed up against the Potomac,
Lee was summoning his deep reserve of calmness and self-
discipline. Storms that had already put the river "beyond ford-
ing stage" were unrelenting and "I shall therefore have to accept
battle if the enemy offers it, whether I wish to or not, and [with]
the result in the hands of the Sovereign Ruler of the Universe,
and known to Him only, I deem it proper to make every arrange-
ment in our power to meet any emergency."

Lee waited for five more days in considerable trepidation, lest his wounded and cornered army, lacking any route for retreat, be overwhelmed and destroyed. He could not have avoided noticing the immensely long wagon train bringing thousands of groaning wounded Confederate soldiers southward, although nowhere did he comment directly on their immense suffering. Instead, he maintained his fortitude by reiterating his belief in both "the blessing of heaven" and "the courage and fortitude of the army," as he wrote Davis on July 10; on the next day, he issued general orders charging his troops to maintain their courage in the face of the most difficult battle, which they all anticipated. Admitting that the "fierce and sanguinary battle" they had fought already had not been "attended with the success that has hitherto crowned your efforts," he reminded them nevertheless that their "heroic spirit . . . has commanded the respect of your enemies, the gratitude of your country, and the admiration of humankind." Now once more into the fray, he urged each of them, for "all that makes life worth having—the freedom of his country, the honor of his people, and the security of his home. . . . Soldiers! your old enemy is before you! Win from him honors worthy of your righteous cause—worthy of your comrades dead on so many illustrious fields."[4]

Privately, Lee was a good deal more sober. On July 12, he wrote to Mary Lee that "our success at Gettysburg was not . . . great. In fact, we failed to drive our enemy from his position" and have withdrawn to the Potomac. "Had the river not unexpectedly risen, all would be well with us. But God in his all wise Providence willed otherwise. . . . I trust that our merciful God, our only hope & refuge, will not desert us in our hour of need, but will deliver us by His almighty hand."[5] By the following night, the rains stopped, the river ebbed, and Lee's chosen people forded back to the promised land of the South. General

George Gordon Meade had been more responsible for this outcome than God, because he delayed any attack until it was too late, much to the fury of Abraham Lincoln and Northern public opinion. (The Army of the Potomac, nearly as devastated in victory as the Confederates in defeat, had been psychologically unprepared to make an immediate attack.) In any event, returning home to Virginia without having to make a stand with a swollen river at the back of his weakened army relieved Lee's deepest fears.

The potential catastrophe after Gettysburg created such enormous immediate anxieties that Lee had no time or energy for much reflection on the battle itself. He suppressed his sense of defeat while focusing on other immediate problems. Self-reproach or harsh criticism of others would have been counterproductive in such a situation. As events began to recede a bit, however, Lee reframed the memory of Gettysburg into a tactical setback from which his army could and would rally because its honor and courage remained intact.

Once he had regained breathing space, Lee amplified his denial of the degree of defeat at Gettysburg. From the Virginia side, he wrote home, "The army has returned to Virginia dear Mary. Its return is rather sooner than I had originally contemplated, but having accomplished what I proposed . . . relieving [Virginia] of the presence of the enemy & drawing his army north of the Potomac, I determined to recross the . . . river." In this analysis, Gettysburg was a simple raid north, and the Confederacy could press on to fight another day. "We are well," he wrote, although it was unclear in this context who "we" were. "I hope we will yet be able to damage our adversaries when they meet us, & that all will go right with us. That it should be so, we must implore the forgiveness of God for our sins, & the continuance of His blessings."[6] Christian resignation, which had been relatively absent from Lee's string of great victories, now reap-peared in especially fervent form, with that overtone of arrogance conversely diminished.

The slaughter at Gettysburg could not vanish from Lee's mind, in part because over the next few weeks Confederate citizens began to react negatively to its enormity, and in part because Lee could not simply dismiss such an event and move on, engineerlike, to the next problem. He became quite defensive, as would have anyone but a saint.

At times, Lee argued that no set of mortals could have done all that the Southern people had expected of his army. For example, he wrote his wife on July 26, "The army has laboured hard, endured much & behaved nobly. It has accomplished all that could have been reasonably expected. It ought not to have been expected to have performed impossibilities or to have fulfilled the anticipations of the thoughtless & unreasonable." The same day, in another letter, Lee expressed self-reproach when he wrote "I fear I required of it impossibilities." But he hedged this insight with the argument that although crossing the Potomac did "draw" the enemy from Virginia, it failed to "detain" them, as God had willed otherwise. The army, he argued, "responded to the call nobly, and though it did not win a victory it conquered a success."[7] With this rather complex and defensive formulation, Lee, after nearly taking responsibility for the defeat, downplayed the loss of a single battle and emphasized the value of the expedition as a whole: He reaffirmed his original purpose as having been a grand raid and not an invasion, which he then considered an overall "success."

Lee could not deny the grievous casualties his men had taken at that terrible battle, and yet he argued that he had rained such heavy blows on the enemy during those three days that he had incapacitated them, thus winning an advantage that compensated for all his losses. The absence of a counterattack was a sort of victory after all. On July 29, he wrote to Jefferson Davis,

"Although our loss has been so heavy, which is a source of constant grief to me, I believe the damage to the enemy has been as great in proportion. This is shown by their feeble operations since."[8] Even though Lee was nearly correct when he wrote that the Union had suffered about as many casualties, they could replenish their ranks, which the Confederacy could not, a factor Lee often lamented though did not mention at this juncture.

Under considerable criticism, not all of it from others, Lee continued to shift his take on the meanings of Gettysburg. On July 31, in his first official report about the battle, he admitted that despite their "gallant" attack on July 3, his men had "fallen back to their original positions with severe loss." In this review, he expended the greatest moral energy on exonerating his army from public criticism. He restated that "more may have been required of them than they were able to perform," using the passive voice to deflect complete acceptance of just who had done the requiring. He continued that his "admiration of their noble qualities and confidence in their ability to cope successfully with the enemy has suffered no abatement from the issue of this protracted and sanguinary conflict."[9]

If, as Lee argued, the army had not been at fault, then by inference at least it must have been their commander who had failed. In a separate, confidential letter written to Jefferson Davis the same day that he filed this first official report, Lee added a far richer and more conflicted analysis about what had and had not gone wrong. Davis had sent Lee a clipping from the Charleston *Mercury*, criticizing the Army of Northern Virginia at Gettysburg, to which Lee replied that as for himself, "I am prepared for . . . criticism, and as far as I am concerned the remarks fall harmless." But as to his soldiers, "no blame can be attached to the army for its failure to accomplish what was projected by me, nor should it be censured for the unreasonable expectations of the public. I am alone to blame, in perhaps expecting too much" of them. This letter contained a measure of self-defense as well as some acceptance of responsibility. Lee then repeated his earlier formula that, if not a "victory," the army had won a "general success," and he could not let go of the notion that the battle itself indeed had been winnable. "I still think if all things could have worked together [victory] would have been accomplished. But with the knowledge I had then . . . I do not know what better course I could have pursued."

Lee then went on to accept Longstreet's prebattle analysis, even while dealing with it as if it had been hindsight. "With my present knowledge, & could I have foreseen that the attack on the last day would have failed . . . I should certainly have tried some different course." And yet the net result of the campaign had turned out about as well as reasonably might have been expected. "What the ultimate result would have been [had we not attacked] is not so clear to me. Our loss has been very heavy, that of the enemy proportionally so. His crippled condition enabled us to retire from the country comparatively unmolested. The unexpected state of the Potomac was our only embarrassment."[10] Gone was any inkling that Lee had anticipated total victory, his scarcely concealed desire prior to the campaign into Pennsylvania.

Criticism had mounted, both in the press and among Confederate politicians and civilians. For example, the Charleston *Mercury* wrote about the whole campaign into Pennsylvania: "It is impossible for an invasion to have been more foolish and disastrous. It was opportune neither in time nor circumstance."

Privately, many of Lee's men were writing that the battle had been a "complete failure," as General Wade Hampton put it to Joseph E. Johnston on July 30. Robert G. H. Kean of the War Department in Richmond concluded in his diary entry for July 26 that the battle had been "the worst disaster which has ever befallen our arms." Kean's analysis was both prescient and harsh: "To fight an enemy superior in numbers at such terrible disadvantage of position in the heart of his own territory, when the freedom of movement gave him the advantage of selecting his own time and place for accepting battle, seems to have been a great military blunder." Kean concluded that "Gettysburg has shaken my faith in Lee as a general." Randolph H. McKim, a young private in the army, expressed this loss of faith quite eloquently when he entered in his diary, "I went into the last battle feeling that victory *must* be ours—that such an army could not be foiled, and that God would certainly declare himself on our side.—*Now* I feel that unless He sees fit to bless our arms, our valor will not avail." McKim summed up both the prebattle belief that one more great battle would win the war and the later sense of utter deflation that was certainly shared by his commander as well as by many, and almost certainly most, soldiers.

Full of disappointment that Lee had ignored his advice, James Longstreet wrote to his uncle that if Lee instead had advanced on Washington and had chosen the ground to await a Union attack, the Army of Northern Virginia would have "destroyed the Federal army, marched into Washington, and dictated our terms."[11] This was Longstreet's reworked reflection of faith in total victory: Lee's tactics had been wrong, not his strategy. Unrealistic though these alternative expectations might have been, they reflected the grand illusions dashed forever by that one battle. Psychologically, Gettysburg was indeed a huge reverse, to whatever degree Lee and his men articulated their senses of loss to each other.

Despite his verbal evasions, Lee shared this awareness of the magnitude of the loss, and he must have noticed some of the discouragement of the men around him, even though they certainly did not confront him. Such feelings led Lee, on August 8, to offer his resignation to Jefferson Davis. As a Stoic, a Christian, and a gentleman, he could absorb such defeat, make sense of Gettysburg, and continue to make war, he reassured Davis. "We must expect reverses, even defeat. They are sent to us to teach us wisdom and prudence, to call forth greater energies, and to prevent our falling into greater disasters. Our people have only to be true and united, to bear manfully the misfortunes incident to war, and all will come right in the end." Although he did not think leaders ought to respond to the criticisms of the masses and the press, Lee was aware that popular opinion, which had turned against him, could not be ignored entirely. "I know how prone we are to censure and how ready to blame others for the non-fulfillment of our expectations. This is unbecoming in a generous people, and I grieve to see its expression." Lee was writing to a man whom he knew to be a fellow sufferer from the slings and arrows of the press and the poison chatterers. Lee, the perfectionist, then admitted to his generalized "inability for the duties of my position. I cannot even accomplish what I myself desire. How can I fulfill the expectations of others?" Therefore, Lee offered himself up as the sacrifice on the democratic altar. "The general remedy for the want of success in a military commander is his removal. . . . I therefore, in all sincerity, request Your Excellency to take measures to supply my place."[12]

How sincere was this offer? Apparently, Lee did not mention it to anyone on his staff or in his family. He hedged by not actually using the word *resignation*—"take measures to supply my place" was a curious euphemism—and he appealed to Davis's sense of his own embattlement amid the din of public censure, of a sort that both men despised as cowardly and ignoble. Lee felt compelled to make the offer, thus acknowledging the public judgment about his recent leadership, while at the same time covertly implying that he was emotionally, intellectually, and spiritually equipped to carry on.

On the other hand, Lee also put into this letter, for the first time, his sense of physical decline, mainly owing to his heart condition, which gave him considerable cause for concern and which might well have diminished his capacity for leadership at Gettysburg. Not usually given to complaint, Lee admitted, "I sensibly feel the growing failure of my bodily strength. I have not yet recovered from the attack I experienced last spring. I am becoming more and more incapable of exertion, and thus making those personal examinations and giving the personal supervision to the operations in the field which I feel to be necessary." As early as the Fredericksburg campaign, Lee had been confined to an ambulance after what appeared to have been a heart attack, an experience that was to be repeated in October 1863, although he sometimes attributed his pain and fatigue to rheumatism in his back, probably a misdiagnosis. His health bounced back between such attacks, but he feared increasing physical decrepitude. He had written to Mary on March 9, 1863, after recovering from his first attack, "My health, I suppose . . . shall never be better. Old age & sorrow is wearing me away, & constant anxiety & labour, day & night, leaves me but little repose."[13] When he went to write his letter of semiresignation to Jefferson Davis, this physical sensibility conditioned his reasoning. He was also articulating the enormous emotional toll he had suffered by demanding such a mountain of self-control amid the carnage he initiated and the grief he swallowed.

As Lee might have anticipated, Davis rejected his offer almost immediately, telling him it would be an "impossibility" to find a better commander. Lee welcomed the response as an act of kind and generous consideration for his "feeble services." He promised to raise the matter no more but directed Davis to continue to feel free to replace him as commander "whenever in your opinion the public service will be advanced." And Lee then offered to return to any post, no matter how humble, of the sort he had held before his unanticipated elevation to command. "I am as willing to serve now as in the beginning in any capacity and at any post where I can do good, the lower the position, the more suitable my ability and the more agreeable to my feelings."[14] Such language replicated the formulations Lee had used when, in the spring of 1862, he had been recalled to Richmond from his failures in South Carolina. Loss triggered anguish and self-abasement in Lee, as if by habit. His sackcloth and ashes, although a passing mood, given both his undeniable pride and the exigencies of his command, marked the return of repressed humility, caused by the defeat at Gettysburg, such as he had not expressed during his annus mirabilis. This dark mood never again entirely lifted, neither during the remainder of the war nor during the rest of his life.

For both Jefferson Davis and Robert E. Lee, the appropriate response to Gettysburg, after the event had sunk in, was to reckon with defeat by calling for a national day of fasting, humiliation, and prayer. By this point in the war, such days of self-criticism had become a convention: Davis called for nine of them during the war. Collective self-scourging was intended to cleanse sinners and wash away the spirit of defeat: Only the heartfelt repenting of individual and collective spiritual impurity could lead to rededication and potential victory. By this means, Confederates coopted the long American tradition of the jeremiad preached to arouse the chosen people from their behavioral and spiritual backsliding and to charge them to renew their mission to build a Redeemer Nation.[15]

Davis set August 21 as the date for reconsidering the meanings of defeat at Gettysburg. For its observance in the Army of Northern Virginia, Lee issued his own proclamation, suspending all but absolutely necessary military duties and commanding every soldier to pray for forgiveness and guidance. "Soldiers! we have sinned against Almighty God," Lee declared. "We have forgotten his signal mercies, and have cultivated a revengeful, haughty, and boastful spirit. We have not remembered that the defenders of a just cause should be pure in His eyes; that 'our times are in his hands,' and we have relied too much on our own arms for the achievement of our independence. God is our only refuge and our strength. Let us humble ourselves before him."[16] Repurification, which Southern Christian soldiers might yet be capable of attaining, would lead the Confederate nation back toward its role as redeeming vanguard.

By this means Lee not only chastised others but, first and foremost, indicted himself for what he believed had been the worms of ambition and contempt that had taken over a considerable portion of his character. He was in this way quite cognizant of the costs his army's victories had brought to his own soul, and he felt a compelling inner need to repurify himself, to reclaim honor from the snares of sinful action. Whereas later generations might dismiss Lee's soul-searching and self-abasement as extremely judgmental and quite unfair, Lee demonstrated through this unambiguous proclamation how he believed he had failed inwardly and therefore why he had been deservedly punished for his sins, just as the Army of Northern Virginia and the Southern people had been justly punished for theirs. This was the most religious component of his complex response to Gettysburg, a form of faith he shared with the other Christian gentlemen in charge of the Confederacy and with at least a certain number of the men in the trenches.

Over time, however, in sorting out the meanings of Gettysburg, Lee came to affix more and more blame on others. His first target was Jeb Stuart, his cousin and cavalry commander. Stuart certainly had let him down hugely in Pennsylvania when, having gone on a vainglorious ride around the Union army, he had been absent without good cause from his primary duty—providing reliable scouting information about the enemy army—during the days that led up to Gettysburg.

As he had with his other major subordinates, Lee had always given Stuart wide military latitude. For example, right after Fredericksburg, he approved of Stuart's loosely defined plans for a raid northward with only the most general of admonitions to be careful. "I will only say that I rely on your judgment in making the attack upon the enemy's camp, and must caution you to be prudent, not to . . . hazard your men without a fair prospect of adequate compensation." Certain intrinsic qualities of the cavalry—the tendencies toward spinning out of control of his own command and stealing civilian property when on wide-ranging scouts—always concerned Lee, but, on personal and class grounds, he trusted Stuart as an exceptional cavalry commander more than he feared such excesses from Stuart's troopers.[17]

Whatever Lee felt toward Stuart about his nonparticipation in the Gettysburg campaign, Lee kept to himself for a month. But on August 5, he burst out in white-hot anger after reading a new set of reports from Stuart's patrols. Most likely, this explosion came not just from his reactions to the reports at hand but from Lee's still raw memories of the events at Gettysburg and his apprehension about Union attacks, which might come soon.

> From the reports of your scouts, they do not appear to me to be as self-possessed as formerly. Their statements are vague, with but few facts to support their suppositions; indeed they seem made up from conjecture, and information derived from citizens and not from their own observation. We shall be let into error if we can't get better. You must endeavour to correct this, and caution them against the consequences. The

squadron of Hampton's brigade that fled the fords of the river with that exaggerated report should be corrected.

As might have been expected, Stuart took great umbrage at this dressing-down, which seemed to reflect Lee's lack of confidence in his most elementary command capabilities.

Two days later, Lee had cooled down enough to write a sort of apology to Stuart—the latest batch of reports from a scout named Stone had been "clear & intelligent," and he accepted Stuart's good opinion of his scouts, "whose labour and exposure I know must be great and whose efforts & information I much value." Lee then repeated his admonition about the reliability of information gathering but in a somewhat warmer voice. "You have only to indicate upon them the necessity of making up their opinions from personal observation & from facts known to them rather than the reports of others."[18]

Normally, Lee would have let his anger go and reverted to kindliness and understanding, but in Stuart's case he did not. The next week, on August 15, he admonished Stuart about the "carelessness . . . in the preservations of arms" that was all too typical of Stuart's command. In a second letter, written August 18, he warned Stuart about the anarchy being fomented by Major John S. Mosby, a quasi-guerrilla captain ostensibly under Stuart's command who, Lee had heard, had threatened to punish civilians and was reputed to be "selling captured goods." What was worse, "it has also been reported to me that many deserters from this army have joined him." Lee gave Mosby the benefit of the doubt, assuming that his men were not operating thus under orders, but he charged Stuart to exercise tighter control over Mosby—by implication faulting Stuart for negligence in this portion of his command. The timing of these admonitions, so soon after Gettysburg and in conjunction with Lee's other criticisms, was no coincidence.[19]

A month later, Lee had apparently cooled down once more, and on September 23 he praised Stuart about a blocking action against the enemy cavalry. "I congratulate you on defeating his plans and arresting his advance. The energy and promptness of yourself and command elicits my high admiration."[20]

In this cooler state, Lee decided to make a major move to place Stuart under permanent control. He assigned Lieutenant Colonel George St. Leger Grenfell from his command as his official assistant inspector general on Stuart's general staff and authorized him both to clean up Stuart's procedures and to report directly back to Lee. Lee had never reined in his major lieutenants in such a fashion, and, taking this innovation as an insult, Stuart responded by assigning Grenfell to a rear echelon. On October 30, Lee put an end to this assertion of independence, when he wrote Stuart politely but frankly that Grenfell was to remain with Stuart's personal staff, where he could "keep you informed of the condition of your men and animals, and the care of the public property of the command. . . . In assigning Col. Grenfell to you, it was of the hope that his experience & capacity would enable him to . . . at all times know the condition of your command . . . the observation of orders . . . the execution of all regulations. . . . If you could furnish him with facilities for moving about as his duties require . . . I should be very glad." Soon enough, following Grenfell's reports, which came directly to him without passing before Stuart's eyes, Lee was sending back detailed instructions to Stuart to correct such matters as improper greasing of the harnesses of artillery horses, brutal treatment of mules, careless filing of proper morning reports, the filth of artillery pieces, and the poor policing of cavalry camps. Although he recalled Grenfell by the end of the year, Lee never really trusted Stuart again, nor did he ever really forgive him for his absence before Gettysburg. However, when Stuart was killed in action on May 12, 1864, Lee mourned his fallen cousin quite effusively.[21]

After his victory at Gettysburg, George Gordon Meade proved a preternaturally cautious commander, who not only failed to follow up his triumph at Gettysburg with an immediate attack on Lee, but only made modest advances before winter set in. Although somewhat of an exaggeration, one could say that the ten months following Gettysburg amounted to a second period of *sitzkrieg* on the eastern front. Relative Union passivity ended only in early May 1864, when the Union Army of the Potomac, under its bold and ruthless new commander, U. S. Grant, began its ferocious Wilderness campaign. This respite gave Lee plenty of time and relative calm in which to rethink Gettysburg, prior to filing his full battle report on January 20, 1864, a document characterized by rather extensive understatement and blaming of others.

Lee discussed events leading up to the battle in the passive voice, almost as if he had not been the author of an intentional strategy. One thing had led to another in almost accidental sequence.

> It had not been intended to deliver a general battle so far from our base unless attacked, but coming unexpectedly upon the whole Federal Army, to withdraw through the mountains with our extensive trains would have been difficult and dangerous. At the same time we were unable to await an attack, as the country was unfavorable for collecting supplies in the presence of the enemy who could restrain our foraging parties by hiding in the mountain passes. . . . A battle

had therefore become in a measure unavoidable, and the success already gained gave hope of a favorable issue.

Lee reiterated that this had been intended as a raid rather than an invasion all along. He argued that topography, not volition, had compelled a fight, and that foraging—clearly one of his original desires—had proved difficult. The most accurate statement was the last, where he asserted that past success had been his most certain guide to making an offensive battle, although he was not clearly referring in this report to earlier battles rather than the opening stages of this particular march.

The lack of conscious military authorship and the rather haphazard decision-making process outlined in this passage quite accurately depicted the risk-taking and opportunism common to much military planning, a great deal of which looks far more intentional in the false light provided by later historians. However, given the conventions of reportage of past martial events, Lee criticized himself unintentionally by using such an analysis—it was as if he had not had much of a plan but had marched north to see what might transpire.

By the end of the second day at Gettysburg, Lee wrote six months later, he had believed victory had been within the Army of Northern Virginia's grasp. "The result of this day's operation induced the belief that with proper concert of action . . . we should ultimately succeed, and it was accordingly determined to continue the attack." Lee's formulation "induced the belief" is quite vague as to exactly who gained a belief in success and implied a community of decision making, when it had been he who had given the orders. As well as diffusing rather than accepting responsibility (such as he had accepted, at least to General McLaws, immediately after the final assault had failed), Lee also set up his blaming mechanism: It was a failure to construct a proper concert of action that had caused the defeat. Lee went on to pin blame quite clearly on James Longstreet. On the morning of the third and final day of the battle, "General Longstreet's dispositions were not completed as early as was expected," but it had been "too late to recall" those units already engaged on the field of battle. The piecemeal quality of the attack, Lee wrote, was due to Longstreet, who was "delayed" by spending far too much time defending his flank and rear before going on the offensive. Lee thus avoided self-criticism about his own lack of clarity.

When Pickett charged, his "troops moved steadily on under a heavy fire of musketry and artillery." However, when the Union artillery opened fire, "our own having nearly exhausted their ammunition in the protracted cannonade that preceded the advance . . . were unable to reply or render the necessary support to the attacking party. Owing to this fact, which was unknown to me when the assault took place," the enemy infantry could advance down the hill in a flanking attack against Pickett's men, who "finally gave way . . . and [were] driven back with heavy loss. The troops were rallied and reformed, but the enemy did not pursue." Thus, in addition to the procrastinating Longstreet, Edward Porter Alexander, the Confederate artillery commander, had been to blame for not informing Lee that he had used up his ammunition. Lee omitted to discuss any failure of his own or his staff in not gathering this crucial information.

The third culprit in Lee's final report was Jeb Stuart. "The movements of the army preceding the battle of Gettysburg had been much embarrassed by the absence of the cavalry," Lee summarized. "In the exercise of the discretion given him . . . Stuart determined to pass around to the rear of the Federal Army and cross the Potomac between it and Washington." However, Union troops blocked that route, so Stuart "was forced to make a wide detour" and was further delayed by the rain-swollen river. "The ranks of the cavalry were much reduced by its long and arduous march, repeated conflicts, and insufficient supplies of food and forage," and they arrived in time only for the second day of battle, which they joined bravely. Stuart therefore had failed in his main duty—to scout the enemy—and this meant that Lee had had to enter battle with insufficient intelligence. In Lee's opinion, Stuart had abused that wide discretion Lee had habitually granted him, and this belief appeared in this report as it had in his earlier dressing-down and reining in of his cousin.

Despite these failures of Longstreet, Alexander, and Stuart, which had been instrumental in the defeat at Gettysburg—and Lee did not offer other causal explanations—the men had fought nobly.

> The privations and hardships of the march and camp were cheerfully encountered, and borne with fortitude unsurpassed by our ancestors in their struggle for independence, while their courage in battle entitles them to rank with the soldiers of any army and any time. Their forbearance and discipline, under strong provocation to retaliate for the cruelty of the enemy to our own citizens, is not their least claim to the respect and admiration of their countrymen and of the world.[22]

Lee's lieutenants had let down their men (and their commander).

As well as blaming specific senior officers, Lee made sure that, given the exigencies of maintaining morale while continuing the war, his report placed his own conduct as well as that of the army as a whole in the most favorable light. When, in August 1863, George E. Pickett filed an angry report on the de-

struction of his division owing to Lee's miscalculations, Lee refused to accept it. "You and your men have crowned yourself
with glory; but we have the enemy to fight, and must carefully,
at this critical moment, guard against dissensions which the reflections in your report would create," Lee wrote Pickett. "I will,
therefore, suggest that you destroy both copy and original [of
your report], substituting one confined to casualties merely. I
hope all will yet be well." Lee suppressed Pickett in the name of
the greater good, which had the effect of protecting his own reputation while continuing to permit Pickett's to suffer. Lee never
fully trusted Pickett after these events, dismissing him from his
command shortly before Appomattox, which did nothing to bol-
ster Pickett's postwar reputation. In return, the brokenhearted
Pickett never forgave Lee.[23]

Finally, in his official report, Lee rather significantly under-
stated Confederate casualties at Gettysburg. The figures he published were 2,592 killed, 12,709 wounded, and 5,150 missing or
captured, for a total of 20,451 of the approximately 75,000 men
present at the battle. Most later historians have put the total
somewhere between 24,000 and 28,000, while Union losses
were 20,049.[24]

Lee settled on his January 20, 1864, version of the meanings
of Gettysburg and never reconsidered them in any basic way. As
late as 1868, two years before his death, he repeated them in a
letter to William M. McDonald, emphasizing in addition that "in
crossing the Potomac I did not propose to invade the North, for
I did not believe that the Army of Northern Virginia was strong
enough. [I believed that it] was entirely too weak a force to
march on Baltimore" or Washington. The battle was "commenced in the absence of correct intelligence," Lee wrote, allud-
ing once more to Jeb Stuart's shortcomings. "Its loss was
occasioned by a combination of circumstances. It was continued
in the effort to overcome the difficulties by which we were sur-

rounded, and it would have been gained, could one determined and united blow been delivered by our whole line." Longstreet had fallen short, Lee repeated. "As it was, victory trembled in the balance for three days, and the battle resulted in the infliction of as great an amount of injury as was received, and in frustrating the Federal campaign for the season."[25] In this reckoning, a tactical loss had become a tactical draw and a strategic stalemate, with the ten months' lull afterward construed as a form of victory.

In the evolution of his writing about the battle—of turning battle into memory—Robert E. Lee thus became the first author of the proposition that at Gettysburg Robert E. Lee did no wrong and that others had been to blame. The corpus of his response had included magnanimity, self-reproach for his previous pride—expressed within the religious framework of a national day of humiliation—and a realistic assessment of the battlefield and the campaign as well, but Lee's thinking developed toward a focus on the failings of others. In this tendency he rather resembled other generals both in this war and in others, as one might expect. Subsequent generations of veterans and historians have spent a great deal of energy exonerating Lee and blaming others, particularly Longstreet, often for political reasons having relatively little to do with the battle itself. More recently, several military historians have revisited the battle, to the detriment of Lee's reputation.[26]

What seems least deniable is that Gettysburg was a great turning point for Lee. Never again did he take the strategic offensive; never again did he maintain the illusion of one total victory; never again was he so sanguine about winning the war. He returned to a more fatalistic sense of the meanings of the war and to a greater humility about himself and his army. Although he regained his equipoise and carried on stoutly after his prideful and victorious year had ended so harshly, doing much to keep the Confederacy going during its darkest hours, never again could he admit the consequences of his audacity nor the size of the defeat at Gettysburg. Neither, finally, could he accept responsibility for his own role in that defeat, nor restate the immensity of what he had attempted and lost during those three bloody days.

Chapter 9

To the Lost Cause

The disaster at Gettysburg ended those illusions of invincibility that had infused the spirit of the Army of Northern Virginia and its commander. After that failure, Lee entered his third phase as warrior, one of grim holding on. His sense of the increasingly desperate condition of his army over the subsequent nineteen months became realistic, verging on defeatism, which he fought off as well as he could. In response, he sought to tighten the reins of both martial discipline and Christian commitment, even as he increasingly mourned for all that was being lost. None of these reactions was unitary or unconflicted: Lee handled oncoming defeat with both calmness and anxiety. He avoided showing the men around him his deepest fears, but they did enter his correspondence, both personal and official, and could not but have been noticed. It took all the stoicism he could summon to remain alert in the field and in command of himself and of others. His efforts were tinctured by ill health—his congenital heart disease weakened him with pain and discomfort even as his military problems worsened—and colored by the long-term impact of the deaths of several of his loved ones, especially that of his favorite daughter, Annie. Taken altogether, these were his severest times of trial.

Back in Virginia after Gettysburg, Lee's army entrenched along the Rapidan River and sat in wait for the Union army. When the attack finally came, a tenacious defense might wear down the enemy's soldiers and its civilian morale, leading to stalemate and the election of a Northern peace party in the November 1864 contest, a victory that sometimes looked like it would come to pass. Much pugnacious spirit had departed Lee after his great Pennsylvania campaign failed, but he resolved to contain the enemy with a more modest and politically realistic defensive posture.

Privately, an anxious Lee could not accept the proposition that God had deserted his worthy servants—surely this prolonged martial trial would result in victory after all. On November 23, 1863, he wrote to his old sweetheart Eliza Stiles with hope, frustration, and determination: "I believe with you that God will release us from the grievous punishment with which he has thought proper to afflict us in his own time. I pray it may be soon! In the meantime we must be patient & all do what we can—Our enemies are strong at every point."[1]

To his soldiers, Lee put the necessity of moral rededication in a more affirmative and grandiloquent light. "Soldiers! You tread with no unequal step the road by which your fathers marched through suffering, privations, and blood to independence," he exhorted his troops on January 22, 1864, urging them to emulate their fathers in "their high resolve to be free, which no trial could shake, no bribe seduce, no danger appall, and be assured that the just God who crowned their efforts with success will, in His own good time, send down His blessing upon yours."[2] During this bleak winter—the time that tried men's souls—at his own Valley Forge on the Rapidan, George Washington's self-appointed heir reminded his men that victory often followed the most terrible defeats for pure men fighting a just cause.

On May 4, 1864, U. S. Grant crossed the Rapidan and launched the most ferocious and prolonged offensive of the war. On May 5–7, Lee used bold and determined tactics to defeat Grant at the Battle of the Wilderness. However, in the most significant strategic development of the war, Grant fought a campaign rather than a single battle. Unlike previous Union generals who had turned back after defeats, Grant moved to the east and the south of Lee's army and attacked again, not once but more or less continuously, at Spotsylvania (May 5–12), at the North Anna (May 23–26), at Cold Harbor (June 1–3), and at Petersburg, just south of Richmond (June 15–21). In each instance, the Army of Northern Virginia defeated the Army of the Potomac, including a slaughter at Cold Harbor that was as one-sided as Fredericksburg had been. In response, Grant never backed down but promised "to fight it out on this line if it takes all summer." After failing to take the Confederate lines and at risk of a mutiny from his troops, who simply could not make another frontal assault, on June 18 Grant settled down to a siege, which was to last eleven months, gradually bleeding the Army of Northern Virginia to death. Lee's generalship was superb during this campaign—his army won every battle—but he was to lose the war.

Even as he parried each of Grant's thrusts, Lee was quite conscious of the potential long-term effects of protracted and static defensive warfare, particularly this close to Richmond, which he believed he could not let fall for political reasons. In early June, he wrote to A. P. Hill, one of his corps commanders,

> the time has arrived, in my opinion, when something more is necessary than adhering to lines and defensive positions. We shall be obliged to go out and prevent the enemy from selecting positions as he chooses. If he is allowed to continue that course we

shall at last be obliged to take refuge behind the works of Richmond and stand a siege, which would be but a work of time. You . . . and all of the corps commanders . . . must be prepared to fight him in the field, to prevent his taking such positions as he desires.[3]

Strong enough to fight Grant to a standstill, Lee's army was no longer sufficiently powerful to resume this more offensive form of defense. The ensuing siege produced exactly the consequences Lee had predicted so clearheadedly: a war of attrition that the Union army could bear but his could not. On June 21, shortly after the siege began, Lee wrote to Jefferson Davis, "I hope your excellency will put no reliance in what I can do individually, for I feel that it will be very little. The enemy has a strong position, & is able to deal us more injury than from any other point he has taken. Still we must try & defeat them. I fear that he will not attack us but advance by regular approaches. He is so situated that I cannot attack him."[4] As had been quite characteristic of Lee since Gettysburg, an underlying negative tone now set in more deeply, a mood that was to increasingly dominate his thought until the end of the war. Gone forever was the pridefulness and contemptuousness that had characterized his attitude during his annus mirabilis. Thus, on August 23 he wrote the secretary of war, "Without some increase of strength, I cannot see how we can escape the military consequences of the enemy's natural numerical superiority," and on September 26 he added to General Braxton Bragg, "If things thus continue, the most serious consequences must result."[5] Previously a man of hopeful if always guarded military spirit, Lee now proved to be something of a pessimistic materialist, particularly after it became clear to him that the chips were down.

During this protracted final stage of the war, Lee's army underwent an agonizing slow-motion implosion.[6] Basic supplies, always short, now shrank to a state that produced permanent aggravation, threatening morale and even fighting capacity. Many members of Lee's army had marched barefoot into Pennsylvania—in fact, the search for shoes (manufactured in Gettysburg) had partly determined where the battle would be fought —and now even fewer had shoes. Over the last twenty months of the war, Lee wrote frequently and with increasing desperation to the quartermaster-general and other logistics officials in Richmond about an absence of soap—which threatened the "health, comfort and respectability" of the troops—a nearly exhausted supply of beef, a lack of "carbines, revolvers, pistols and saddles, and other accouterments of mounted men" for the cavalry, and the perpetual lack of "serviceable shoes," sometimes as few as fifty pair per regiment, each of which had anywhere from five hundred to one thousand men. As for beef, Lee wrote that he had been "mortified to find out that when any scarcity existed, this was the only army in which it is found necessary to reduce the rations." Troops on garrison duty ought to be able to manage "on lighter diet than troops in the field," Lee insisted, and he urged that at the very least, if there was not enough beef, "all [armies] ought to fare alike" in order to "stop complaint" and produce "more contentment." As for arms and mounts for the cavalry, Lee argued that "those [civilians] who are reluctant to part with their arms and equipments [should be warned] that by keeping them they diminish the ability of the army to defend their property." Concerning food, civilians ought to be told that they could either "support an army that has borne and done so much in their behalf, or retain these stores to maintain the army of the enemy engaged in their subjugation" after their selfishness had helped cause defeat.[7]

Because civilians evidently could not be badgered or shamed into sharing scarce goods, Lee eventually became willing to stretch his patriotic sensibility far enough to countenance establishing a system of trading with the enemy (which in part would just institutionalize and control an already flourishing illegal trade). On December 14, 1864, he wrote to the governor of North Carolina that he had "no objection to our people exchanging cotton etc. for necessaries, but it should be placed under proper restrictions . . . not tolerated for purposes of speculation [but only] for the army and our needy population." After the loss of the last major Atlantic port, Wilmington, North Carolina, on January 15, 1865, Lee wrote Davis that it was now urgent "to extend and systematize the exchange of our cotton, tobacco and naval stores for articles of necessity." He then outlined such a system in considerable detail. Lee was so hard-pressed that he was willing to abandon patriotism for greed if it would supply his army any better. "The interest and cupidity of individuals will be found far more effectual in overcoming the difficulties that beset the traffic, than the most energetic efforts of regular government agents stimulated only by the desire to do their official duty." Lee had rarely put the motive of self-interest above disinterested duty, so, pushed as he was by extremely difficult logistical demands, this was a considerable departure into modern values for him. In the name of victory over the corrupt and materialistic North, General Lee jettisoned the traditional moral economy and prepared to greet the amoral free market.[8]

Though willing to alter his values to accommodate supply gathering from civilians, Lee demanded discipline, discipline, and more discipline from the officers and men within his army as times grew tougher. He hectored both Richmond and his own soldiers with a more or less steady stream of admonitions, and he imposed stringent reforms.

Recruitment, always a problem, became even more urgent as the siege of Petersburg ground away at his army. "Unless some measures can be devised to replace our losses, the consequences may be disastrous," he wrote the secretary of war on August 23, 1864. "I think that there must be more men in the country liable to military duty than the small number of recruits received would seem to indicate," he insisted. He thought that the number of agricultural deferments in particular could be slashed, although he did not specifically discuss the deferments for holders of more than twenty slaves, which embittered poor whites in his army and their families back home. A few thousand more from the ranks of such excused men could hold the stronger parts of the line, Lee argued, while veteran troops could then venture out on the attack.[9]

Lee was convinced that other forms of military shirking had become institutionalized, as in western Virginia, where guerrilla units had been organized behind enemy lines. Set up on a local basis, such companies caused "desertion from the general service. Men go within the enemy's lines, either really or nominally, with the connivance or invitation of the officers, to enter these organizations," where their main tasks often seemed to be pilfering from civilians for their own benefit rather than serving any larger Confederate military purpose.[10]

Even within regular units right under Lee's nose, disorder was almost endemic. "What our officers most lack is the pains & labour of incubating discipline," Lee insisted to Jefferson Davis on August 13, 1864. "It is a painful tedious process, & is not apt to win popular favour." Not only had many officers eased up on their men in a most unprofessional manner in order to curry their favor, they would not take the first step and impose discipline on themselves. "Many officers have too many selfish views to promote to induce them to undertake the task of instructing & disciplining their Commands. To succeed it is necessary to set the example, & this necessarily confines them to their duties, their camp & mess, which is disagreeable & deprives them of pleasant visits, dinners, &c."[11] All that gracious Southern hospitality, charming in peacetime, became dysfunctional in war; Lee knew he had a huge task in attempting to turn gentleman sybarites into ascetic warriors.

But try he did, time after time. On February 22, 1865, in one of his more elaborate final attempts to re-create a winning army, Lee, who had become commander in chief of all the Confederate armies, circulated general orders about professionalizing the service. "Many opportunities have been lost and hundreds of valuable lives uselessly sacrificed for want of a strict observance of discipline," Lee told his general officers. Victory went to "discipline and courage far more frequently than [to] numbers and resources," Lee, who lacked numbers and resources, now argued. For triumph, hyperdiscipline would be required. "The greatest number of casualties occur when men become scattered, and especially when they retreat in confusion. . . . A few men, retaining their organization and acting in concert, accomplish far more . . . than a larger number scattered and disorganized." Appearances counted: "A steady unbroken line is more formidable to the enemy and renders his aim less accurate and his fire less effective." At the core of his policy was "preserving order," which would require "constant watchfulness" among officers, because "men must be habituated to obey." In the eleventh hour of the war, only a heightening of such discipline—upon men who were by nature and culture unruly—might rescue the South. To this end, the army had eliminated popular election of officers, and now Lee published orders about the means of choosing them through a "thorough examination by competent officers selected by the corps commander" and appointments to noncommissioned-officer slots "from those soldiers of the company most distinguished for courage, discipline, and attention to duty." These new sergeants were to march two paces behind the rear rank of their ten-man squads "with loaded guns and fixed bayonets," enforcing obedience by using "such degree of force as may be necessary. If any refuse to advance, or disobey orders, or leave the ranks to plunder or to retreat, the [noncommissioned officers] will promptly cut down or fire upon the delinquents." Any officers or noncommissioned officers who failed to impose such discipline were to be broken to the ranks.[12]

Such draconian orders, new to the Confederate army if not to martial history, were clear measures both of Lee's frustration and of his toughness in the face of immense military problems. Somehow, if he could make Spartans out of country boys and lazy gentlemen, he might still be able to construct an elite corps that could stand in the pass against the barbarian hordes.

But with these harsh measures, Lee also indicated his awareness that his army was melting away. During the last stage of the war, seeing that the end was in sight, most of his soldiers deserted. They left not out of cowardice, for most of them had shown their mettle at Gettysburg and the Wilderness, but because they had had enough and quite often because their wives, mothers, and sisters called them home, telling them they had already done their duty. Lee's letters were filled with his knowledge of this mass departure, on which he reflected with both sadness and anger. Desertion was not new, of course, although it increased vastly during the last six months of trench warfare at Petersburg. From a relative trickle when the Army of Northern Virginia was winning its great victories, the problem had accelerated right after Gettysburg.

In coming to terms with desertion, Jefferson Davis, doubtless under political pressure from Confederate congressmen and parents, tended to leniency and Lee to use of the firing squad. When Davis periodically issued pardons to such men, Lee urged him to return to stringent measures. "Great dissatisfaction is reported among the good men in the army at the apparent impunity of deserters," Lee wrote Davis on August 17,

1863. "I would now respectfully submit to Your Excellency the opinion that all has been done which forbearance and mercy call for, and that nothing will remedy this great evil which so much endangers our cause except the rigid enforcement of the death penalty." In a follow-up letter, Lee observed that earlier in the war "it was found that stringent measures alone would keep the army together" and that "after a few executions a number of the men were pardoned, and the consequence was a recurrence of desertion to an alarming degree. A return to sterner discipline was found to be absolutely necessary."[13]

This disagreement between Davis and Lee persisted until almost the end of the war. Although he did not meet Davis halfway, Lee did bend to the extent of agreeing to suspend the death penalty when a deserter voluntarily returned to his unit and took up his rifle. On the whole, however, his position remained that when in any doubt, deserters should be shot.

One of Lee's clearest enunciations of his rigorous stance came in a letter to Davis on April 13, 1864: "My views are based upon those considerations of policy which experience has satisfied me to be sound, and which are adverse to leniency, except in cases showing some reason for mitigation." Prior good conduct in itself was not such a ground. Lee was "certain that a relaxation of the sternness of discipline as a mere act of indulgence, unsupported by good reasons, is followed by an increase of the number of offenders. The escape of one criminal encourages others," as did general proclamations of amnesty or frequent acts of individual clemency, both of which Davis used. Better to err on the side of shooting too many than to encourage others to desert by softness; as for negative encouragement, in the past "military executions" had "a very beneficial influence," which ought to point the way to the general rule for the future.[14]

During that demoralizing winter of trench warfare in 1864–1865, when his men began deserting in droves, Lee finally began to consider the reasons for the phenomenon instead of merely chalking it up to moral turpitude, which he believed he could overcome with brute force. "I have endeavored to ascertain the causes [of the] alarming frequency of desertions," he wrote to the secretary of war on January 27, 1865, "and think that an insufficiency of food and nonpayment of the troops have more to do with the dissatisfaction . . . than anything else. All commanding officers concur in this opinion." All Lee could imagine as a remedy was greater efficiency in the commissary bureaucracy, which might lessen the genuine "suffering for want of food."[15] As causes of desertion, to scarce provisions Lee added continuous duty in the trenches, which was endlessly dreary and unhealthy as well as dangerous, and appeals from the women back home. He wrote on February 24, 1865, that "the men are influenced very much by the representations of their friends at home, who appear to have become very despondent as to our success. They think the cause desperate and write to the soldiers, advising them to take care of themselves, assuring them that if they will return home the bands of deserters so far outnumber the home guards that they will be in no danger of arrest."[16] Interestingly enough, Lee did not propose censoring the mails.

Lee's analysis of the causes of desertion was quite prescient. The major problem was that he could imagine no remedy to the lack of pay and supplies nor to the siren appeals from back home. Lee's final call for executions had come on November 18, 1864, when he wrote the secretary of war that "desertion is increasing in the army notwithstanding all my efforts to stop it. I think a rigid execution of the law is [best] in the end. The great want in our army is firm discipline."[17] But when the number of decampments continued to increase exponentially, Lee simply could not shoot every deserter, neither as a practical matter nor as a morally acceptable alternative. He might have been a martinet when shooting selected deserters had effectively stanched the flow, but he could hardly permit himself to become that cold and voracious monster who alone could stem the cresting flood with mass executions.

The problem had become so general and obvious that Lee himself proposed issuing a general clemency order. Davis concurred. Real men, Lee insisted in his order, dated February 11, 1865, "cannot barter manhood for peace nor the right of self-government for life or property. But justice to them requires a sterner admonition to those who have abandoned their comrades in the hour of peril." Lee then offered a final chance for deserters to reclaim their moral manhood: "A last opportunity is afforded them to wipe out the disgrace and escape the punishment of their crimes." General Order Number 2 gave deserters twenty days to return to their commands. To Lee, this order was a highly undesirable expedient and a great concession to the spineless. He inserted in it a provision that all who deserted after the publication of this general clemency "shall receive quick and merited punishment," which palliated his resentment about giving in to the criminally undisciplined.[18]

Magnanimous or not, the policy did not work. Desertions increased rather than decreased after publication of this order, which his men may well have understood to have been an act of desperation on his part, which, of course, it was. "These desertions have a very bad effect upon the troops who remain and give rise to painful apprehension," Lee wrote to the secretary of war on February 24, 1865, without clarifying whether it was the other men or he himself who felt the deepest anxiety. And on February 28, he conceded that it was not just shirkers and scoundrels who were departing. The pattern of defections, "which, unless it can be changed, will bring us calamity," Lee concluded, came now from among "troops who have acted so nobly and borne so much."[19] Lee could no longer deny that the Confederacy had reached its twilight.

In the face of so much defeat, and given his martial value structure, Lee used harsh discipline as a matter of course for as long as it seemed at least potentially effective. And yet he never employed brute force as an end in itself, nor did he ever entirely uncouple it from that patriotic Christian religiosity that was the Confederacy's bedrock faith: that it might become a Christian commonwealth superior to the debased and materialist North. This ecumenical Protestantism with millenarian overtones was employed to place current defeat in the context of a final victory. As thick clouds darkened the Confederate sky toward the end of the war, Lee reverted more and more to religious formulations of a sort characteristic of his whole life, until he had forgotten himself in the pride of victory before Gettysburg brought him back down. He also encouraged those periodic revivals that swept the Confederate army, especially during the spring of 1864.[20]

One useful way to interpret such rediscovered piety is as part of a revitalization movement, a collective surge of belief during worsening times, based on the perfervid hope that God will surely reward the purest of heart among his servants, if only they worship, serve, and sacrifice to him deeply enough, whatever events and material realities portend to the contrary. Such movements often appear to outsiders to be just so much delusional whistling in the dark, but for those thus engaged they can lend the courage not just to carry on but to redouble efforts in the face of all odds by reinforcing hope for ultimate deliverance. Whether Lee, who had the prestige to call for a surrender, ought to have given up several months before he did to save the South needless suffering is an interesting counterfactual moral question that historians have raised. In point of fact, it was this

heightened Christian faith tied to martial grit, more than anything else, that disallowed even thinking about surrender for
Confederate leaders such as Lee until it became completely obvious as the only alternative.

Lee did everything in his power to aid in the reinforcement
of religiosity. Early in the war, he had noted to his daughter
Annie that "one of the miseries of war is that there is no Sabbath, and the currents of work and strife have no cessation. How
can we be pardoned for our offenses!" Of course, one could not
count on the enemy to take Sunday off, but the absence of a
proper Sunday continued to rankle Lee. Therefore, in February
1864, with his army wintered down on the Rapidan River, he issued general orders to restore as much of the Sabbath as possible, as "obligation of a proper observance of the Sabbath" was
"not only a moral and religious duty" but contributed to the "personal health and well-being of the troops." Lee did not mention
that spiritually reinforced soldiers fought harder and more willingly. He had "learned with great pleasure that in many brigades
convenient houses of worship had been erected," and therefore
his orders reinforced Sunday observances the men already had
initiated. To that end, he urged that all but the most essential duties be "suspended" on Sunday, including daily inspections, and
that commanding officers should maintain "order and quiet
around the places of worship, and prohibit anything that may
tend to disturb or interrupt religious exercises."[21] Although Lee
did not require attendance, he did everything he could to facili-
tate it.

From that winter until the end of the conflict, reaffirmations
of faith characterized Lee's official correspondence as frequently as his reiterations of the necessity for martial discipline.
Indeed, these two parts of his belief structure were mutually reinforcing, together forming a kind of subdued utopian expectation, in which bad events were interpreted as but final tests of a

faith that would induce a messianic resolution if soldiers learned to tie renewed faith to increasingly disciplined military service. So frequent were both types of expression that one can consider them parts of a larger ritual: what had to be done to secure victory in the face of an increasingly powerful enemy when one's own resources of men and material were dwindling.

Several phrases became standard in Lee's depictions of military advances and setbacks, motifs he used dozens of times. "The blessings of God upon your undaunted courage will bestow peace and independence to a grateful people," he wrote troops who had reenlisted in 1864. During the Wilderness campaign, he peppered his dispatches with such sentences as "every advance on [the enemy's] part, thanks to a merciful God, has been repulsed" and "I am the more grateful to the Giver of all victory that our loss is small," a formulation he used frequently. During the siege at Petersburg, the rituals redoubled. Lee noted a victory by Nathan Bedford Forrest in Mississippi in June 1864 by writing to his fellow believer Jefferson Davis that it showed "that we are not forsaken by a gracious Providence. We have only to do our whole duty, and everything will be well." And, in December 1864, after discussing the dangers of Sherman's advance in the west and the growing risks posed by Grant on his own front, Lee closed a letter to Davis, "with a firm reliance in our merciful God that he will cause all things to work together for our good, I remain with great respect, your obedient servant."[22] Surely there had to be an order to things, surely God was not blind. This is but a small sample of what amounted to prayers embedded in military missives.

In intimate letters to his wife, Lee was even more fervent in his prayers. On October 9, 1864, celebrating Mary's fifty-sixth birthday, Lee wrote, "How sparingly have ... afflictions ... been inflicted in comparison with His blessings. I join heartily in your prayer that we may suffer everything rather than depart from him!" That was the main point of doing battle for the Lord: to prove faith whatever the adversity or the outcome. "Reverses . . . must come, to show us our weaknesses, our dependence, & to call forth renewed exertion." Faith urged action. "Our enemy is very numerous & still increasing & is able by his superiority of numbers to move at pleasure. Still I trust he may not be permitted to have everything his own way & that his course will at last have an end."[23] Such was Lee's affirmation of faith at a terrible juncture; while swearing to continue to act with confidence, he acknowledged inwardly that defeat was near, something that he tried to avoid dwelling upon by frequently reiterating affirmation of God's providence.

Lee could continue to struggle forcefully until the end not merely because he believed in a merciful deity guiding this life but because he transparently and warmly believed in the existence of a literal heaven, a far better place to which all Christians would go after the travails of earthly life had ended. For him, death was no void but a purified and permanent home. This belief reduced and helped explain the terrors of war, as it did the sufferings of everyday life, at a time when both parents and children frequently died untimely deaths. After death would come an ever-peaceful ingathering of the translated army and transported families.

From the start of the war, Lee had access to conventional formulas for explaining and dignifying death, which he wrote to the families and comrades of fallen soldiers. To the father of his young cousin Randolph Fairfax of Richmond, who was killed at Fredericksburg, Lee offered several of his usual phrases of commemoration. Fairfax had embodied "patriotism, self-denial and manliness of character." Now he had been "translated to a better world, for which his purity and piety eminently fitted him." His pain in living had ceased forever. "You do not need to be told how great is his gain. It is the living for whom I sorrow." When

Colonel Thomas R. R. Cobb, son of General Howell Cobb of Georgia, fell in battle, Lee assured the father about his son's "immortal name" and "unshaken courage and fortitude." For more senior figures, Lee added the consolation that not only had they reached heaven but their example could shine down through history for others. When General Maxey Gregg was killed, Lee wrote to the governor of his home state that South Carolina had lost a "gallant" officer, who had been illuminated by "disinterested patriotism" and "unselfish devotion. . . . The death of such a man is a costly sacrifice, for it is to men of his high integrity and commanding intellect that the country must look to give character to her councils, that she may be respected and honored by all nations."[24]

In Lee's ranking, the manly military virtues of fallen comrades were to be venerated but even more important was purity of soul. Thus, after Jeb Stuart was killed in May 1864, Lee issued a general order that declared that "to military capacity of a high order and all the nobler virtues of a soldier, he added the brighter graces of a pure life, guided and sustained by a Christian's faith and hope." Removed by the "mysterious hand of an Allwise God," Stuart could serve as a reminder to his comrades in arms through "the proud recollection of his deeds, and the inspiring influence of his example." Similarly, when Stonewall Jackson had been killed a year earlier, Lee wrote that all officers and soldiers ought to "emulate his invincible determination . . . indomitable courage and unshaken confidence," while to his brother Carter he added that Jackson's spirit "I trust will be diffused over the whole Confederacy."[25] Spirit would rise to rest with God, but it could also move across the Southern landscape, to be ingested by the living to their patriotic benefit.

As the war entered its final phase in the trenches before Petersburg, Lee's faith in the transformative value of noble soldierly deaths receded. His set of long-held beliefs now focused even more rigorously on the next life. Thus, when Wade Hampton's son was killed in October 1864, Lee wrote the father, "I know how much you must suffer. Yet think of the great gain to him, how changed his condition, how bright his future. We must labour on in the course before us, but . . . he is now safe from all harm & all evil."[26] Lee no longer stressed the reinforcement of the spirit of the living, which would lead the Confederacy on to victory and independence. Now, at best, the examples of the dead could help God's suffering servants live on until that blessed day when they too would be transformed. Lee expressed considerable longing for death and deliverance by this point in the war.

Of course, all these were ritualistic formulas, unoriginal to Lee but gathered by generations of his predecessors and deployed by him as a matter of convention. It is noteworthy that evangelical women were more likely to write this way than men. More often than men, women wished openly for death as they found worldly existence trying and distracting from their ultimate goal of spiritual reunification. These were the formal, even stylized chants Lee obviously believed appropriate to offer survivors as matters of consolation. And yet they also rang with sincerity—soldiers were created to fight, kill, and if need be die in the service of their values. Unshaken in these ancient warrior values and focusing on the afterlife, Lee could equip himself and others both to carry on the struggle and to prepare for the unpredictable but always imminent moment when bullets might strike them down.

If his military death pronouncements were rather stylized emotionally, Lee's more private discussions of death with his family expressed rawer feelings. For example, in the midst of reconstructing his shattered army after Gettysburg, Lee wrote to his daughter-in-law Charlotte, Fitzhugh's wife, with both sorrow and determination, "the loss of our gallant officers and men . . . causes me to weep tears of blood and to wish that I never could hear the sound of a gun again. My only consolation is that they are happier and we are left to be pitied."[27] In his official correspondence, Lee never used such vivid metaphors, and if in a sense this letter also is conventional, nevertheless it indicates something of the deep grief and desire for transcendence, coupled with dedication to the war effort, that had become characteristic of Lee. The Civil War had extracted an enormous price from his soul.

Victorian-era Americans such as Lee, during peacetime as well as wartime, were far more acquainted with death than have been later generations, as medical science has caused death rates to drop and life expectancy to rise so dramatically. The Victorians dealt with death in a more positive way than do we, not in the least, of course, because they were impelled to do so by so many more losses. In his immediate family alone, Lee had lost his father in 1818, when he was eleven (although Light Horse Harry had departed home forever four years before that, which must have been a kind of death in life for his little boy); his mother in 1829, when he was twenty-two; Mary Custis, his treasured mother-in-law in 1853; and, in 1856, his younger sister, Mildred. The fullest record of Lee's reactions to these deaths exists in the case of Mildred, elaborated in a manner typical then but unusual now.

Lee was in the wilds of the Texas frontier when he heard of his Parisian sister's death from her son, Edward Lee Childe. Lee wrote that he could measure Edward's feelings by his own, which were "miserable . . . God knows how I cherish her memory." There she had been in far-off Paris, and he could feel "the pain of separation from all that was dear to her in the world" back in Virginia. Fighting Indians in Texas, he too was far from the family and the Old Dominion, which produced a kind of commensurate pain to the one he felt for Mildred, which he knew Edward was sharing. "The separation from my dear wife & children is very grievous to me," he wrote Edward, "& I do not know how long I can stand it. I fear it will eventually drive me from the service." As for his darling sister, "A thousand regrets continually besiege me at my long separation from her, & the hope with which I constantly beguiled myself of an ultimate re-union, is now my torture." He felt terrible that he had not seen her in so many years and that their long separation in this life had become infinite. "But I must trust in the mercy of our father in Heaven to unite us in that world where we shall know no sep-aration, no misery!" This was not merely an abstraction or a symbol for Victorian-era Americans such as Lee but a literal and absolute belief. Anguished feelings of separation and grief were more than matched by faith in ultimate reunion.

Certain that Mildred was now in heaven, Lee could reassure his nephew that "I now sorrow for the living, not the dead. I do not even wish her to return to this world of pain & care. In the highest mansions of a glorious heaven she will be forever happy." And up there she would join Mary Custis, about whom he had written to Markie Williams three years earlier that "for every tear that has been shed on earth, there was a smile in heaven when she entered." Now Mary Custis in turn would smile on Mildred Lee when she greeted her, and her still living kin also had to focus on that reunification that would come all too soon. "It is necessary that our hearts be withdrawn from this world, & our treasures be transferred to that where they may shine forever."[28]

This set of mourning rituals, coupled to his military experi-ence and his stoic determination, prepared Lee, to some extent at least, to handle the grief that the carnage of war produced in him. Still, he must have mourned for all those men who were killed under his command—not just his angina but war, too, aged him at a dreadful pace. Lee also suffered a series of personal tragedies during the war. Right after Gettysburg, he heard of the "irreparable loss" suffered by Eliza Stiles, his long-ago sweetheart. "Your loss is mine too, for your sweet child was as dear to me as my own daughters," he wrote Eliza, although he added that he was certain that God had "taken her unto himself." Earlier and closer to home, in June 1862, Fitzhugh and Charlotte's firstborn son died; although Lee wrote Mary that he felt a "void" in his heart, he also discussed his compensatory faith in his little grandson's "merciful transition" to heaven. Six months later, when Charlotte lost her newborn baby, Lee wrote her about that "void" while consoling her that she now had "two sweet angels in heaven." And a year after that, when Charlotte herself died, Lee wrote his wife that he had loved Charlotte with a father's love and that he would grieve for her, but also that it was a "glorious thought . . . that she has joined her little cherubs," where some day all the Lees would "unite in that haven of rest, where trouble & sorrow never enters."[29]

But the most grievous loss of all during the war for Lee was that of his daughter Annie, who died of typhoid fever on October 20, 1862, at far-off Saint Mary's Academy, near Raleigh, North Carolina, chosen as a safe haven from the war. Once again, Lee wrote his wife that he felt a special "anguish" about "Sweet Annie" because of his earthly separation from her. "To know that I shall never see her again on earth, that her place in our circle which I always hope one day to rejoin is forever vacant, is agonizing in the extreme. . . . God . . . has taken the purest & best." And yet, as he wrote to his youngest daughter, Mildred, who was also enrolled at Saint Mary's, "the heavy blow that has been dealt to us was sent in mercy & kindness to her."

There she now was, a "happy angel in Heaven," where one day all the Lees would be "summoned" to join her, his mother and father, Mary Custis, and all the rest to come.

In the spring of 1870, Lee visited Annie's grave in North Carolina, as preparation for a reunification that could not be distant and to counteract some of that terrible feeling of loss and separation that had remained with him since her death in 1862. "I wish to visit before I die my dear Annie's grave," Lee wrote Mildred, aware that his health was declining rapidly. "I wish to see how calmly she sleeps away from us all, with her dear hands folded over her heart as if in mute prayer while her pure spirit is traversing the land of the Blessed."[30]

Annie's death had been the worst, yet during the war he had tried not to dwell on it but rather to link it to all the deaths of his soldiers in a manner that would lead to rededication to the struggle rather than removal from it. "At another time I might have been overwhelmed at the loss of that dear child who never gave me ought but pleasure," he wrote one of his female cousins on April 20, 1863, shortly before the smashing victory at Chancellorsville. "But now individual grief is almost absorbed in universal affliction, tempered by the conviction that there is but one thing to be accomplished. When that is done all will be well."[31]

War escalated death and heightened the necessity for those mourning rituals culturally available to Lee. In order to remain engaged militarily, such a general simply could not open his heart to the tragedies of thousands of freshly slaughtered corpses, and therefore he rehumanized himself by mourning in immediate, personal, often familial ways. Though coming to terms with tragedy in this way, Lee's ultimate purpose was not grieving but affirmation of continued war based on denial of the finality of death. In keeping with endless generations of generals, Lee had urgent reasons to ask, with Saint Paul, "O death, where is thy sting? O grave, where is thy victory?"[32]

During the last few months of the war, Lee's sadness grew so profound that his protestations about the attractions of heaven as a refuge gained increasing certainty for him. Although he never carefully thought through all the meanings of William T. Sherman's inexorable advance on Atlanta, which fell on September 1, 1864, Lee did understand the impact of the reelection of Abraham Lincoln that November, which Sherman's actions had delivered. The most profound resignation characterized the letter he wrote to his wife on November 14. "I must take it for granted we must . . . make up our minds for another four years of war. I trust our merciful God will sustain us & give us strength & courage to bear unrepiningly the chastisement & trials he may deem fit to cleanse us of our sins & make us worthy to become his servants."[33] Not coincidentally, after Lincoln's reelection, desertions soared, as the men in the trenches absorbed the ramifications of war without victory and without end.

Even this absolutely joyless resolution about four more years of unrelenting struggle was unrealistic under the military circumstances; Lee's understanding of the disintegration of his army subsequently veered between plans for somehow holding on until something better turned up and a fairly cogent assessment of the Confederate collapse. As Sherman began his march through South Carolina in January 1865, following the fall of Savannah at Christmastime, Lee wrote to William P. Miles, a leading South Carolina congressman, that he would not weaken his army to create a blocking force to his south. "If the people in South Carolina & Georgia would turn out in all their strength, aided by the troops now in that department, the advance of Sherman ought to be checked," Lee concluded, with a nearly total lack of plausibility, as if a *levée en masse* such as had never before been accomplished in the war could save the day against Sherman's numerous battle-tested veterans.

Even after Union troops had razed and burned Columbia, South Carolina, Lee hoped that Sherman would not continue to advance at such an incredible rate. "I do not see how Sherman can make the march anticipated," Lee wrote to the secretary of war on February 19, "but he seems to have everything his own way." Lee simply could not think through the consequences of Sherman's advance very coherently, so overwhelmed was he by his own massive problems.

At long last, however, expressing his fears of an imminent "calamity," Lee proposed to leave Petersburg and Richmond. "I fear it may be necessary to abandon all our cities, & preparation should be made for this contingency," Lee wrote the secretary of war. He suggested that the only hope would be to unite his army with that of Joseph Johnston, then in North Carolina, "as separately they do not seem to be able to make headway against the enemy." Lee suggested that to this end provisions be accumulated in southwestern Virginia and that every available male citizen in the remaining territory be conscripted, something no one could have managed this late in the war. And at this time, Lee wrote his wife, who was living in Richmond, that the enemy was "advancing and having everything his own way. [God] does not always give the battle to the strong, I pray that we shall not be overwhelmed. I shall however endeavour to do my duty & fight to the last." Little hope remained within Lee that his desperate campaign might work.

Admitting that Richmond would fall, previously politically unthinkable for Lee, showed how desperate he had become. In the grip of this apprehension, he wrote Mary on March 18 that she had better plan to leave the Confederate capital even though "I know no place where you would be entirely secure from the evils of war. The whole country is liable to be overrun ... & even in the most secluded place you may . . . be intercepted."[34] The Union monsters were spreading their evil everywhere through the South, and Lee was powerless to cut off their tentacles.

One of Lee's final acts while he remained at Petersburg was to cashier General Jubal A. Early, whose opposition in the Shenandoah Valley of Virginia to a rampaging Union army under Philip Sheridan had been entirely ineffective. Lee insisted to Early that "my own confidence in your ability, zeal, and devotion to the cause is unimpaired," but he felt compelled to "yield my opinion" and bow to the "current of [public] opinion," which had lost patience with Early. The people demanded a commander who would be "more likely to develop the strength and resources of the country and inspire the soldiers with confidence." Lee admitted that he had to "defer to . . . those to whom alone we can look for support."[35] In other words, Lee was tossing Early to the mounting legions of critics of the Confederate military effort: Almost always resistant to the blandishments of democratic opinion, in this case Lee caved in, which was not precisely to his honor but may have bought him a bit of time before all that public anger would have turned directly on him. Ironically, after the war Early not only forgave him but became the publicist most responsible for posthumously beatifying his old commander.

Still, though Lee was willing to fire Jubal Early for reasons of expediency and was prepared to abandon Richmond, he was not ready to quit the war. After he tried and failed one last time to break through Grant's encroaching lines at Petersburg on March 25, he wrote to Jefferson Davis that "the greatest calamity that can befall us, is the destruction of our armies. If they can be maintained, we may recover from our reverses, but if lost we have no resource."[36] The final remainders of the Confederate nation would be the remnants of its armies.

Lee was extremely tough until the end, although his plans

for joining Johnston somewhere in western Virginia to produce a major reversal of fortune were highly unrealistic. Blowing up remaining Confederate supplies and burning official records, thereby beginning a fire that consumed much of the city, Lee abandoned Richmond on the night of April 2 and, with the rag-tag remnants of his army, fled westward.

On April 6, after a brief battle, much of his remaining force, perhaps seven thousand men, surrendered. Two days later, Philip Sheridan raced around the residue, which led to the final surrender on April 9. By this point, a Union army of perhaps eighty thousand men captured the fewer than twenty thousand men left to Lee, about half of the number that had left Peters-burg a week earlier. Those not captured had already gone home, joining the flood of deserters from the previous six months.

In a sense, the vast majority of the men had surrendered be-fore their commander formalized their acts. Discipline, piety, and honor to their beloved commander had counted for less than the common sense of the situation, which the men grasped well before their general in chief was willing to admit to it. In the final analysis, no Confederate had been more single-mindedly devoted to duty and the sacrifices duty entailed than Lee.

Back in Richmond, ten days after the surrender, Lee wrote to Jefferson Davis, who was somewhere in flight southward, that it had been Confederate soldiers and Southern civilians who had failed the cause at the last hour.

> The operations which occurred while the troops were in the entrenchments in front of Richmond and Pe-tersburg were not marked by the boldness and deci-sion which formerly characterized them. Except in particular instances, they were feeble, and a want of confidence seemed to possess the officers and men.

> This condition, I think, was produced by the state of
> feeling in the country, and the communications re-
> ceived by the men from their homes, urging their re-
> turn and abandonment of the field.[37]

By contrast, to his own satisfaction, Lee, who had never pan-
icked during the terrible final campaign of the war, remained
steely and internally undefeated.

After another month of rest and reflection, Lee defined his
surrender as yet another great spiritual trial. "God has thought it
fit to afflict us most deeply and his chastening hand is not yet
stayed. How great must be our sins and how unrelenting our obduracy. We have only to submit to His gracious will and pray for
His healing mercy." And then Lee added a flicker of that personal obduracy of which he had never fully repented. "Heaven's
power could not long have withstood the overwhelming force
opposed," and so, by inference, how could he? Lee then submitted to the surrender, however unattractive it was to his pride. "It
is . . . useless to look back now that the South is willing to have
peace," which he hoped would be a just and permanent peace,
based on the "affections and interests" of the whole reunited
country, an end toward which, he wrote, "all good men should
labour."[38]

And yet, even in the general order that he had issued on
April 10, thanking and disbanding what was left of his army,
Lee had embedded a political position that marked the beginning not of Southern capitulation but of Southern resistance to
postwar Northern dominance. Offering his men his "increasing
admiration for your constancy and devotion to your country," he
assured them that such untarnished "valor and devotion" should
not have ended in their "useless sacrifice" and that this had been
the reason he had surrendered. Lee opened his general order by
asserting, in a sentence that became legendary, "After four years

of arduous service, marked by unsurpassed courage and fortitude, the Army of Northern Virginia has been compelled to
yield to overwhelming numbers and resources."[39] With such
language, the goal of independence, and indeed the whole moral
weight of the Confederate cause, flew free from a physical defeat that was materially determined. The body had been
crushed, but the spirit remained untarnished.

In many ways, there was nothing new about Lee's position
on the overwhelming quality of Northern manpower and material—he had been saying exactly that repeatedly since late 1861.
Indeed, all his stress on discipline and godliness was intended to
produce an elite army that could defeat an enormous enemy
that lacked the essence of duty and piety. In this sense, Lee had
always been an idealist at war.

But now defeat politically recontextualized Lee's position; in
the shadow of Appomattox, his argument both assuaged Southern honor and forwarded beliefs that, military setbacks notwithstanding, Southerners had been right all along and that their
essential righteousness would never disappear. The Confederacy was never defeated inwardly but only overwhelmed by the
brutish Northern leviathan. At the McLean House, suffering the
physical death of military surrender, the Confederacy became
immortal. Exactly here can one find the essential moment of ori-
gin of the "lost cause," of which Robert E. Lee was the effective
first father, George Washington clothed in an ironic dress uniform after all. Others would make use of that argument and of
the saintly General Lee they depicted after his death in 1870 to
lead a political counterrevolution that, by 1876, retook political
control of their section of the nation when they coupled Lee's
formulation of undefeated Southern identity to white supremacy, a project in which Lee himself participated after the
war. Southern white nationalism arose from the ashes of the
lost cause to a considerable extent because of the prideful spirit

Lee both articulated and embodied. He was the sacrificial lamb, the Confederate Christ on the cross at Appomattox who then was resurrected by others in the spirit and the body politic. Before he died, he also became the soft-spoken but implacable foe of submission and conciliation.[40]

Chapter 10

THE WAR HE REFUSED

*R*obert E. Lee had been so loath to relinquish the Confederate capital at Richmond that when he finally departed, it was too late to ward off the final defeat of the Army of Northern Virginia for long. Through fighting so long to preserve it, he and his soldiers, backed by Southern public opinion, had turned Richmond into a sacred place, the indisputable symbolic apex of Confederate independence in which Confederate collective honor inhered.

Despite his ability to improvise in often brilliantly unorthodox ways on the battlefield earlier in the war, Lee's martial conventionality narrowed the range of political and strategic alternatives he considered, not just in defending Richmond but in conducting the war more generally. On issues of race, including the possible use of black soldiers, and on the option of fighting a guerrilla war rather than a conventional one, Lee retarded or rejected options that other Confederates proposed. Such alternatives might not have worked, but Lee's hesitation or refusal to pursue potentially effective military avenues that strained his senses of Southern tradition, honor, and civilized Christian behavior had an impact on the war.

Men of Lee's social class fought for white independence

predicated on the preservation of slavery. At first, in large measure to retain the loyalty of slave owners in the border states, Union leaders balked at making abolition an explicit war aim, buying into the notion that reunion could be achieved with slavery still in place. But as the war continued, Union policy shifted until, with the Emancipation Proclamation of 1862, followed in early 1863 by the first mass enlistment of black troops in the Union army, Confederates would have to give up their slaves along with their claims to nationhood in order to end the war. They had not wanted to admit that slavery was as important as independence, something the shift in Union policy uncovered.

Especially during the last year of the war, a significant minority of Confederate officers and politicians began to emphasize independence and to reconsider slavery, albeit in a hesitant manner. Some of them, including Lee, came to believe that in the context of depleted white manpower and effective Northern utilization of ex-slaves as soldiers, they could end slavery and fight for independence with black soldiers on their side. The almost total lack of interest in this scheme by both Southern masters and the slaves themselves indicated that the notion of black Confederate soldiers was only a hollow fantasy prompted by the prolonged catastrophe of defeat. However, this project, which was finally articulated into legislation (ineffective in practice), revealed some of the contradictions upon which white Southerners had been attempting to build their nation.

Managing slavery while fighting a war was a major problem for all Confederate masters, and Lee was far from exempted personally. Taking considerable time and energy away from running his huge army, Lee struggled to deal fairly with the Custis slaves in consideration of the January 1, 1863, deadline for their manumission, as stated in his father-in-law's will. Arlington was gone and almost all the slaves there had scattered beyond Lee's reach, many to the North. Despite Union raids, however, many slaves remained on the other Custis estates, White House and Romancoke, which had been deeded to Fitzhugh and Robert, Jr.

As the date for manumission approached, Lee made plans to free the slaves, but he was also concerned about the debts on the estates, which threatened to impoverish his sons. Therefore, he equivocated. In January 1862, he wrote Custis, "Unless the legacies are considered in the light of a debt of the estate, the people must be emancipated at the end of this year. If the legacies form a part of the debt of the estate then they must help to pay it by their work." The sooner the debt was cleared the sooner "the boys will get their property & the people their freedom." He proposed gathering revenue from hiring out the slaves, which would create a sinking fund to be applied to the debts: Slavery would continue until the slaves had in effect purchased the freedom already granted to them in the Custis will. Despite the problem of debt and the chaos of war, Lee insisted that "we must try, as well as the condition of things permit, to carry out your dear Grandfather's wishes," even while he proposed to undercut what had been offered as an unconditional grant to the slaves in the will.[1]

Under the pressure of Union advances, Lee abandoned this form for his funding scheme. After telling Fitzhugh that "if the war continues I do not see how this can be accomplished," Lee modified his project, shifting the proceeds gained by hiring out the slaves from reducing the debt to their own postmanumission accounts, as it were. "They can be hired out & the fund raised applied to their establishment hereafter," Lee now argued. Given the wartime economic exigencies faced by his sons, Lee wrote that "if . . . you cannot otherwise carry on your farm, they might continue as they are until circumstances permit me to emancipate them." Then Lee, who was at least as interested in his sons' solvency as in their slaves' freedom, argued that he was thinking only of the welfare of the slaves. "If emancipated under present conditions, even if I could accomplish it, I do not see what would become of them. I think it better therefore to continue them as they are the present year." Lee was torn about this issue, wanting to do the right thing by his sons and also, eventually, by his slaves. Thus, he reiterated with considerable ambivalence, "If circumstances permit their emancipation I must do it. If not & you do not require them on the farm then to hire them out all that can be hired & emancipate them as soon as it can be done."[2]

During the summer of 1862, Union troops raided Fitzhugh's White House plantation, leaving it desolated. Afterward, Mary Lee reported to Charlotte, Fitzhugh's wife, that, according to the overseer, who had been there, many slaves had been taken off the plantation under false pretenses. "Tell Mammy her husband is there. Clairborne & Colbert & Bob Cryden & Dinah & some few others" remained. "The rest were deluded off with the most infamous lies & were taken in the boats, men women & children. Poor creatures [perhaps] to starve this winter." One week later, Union forces also raided Romancoke, and once again Mary Lee reported that many slaves had been spirited away, although others remained. "Severl have been sick from wearing yankee clothes, one man has died in consequence." When the overseer, Mr. Collins, gave Mary Lee his report, he also told her that many of the boys, women, and old men who remained "rejoiced when he told them he would let their masters know about them."[3] Yankees would only exploit and destroy the people they professed to free, while kindly old Southern masters knew how to care for their charges, Collins wished to believe, and Mary Lee agreed.

Within slavery or not, white benevolence was still undermined by black indifference, both the Lees believed. Indeed, even when he discussed finding the dispersed slaves in order to hand them their emancipation papers as the great date ap-

proached, Lee could barely contain his annoyance at what he believed to be the laziness of the family retainers. "I want a good
servant badly," he wrote Mary from Fredericksburg, shortly before the Union attack in December 1862, "but I do not think it is
worth while to commence with Fleming at this late date. He
would have to learn a good deal before he would be useful & . . .
I wish to liberate all of them." Fleming made him think of other
slaves whom he believed he had been treating very well despite
their no-account natures, including his current valet, whom he
intended to free at the end of the month. "Perry is very willing &
I believe does as well as he can. You know he is slow & inefficient. . . . He is also very fond of his blankets in the morning.
The time I most require him out. He is not very strong either. I
hope he will do well when he leaves me & gets in the service of
some good person who will take care of him."[4]

Facing black freedom, Lee fully articulated his exasperation
about blacks in the context of his continuing concern for their
welfare once they left the protective confines of slavery. Freedom was not the natural state for these perpetual children, Lee
believed, and for him and others of his background the anticipation of emancipation was sufficiently upsetting to produce
derogatory formulations of a sort he had rarely written when
blacks were securely in what he saw as their place.

As emancipation day neared, Lee's commitment to freeing
as many slaves as he could grew, even as his doubts about their
capacity for independence continued, mixed with a genuine
worry over their well-being. On December 16, he wrote Mary, "as
regards the liberation of the people, I wish to progress in it as far
as I can." Evidently, the Lees had brought at least a few slaves
with them when Mary had fled Arlington. "Those hired in Richmond can still find employment there if they choose," Lee now
wrote, making it clear that he would free those household slaves
immediately. "Those in the country [at White House and Ro-

mancoke] can do the same or remain on the farms. I hope they will all do well & behave themselves. I should like to attend to all their wants & see them placed to the best advantage. But that is impossible. All that choose can leave the State before the war closes."[5] Five days later, his thinking had clarified further. "Those [in Richmond] that are hired out can . . . be furnished with their free papers & hire themselves out. Those on the farms I will issue free papers to as soon as I can see that they can get a support." He would not abandon them to the wilderness; however, it was precisely through this protective paternalist position that Lee backtracked on manumission. "As long as they remain on the farms they must continue as they are. Any who wish to leave can do so. The men could no doubt find homes, but what are the women & children to do?" The overseer was charged with staying put to "take care of the people till I can dispose of them." In other words, Lee would continue to hold those slaves in bonds who were not prepared to fend for themselves. And he added a few days later that he would issue free papers to slaves who had already left—"those that have been carried away," as he put it—if they ever came calling, an unlikely eventuality.[6]

Lee did not seem to consider the likelihood that most of these slaves must have left not only voluntarily but eagerly, thereby emancipating themselves without waiting for their master's fiat. As was true of his wife, Robert E. Lee could not believe in his heart of hearts that the faithful slaves had been other than kidnapped by the perfidious Yankees.

Somewhat to Lee's surprise and certainly to his growing annoyance, not all the slaves took up their free papers and left the plantations. By the next winter, he was getting fed up with their continued dependence. In the fall of 1863, he wrote Mary that he had directed overseer Collins "as soon as he could get in the small crop this fall . . . to emancipate them. They can then hire themselves out and support themselves." Evidently, Lee believed that certain able-bodied black men were in fact malingering under his care. "Their families if they choose or until they can do better can remain at their present homes. I do not know what to do better for them." The enemy had stolen all the livestock, and the crop was small, and "there is no certainty if they remain of making enough to live on."[7] Lee felt himself left with unproductive mouths to feed.

Far from making money for him, the Custis legacy was costing him more than it brought in—a practical reason to speed the slaves into freedom. Indeed, Lee was beginning to resent these dependents quite a lot. After a couple more months, when many continued to stay on the plantations, Lee wrote in irritation to Mary, "I much prefer their receiving their free papers & seeking their fortune. . . . I do not see why they can not be freed & hire themselves out as others do. . . . I am afraid there is some desire on the part of the community to continue them[selves] in slavery, which I must resist."[8] Here, presented in a very annoying manner, was proof positive of the benefits of slavery for the slaves. That northern Virginia was too torn up, burned over, and dangerous for fortune seeking, security, and freely contracted employment Lee did not discuss. He was willing to be the emancipator, and the slaves ought to be willing to enter the adventure of freedom.

When some slaves still remained late into 1864, and Mary Lee asked his help with old Isaiah Patterson, Lee complained to her with a sarcasm unusual to him, "I have a great consideration for my African fellow citizens, but must have some for their white brethren."[9] Rather preoccupied fighting the war, he had had enough of his obligations to the Custis slaves and wanted to cut their ties with him. Paternalism had its limits even for the most patient paternalist.

While freeing his own slaves in this halting way, Lee fought a war to continue slavery. Plantation slaves, who offered a potential threat to the Confederacy, had to be controlled by the presence of white masters or overseers, which exacted considerable white manpower resources drawn from the limited pool that otherwise might have been applied to the war effort. In addition, exempting the wealthier planters or their delegates from military service made many poor whites bitter about the rich man's war and poor man's fight, as they called it. This class resentment exacted a deep set of political costs within the Confederacy and almost certainly accelerated the waves of desertion toward the end of the war. Yet if Southerners had not continued to carry the costs of the peculiar institution (as well, of course, continuing to benefit from low-cost, unfree labor), what would their quest for nationhood have meant? And so, until very late in the war, they fought for independence inextricably bound to the continuation of white dominance within the slave system.

In common with most of the Confederate leadership, Lee rarely mentioned out loud the dangers posed by the fifth column of slaves behind Confederate lines. Wherever the Union armed forces raided the South, however, Lee was well aware that slaves often brought valuable information to the Northern army to which thousands of them fled when given half a chance. When Union gunboats threatened to penetrate up the Rappahannock River in May 1863, for example, Lee wrote to the Virginia cavalry commander defending the mouth of that river that he must make defensive warfare in utmost secrecy. "The chief source of information to the enemy is through our negroes," Lee wrote. "They are easily deceived by proper caution. Secrecy, diligence, and constant attention must always be practiced."[10] Lee expressed a certain contempt for the gullible slaves and a belief that intelligent white men could always control them while at the same time stressing the advantages their information might offer the enemy. This amounted to a contradictory message about the intelligence of black people.

As for larger concerns about the potential for a slave insurrection, Lee, again in keeping with unstated Confederate policy, remained nearly silent. Indeed, when North Carolina governor Zebulon Vance captured a Union mail packet that included a letter from a Northern citizen proposing an organized uprising all over the South for the night of August 1, 1863, Lee suggested that Vance take proper precautions but do nothing to notify the larger public about "this diabolical project." Not wishing to give free publicity to the idea nor to frighten white civilians, Lee also did not appear deeply concerned about such schemes, which indicated that he was secure in his faith that slaves would remain subordinate if normal precautions were taken.[11]

For Lee, the single greatest problem presented by slavery came not from the slaves themselves but from the negative political meanings the peculiar institution held when it was linked in the eyes of Europeans to the Southern struggle for independence. After his army bogged down in the Petersburg trenches, Lee spelled out his analysis to Jefferson Davis:

> As far as I have been able to judge, this war presents to the European world but two aspects. A contest in which one party is contending for abstract slavery & the other against it. The existence of vital rights involved does not seem to be understood or appreciated. As long as this lasts we can expect neither sympathy nor aid. Nor can we expect the policy of any government towards us to be governed by any other consideration than that of self interest. Our safety depends upon ourselves alone.

Here Lee asserted what many Confederates wished to believe late in the war and what many Southern apologists have contended ever since the war ended, that independence and not slavery was the "vital right" for which the Confederacy fought.

Such a position refused to posit the inescapable next issue—that had slavery not existed there would have been no need for secession and war and that therefore the central point of independence was the freedom to continue slavery. Yet in this letter, Lee asserted this self-deceiving political position within a statement of his clear realization that whatever Confederates wanted to believe about the distinction between slavery and Southern independence, Europeans concluded otherwise. This was doubtlessly regrettable, Lee acknowledged, but it was an indisputable fact that would preclude British or French intervention on behalf of the Confederacy—the enemy of the aggressive Yankees, who were the Europeans' true competitors—as their publics would not permit any overt defense of the institution of slavery, long since abolished in European empires.

On September 22, 1862, Abraham Lincoln further stood off would-be European interventionists by issuing the Emancipation Proclamation: With abolition now a declared Union war goal, intervention would amount to a defense of slavery. The Proclamation also meant that if the Confederates were to surrender with the Republicans in power, they would agree to the elimination of slavery; this guaranteed that they would fight until totally defeated. This was the fundamental reason Lincoln's reelection in 1864 was so devastating to Confederate morale. Unlike many Confederate diplomats and politicians, Lee was quite clearheaded in his realization of the Southern isolation from world opinion solidified by Lincoln's victory. Even before that catastrophic political event, Lee wrote Davis that only if they could "defeat or drive the enemy from the field, we shall have peace," sensing the enormous geopolitical dangers siege warfare already had brought him. Slavery had become the inescapable iron collar around the Confederate neck.[12]

Northern emancipation also led, by the beginning of 1863, to the recruitment of black troops into the Union army, nearly two hundred thousand men by the end of the war. While the Confederacy lost irreplaceable white manpower, the enemy army expanded, in considerable measure from the ranks of escaped slaves, who formed the vast majority of that new black Union soldiery—a dramatic Union gain that was at the same time an indisputable Southern loss, both symbolically and materially.

Blacks in arms fighting for their own freedom against their former masters were anathema to slaveholders, violating their deepest belief concerning black inferiority, of the sort Lee expressed, for example, when he discussed the endless dependency of the Custis slaves. White men ought to have sole possession of military weapons and martial honor—the very core of manhood. To enlist and arm black men was indeed to turn the world upside down.

In his few comments on black Union troops, Lee expressed the normal Confederate contempt for them. For example, on September 20, 1863, Lee warned Jefferson Davis about the gathering in Union-occupied Norfolk of "negro troops and cavalry," said to be preparing for a raid on the Weldon railroad junction. "I do not apprehend that these negro regiments will prove a very formidable body, though unopposed they might do us great damage," Lee concluded. To give another example, on June 26, 1864, Lee proposed to Davis a lightning clandestine attack— what later generations would call a commando raid—into Maryland to free the thousands of Confederate prisoners at Point Lookout. "I have understood that most of the garrison at Point Lookout was composed of negroes," Lee argued. "I should suppose that the commander of such troops would be poor and feeble. A stubborn resistance, therefore, may not reasonably be expected." A crack company of real and true white Confederate troops ought to be able to achieve the liberation of prisoners who were guarded only by inferior stock.[13] Davis ignored this extremely risky proposal, which was based more on contempt for the black sentinels than on the likelihood of success of a raid so far behind Union lines. Perhaps it was Lee's racial antipathy that led him to suggest such an audacious plan, one far more characteristic of his thinking before Gettysburg than this late in the war.

Confederate hatred for black Union troops spilled over most lethally on the issue of treatment of prisoners of war. In several instances, Confederate troops shot down black troops rather than accept their surrender. In the two most fully recorded cases—at Poison Springs, Arkansas, and Fort Pillow, Tennessee—several hundred blacks were slaughtered after throwing down their arms; many instances of the killing of smaller groups and of black retaliation went unrecorded in official reports. As for Lee's army, recent scholarship has described the massacre of black troops attempting to surrender at the battle of the Crater, on the Petersburg front on July 30, 1864, in which many Confederate soldiers participated. As North Carolina major Matthew Love described the scene in a letter to his mother, his regiment refused to take prisoners and "such slaughter I have not witnessed upon any battlefield anywhere. Their men were principally negroes and we shot them down until we got near enough and then run them through with the bayonet. . . . We was not very particular whether we captured or killed them, the only thing we did not like to be pestered burying the heathens."[14] If General Lee knew of this significant incident, he did not respond to it.

The capture of black troops, which occurred more frequently than their murder, led to the breakdown of the prisoner-of-war exchange cartel, which had been a system of returning prisoners rather than imprisoning them. This policy shift, inaugurated by the Confederates, which led to the horrors of Andersonville and Northern prisoner stockades late in the war, injured

the South far more than the North, because captured Union soldiers could be otherwise replaced—often by blacks—while the
Southern manpower pool was nearing exhaustion. The reason
for the breakdown was the Confederate insistence that ex-slaves
were not free and equal prisoners. If they had escaped from
bondage to join the Union army, they would be returned to it
when captured.

In the fall of 1864, Robert E. Lee articulated this policy in an
exchange of letters with U. S. Grant. On October 1, Lee wrote
Grant that "with a view of alleviating the sufferings of our soldiers," he proposed an exchange of prisoners to the two armies
operating in Virginia, "man for man . . . upon the basis established by the [prior] cartel." Grant immediately inquired about
the status of black United States troops. "Before further negotia-
tions are had upon the subject I would ask if you propose deliv-
ering these men the same as white soldiers?" Lee responded that
"I intended to include all captured soldiers of the United States
of whatever nation or color. Deserters from our service and negroes belonging to our citizens are not considered subjects of
exchange." Grant would not accept this, and he told Lee that the
United States government "is bound to secure to all persons received into her armies the rights due to soldiers. This being denied by you in the persons of such men as have escaped from
Southern masters induces me to decline making the exchanges
you ask." Grant then asked for further clarification from Southern legal officials, and soon Lee made it crystal clear: "I have no
objection to . . . exchanging prisoners, man for man, free negroes included. Recaptured slaves of Confederate citizens will
not be exchanged."[15]

Grant insisted that by becoming Union soldiers, escaped
slaves had become persons to be treated equally with all other
captured troops. After he had been fully briefed by the Rich-

mond authorities, Lee argued back to Grant, quite to the contrary, that Negro slaves "who through compulsion, persuasion, or of their own accord leave their owners and are placed in the military . . . service of the United States [remain] a species of property. . . . The capture or abduction of a slave does not impair the right of the owner to such a slave, but that right . . . attaches to him immediately upon recapture [and] will be restored like other recaptured property to those entitled to them."[16] Lee wrote that he would treat free black Union prisoners just like white men, thus asserting a kind of color blindness. However, as for escaped slaves, the rights of property—the nonpersonhood of black slaves—superseded any consideration of them as Union soldiers. This belief led Lee to employ captured ex-slave Union soldiers in digging trenches around Petersburg, to which Grant responded by putting white Confederate prisoners at the same risk reinforcing his trenches. While arguing that he had not exposed black prisoners to fire, which was not precisely true, Lee withdrew them, without abandoning the proposition that he had every right to use them this way.

In response, Grant then withdrew Confederate prisoners from such dangerous duty, and wrote Lee that

> I shall always regret the necessity of retaliating for wrong done our soldiers, but regard it as my duty to protect all persons received into the army of the United States, regardless of color or nationality. . . . All prisoners of war falling into my hands shall receive the kindest possible treatment . . . unless I have good authority for believing that any number of our men are being treated otherwise. Then, painful as it may be to me, I shall inflict like treatment on an equal number of Confederate prisoners.[17]

In effect, Lee had conceded that he would not use escaped black Union prisoners as he used other slaves, but neither would he send them back as prisoners of war: Things they had been; things they remained. Because of this impasse, the exchange cartel was never repaired and tens of thousands of prisoners of war, on both sides, mainly white, died of cholera and typhoid fever in hellish prison camps.

Confederate atrocities against black prisoners and their white officers continued as well. Late in the war, after Lee had been named general in chief, and in theory had control of all Southern armies, Grant sent him an eyewitness account written by a white lieutenant of a black infantry regiment in Tennessee. This lieutenant had been shot in the head and left for dead after being captured by Confederate soldiers who also murdered two white officers in his unit. This was the most irrefutable case Grant could find of such Confederate behavior, and he threw it in Lee's face. "I have no reason for believing this course has been persistently followed . . . yet I believe it has been the practice with many officers and men in the Confederate Army to kill all such officers as may fall into their hands." Grant did not accuse Lee of issuing a policy directive to commit such murders, but he did insist that Lee now issue orders prohibiting such practices in the future.

Lee replied that in this instance "I know nothing of the facts," nor did he have "the means of ascertaining them." If true, the act was done without authority and at variance with Confederate rules.

> It was probably one of those acts of unauthorized violence proceeding from individual passions, which it is difficult to prevent, but which are not the less to be lamented. Many similar outrages committed upon the persons of Confederate soldiers and civilians by per-

sons in the Federal service have been reported to me, which I trust admit of the same explanation. I endeavour by every means in my power to prevent such violations of the rules of civilized warfare, which only tend to inflame feelings already unfortunately too much embittered, and which unavoidably reflect upon the party to which the perpetrators belong.[18]

Lee, the stoic at war, argued that combatants ought to rein in their angry feelings, which did not demonstrate much realism about warfare, the means of which sometimes included the shooting of prisoners, about which he maintained cool detachment.

Both Grant and Lee were playing to public opinion in this exchange, which, of course, led to no resolution. However, this correspondence was a clear indicator of the reception accorded black Union troops in Southern eyes. Many black troops and some of their white officers were indeed killed rather than captured—an escalation of violence away from general practice earlier in the war. This was the ultimate Southern action growing out of the belief in the nonpersonhood of black slaves, and, although it is impossible to discover just how widespread it became, it was an appalling precursor to the murderous night riding that white Southerners used to counter Reconstruction and put blacks back in their "places."

As white manpower diminished due to death, injury, and desertion, and in the face of Union employment of ex-slaves as soldiers, Lee began to look, in considerable desperation, toward engaging blacks in the Confederate war effort. In a rather extended disquisition on human resources that he wrote to Jefferson Davis on September 2, 1864, Lee analyzed alternatives. White power might be augmented by severely curtailing military exemptions for slave managers and owners and by ending the fairly widespread practice of detailing troops to bring in the harvests. After all, Lee wrote, "if they remain at home their produce will only benefit the enemy, as our armies will be insufficient to defend them." Old men and young boys currently kept on reserve as a home force should be brought to the front, taking the places in the trenches of veteran troops who then could go on the attack. But most seriously, Lee pushed for the far greater use of black men at the front, thereby "relieving all able-bodied white men employed as teamsters, cooks, mechanics and laborers, and supplying their places with negroes. I think every measure should be taken at once to substitute negroes for whites . . . wherever [they] can be used." Then Lee concluded with realism bordering on cynicism, "It seems to me that we must choose between employing negroes ourselves or having them employed against us." Not that he thought better of blacks, but he was desperate for any source of labor.[19]

There was nothing new about the use of black labor on fortifications—slaves had long been leased for such uses, and a February 27, 1864, law allowed for the impressment of slave labor by the army if masters did not volunteer them, though this law had not been much employed.[20] In the fall of 1864, Lee tried to implement such impressment. He called upon Richmond for five thousand black draftees to be used in cutting wood, building railroads, and in general creating a mobile, quasi-military work corps. "I am confident that our people will contribute this species of property with as much willingness as they have all others, and no time should be lost in procuring the great addition to our resources which the use of our negroes can afford us," Lee wrote the secretary of war, who responded positively.[21]

In order to control such a corps and induce them to work hard, Lee proposed to the Richmond bureaucracy a gang system, much like that used on cotton plantations, superintended by experienced managers characterized by "probity, energy and intelligence. Every precaution should be taken to insure proper and kind treatment of the negroes to render them contented in their service," Lee wrote, in the fashion of progressive slave masters. Harsh discipline, when necessary, ought to come not from whip-wielding foremen but only after referral to senior managers, and "there should be a system of rewards, too, for good conduct and industry, these rewards to be paid to the meritorious over and above the hire paid to their masters." Lest anyone in Richmond think Lee was proposing a halfway house to free labor, Lee added, "most of the negroes are accustomed to something of this sort on the plantations." When the Engineering Bureau drafted its regulations, however, it omitted reference to wages of any sort.[22]

However evolved the plans for this black labor corps in Lee's mind and on the Confederate drawing board, they did not work. As Lee knew nearly from the start of this effort, in the face of opposition from masters the War Department would not enforce the impressment legislation and thus could not produce anything approaching the number of laborers Lee required. By December 20, 1864, Lee wrote in considerable frustration to the secretary of war, that of the request for five thousand workers "two thousand is the greatest number which ever reported, and those in small bodies at different intervals. . . . A large number of them have deserted. . . . I cannot state the present strength of the force, but think it cannot exceed 1200." Lee then called for five thousand more black men, of whom, he reported to the governor of Virginia on February 9, 1865, only 502 ever reported. The system had failed, and therefore, "the troops are kept constantly employed in repairing the ravages of the winter storms & cutting wood, procuring supplies. . . . They cannot be called off from the lines of entrenchment & do the work for which I desired the negro force."[23]

Earlier, as they watched the enlistment of a black Union

army even while their own pool of white conscripts decreased, some Confederate leaders had broached the forbidden topic of creating their own black corps, not merely of laborers but of soldiers. The first major figure to forward such a plan was Major General Patrick Cleburne, an Irish immigrant and division commander in the Army of the Tennessee. On January 2, 1864, Cleburne and several of his subordinates urged the rest of the western army to organize a reserve corps composed "of the most courageous of our slaves," to whom freedom would be guaranteed in exchange for fighting. Cleburne believed that his proposal would not only entice slaves to enlist in the Confederate army but also win new sympathy in Europe by taking away the slavery issue from the Northern political and military forces that would thus be exposed in the eyes of the world as rapacious conquerors. Realizing that an open discussion of this issue would split the master class, Jefferson Davis hurriedly suppressed circulation of this proposal, which therefore did not become known to the Southern public.[24]

As the bloody summer of 1864 led into the black autumn of the Petersburg trenches, Jefferson Davis himself began to realize that he had to employ slave men in the war effort, as all else was failing. Therefore, on November 7, in his annual message to the Confederate Congress, Davis moved toward the military use of blacks. Realizing that the February 27 impressment act had not worked well, Davis went well beyond Robert E. Lee's proposals for strengthening implementation of that project. Davis wrote that the law on the books dealt with slave laborers "merely as property," something Lee had not challenged; now Davis argued that "the slave, however, bears another relation with the State— that of a person." In this light, Davis proposed to enlist the "zealous discharge of duty" on the part of the labor corps through promising them their freedom, albeit after their service rather than before it. Davis did not propose to arm the blacks, not at least at first, but he wrote that should the white population prove insufficient to fight the war and "should the alternative ever be presented of subjugation or of the employment of the slave as a soldier, there seems no reason to doubt what should be our decision," an oblique way of calling for black troops.[25]

However delicately, Davis had addressed the nub of the question: Black Confederate soldiers possibly would fight (as were their Union brethren already) as persons, not as the things to which slavery reduced them. Considering them as persons meant rejecting their prior definition, upon which slavery and the Confederacy had been based. Not surprisingly, therefore, Davis's proposal aroused a mighty debate in the South. By articulating in public the proposition of both arming and freeing blacks, he had pointed to the deepest contradictions in the ultimate purposes of the Confederacy.

Powerful men opposed this conversion of property into persons as utterly opposite to the Confederate rebellion, which had been intended to keep property as property. "If slaves will make good soldiers our whole theory of slavery is wrong," thundered the influential Georgian politician and general Howell Cobb. "But they won't make soldiers. As a class they are wanting of every qualification of a soldier," which was to say moral manhood. Most of the men in Lee's ranks agreed with Cobb.[26]

In the face of such opposition, the more "progressive" Confederates pressed on, so desperate was the military situation. Finally, on February 10, 1865, Congressman Ethelbert Barksdale of Mississippi introduced an act to enlist blacks. He and others called on Robert E. Lee, whom they viewed as the moral leader of the South, to come on board.

Doubtlessly realizing the divisiveness of this issue, Lee had held aloof from declaring himself in favor of arming blacks for several months longer than Jefferson Davis had. On January 11, in confidence, he wrote to State Senator Andrew Hunter of Virginia that, given the paucity of white manpower and the power of the enemy, "we must decide whether slavery shall be extinguished by our enemies and the slaves be used against us, or use them ourselves at the risk of the effects which may be produced upon our social institutions. My own opinion is that we should employ them without delay." As was true of all men, engaging "the personal interest of the soldiers in the issue of the contest" would be the best possible means to enlist their "fidelity." Therefore, Lee urged "giving immediate freedom to all who enlist and freedom at the end of the war to [their] families." Lee argued for immediate emancipation not out of idealism but on practical grounds. "We should not expect slaves to fight for prospective freedom when they can secure it at once by going to the enemy, in whose service they will incur no greater risk than in ours."

If in this private communication Lee was apparently accepting the principle of black personhood, nevertheless he made it clear to Hunter that he was not suggesting racial equality and that he continued to have little doubt that whites would be able to dominate black men in freedom as they had in slavery. "I believe that with proper regulations they can be made efficient soldiers. They possess the physical qualifications in an eminent degree. Long habits of obedience and subordination, coupled with the moral influence which in our country the white man possesses over the black, furnish an excellent foundation for that discipline which is the best guarantee of military efficiency."[27] Secure in his belief in white supremacy, Lee was willing, in the eleventh hour, to consider freeing and arming the slaves, even with a certain equanimity. He was confident that he could control and discipline black troops, once their fidelity was secured by freedom.

Only rumors of these views reached the Confederate newspapers before February 18, when Lee replied to the request of Congressman Barksdale for a public statement in support of black troops. In this letter, Lee repeated much of what he had said to Hunter, proposing immediate emancipation and repeating his faith in those "habits of obedience [that] constitute a good foundation for discipline," which would make adequate soldiers of blacks. Lee also stressed the lack of practical alternatives to this project, for "our white population" was suffering grievously and was now inadequate in number to carry on much longer, and the enemy "will certainly use [Negroes] against us if he can get possession of them." Lee concluded that "I cannot see the wisdom of holding them to await his arrival, when we may, by timely action and judicious management, use them to arrest his progress."[28]

When they heard of their commander's support of this plan, most of Lee's soldiers were outraged. Reading of it for the first time in the papers, one Virginia artilleryman recorded in his diary, "from today, I date the history of our downfall as a nation," and others responded by deserting such a redefined Confederate cause, or at least by using it to justify an act they already intended. A North Carolinian wrote home, "Mother I did not volunteer my services to fight for a free negroes country but to fight for a free white mans free country & I do not think I love my country well enough to fight with black soldiers."[29] Robert E. Lee was out of touch with the opinion of his men on this issue, or else he was so obsessed with the need for fresh troops that he pressed on despite knowledge of their likely response.

Even with the support of Robert E. Lee, a bill for black soldiers passed the Confederate Senate on March 13 only after a long and bitter debate, by nine votes to eight, and only after it was stripped of any mention of emancipation. However, on March 23, the Confederate War Department slipped emancipation back into their regulations implementing black enlistment.

Finally having joined in this campaign, Lee was keen to get going. Even before Congress had acted, he was pushing Davis to carry the law into effect as soon as possible. "It will probably be impossible to get a large force of this kind in condition to be of service during the present campaign," he wrote Davis on March 10, "but I think no time should be lost in trying to collect all we can. I attach great importance to the result of the first experiment with these troops, and think that if it prove successful, it will greatly lessen the difficulty of putting the law into operation." Pushing as far as his imagination could carry him, on March 24 he called on Davis to immediately seize and enlist all Negroes, free and slave, between the ages of eighteen and forty-five. "The services of these men are now necessary to enable us to oppose the enemy."[30] Desperation had led Lee to abandon states' rights and the sanctity of property for national power and black emancipation, thus contradicting two constitutional foundations of the Confederate revolution.

And even then, nothing much happened. On March 27, Lee complained to the War Department that he had not yet seen the published bill, much less heard of any action. He was prepared to send out some junior officers who had volunteered to recruit black soldiers, but he was also aware that the "enemies of the system" were busily doing all they could to "thwart" such efforts. It was clear that whatever the badly divided Congress had done, public opinion had not been converted. "If the [Virginia] authorities can do nothing to get those negroes who are willing to join the army but whose masters refuse their consent, there is no authority to do it at all," Lee wrote on March 27 to General Richard S. Ewell, who was in charge of the project in Richmond.

All Lee could do was fulminate about the insubordination of the master class. "What benefit they expect their negroes to be to them if the enemy occupy the country, it is impossible to say." Lee suggested that the state simply seize slave soldiers from their unwilling masters, but only if "the negroes should know that their service is voluntary. . . . While of course due respect and subordination must be expected" from them, in return they should be treated like "any other soldiers. . . . Harshness and contemptuous or offensive language or conduct to them must be forbidden and they should be made to forget as soon as possible that they were regarded as menials." Lee spoke as one Southern gentleman to another in the traditional language of command, although in a radically shifted context. "You will readily understand & know how to [cultivate] their good will & elevate the tone & character of the men."[31] Now that he had accepted the proposition, it seemed quite plausible to him, within the realm of his paternalist values.

These amounted to suggestions, after all was said and done, for training phantom troops: While thousands of Virginia slaves freed themselves by fleeing northward and then joined the Union army, few volunteered to be Confederate soldiers, and even fewer masters cooperated. Two or three dozen black recruits did begin to drill, without arms, in the Richmond streets during the last week of March. On March 30, Lee dictated a letter to Ewell that he "regret[ted] very much to learn that owners refuse to allow their slaves to enlist. [I] deem it of great importance that some of this force should be put in the field as soon as possible." Lee pushed Ewell both to "press this view upon the owners" and to take up the "vital" task himself with "energetic and intelligent effort." As the Confederacy collapsed, masters simply refused to join this revolutionary twilight project. Nevertheless, on April 2, the last afternoon before Petersburg and Richmond fell, Lee was still peppering Jefferson Davis with plans to detach some his officers in order to recruit black troops.[32] At the time, Davis was packing his valises and preparing to flee.

Following rather than leading the more innovative among the badly divided Confederate leadership, Lee finally accepted the proposition of free black troops but far too late to make any effective use of them. Indeed, the whole proposal was an absurd pipe dream in assuming that blacks would ever fight for their former masters rather than the enemies of their former masters, and that whites might really be willing to end slavery in the name of independence. Perhaps the deeper meaning of this project was that honor-bound gentlemen such as Lee found it hard to accept, as their republic crumbled, that they had really fought and suffered and died for slavery as opposed to nationhood. However wildly implausible and politically self-contradictory, this weird plan and Lee's considerable interest in it as his nation expired showed that he could at least imagine a war fought in a radically different way.

On the other hand, as the Confederate war effort collapsed, Lee rejected the alternative of guerrilla warfare as a means to prolong Confederate resistance. Although he was confident he could control black troops attached to his army, he was at least equally certain he could not control guerrillas, who would have been drawn mainly from the poor white population. By opposing even the possibility of guerrilla warfare, Lee exposed his deep-seated distrust of the white lower orders, an attitude he sometimes managed to mask.

As in the case of Jeb Stuart after the battle of Gettysburg, Lee's opinion of cavalry, much less guerrillas, was low at best. Cavalry forces were designed to ride off from the infantry into enemy country to collect intelligence and rip up the infrastructure of the other side. Lee the disciplinarian believed that such units were altogether too attractive to the romantic swashbucklers among both the gentlemen and the nomadic poor whites under his command. No reader of Sir Walter Scott, Lee demanded subordination and order from his men, and the cavalry was always going away from his control, off in the direction of indiscipline and self-gratification. To take just one of many examples of his fretting about this service, on August 1, 1863, Lee

supported the promotions of Wade Hampton and of his own
nephew, also named Fitzhugh Lee, to the rank of major general
in the cavalry, but he added to Jefferson Davis that "I should admire both more if they were more rigid in their discipline. But
I know how difficult it is to establish rigid discipline in our
armies," by which Lee implied that the cavalry in particular was
endemically undisciplined.[33]

Throughout the last phase of the war, Lee noted that many
men ran off to join new cavalry units. On January 20, 1864, Lee
advised Jefferson Davis that many Louisianians among his command were deserting to join General John H. Morgan, the daring
cavalry raider who operated in Kentucky and Tennessee. And on
August 14, he wrote to the secretary of war of a similar case
among the Ninth Alabama Infantry Regiment. "The deserters
are supposed to be making their way home with the intention of
joining some cavalry commands that are being organized in Alabama," Lee warned. "Steps should be at once instituted to punish all officers who receive deserters into their commands," he
insisted. The Richmond authorities should forthwith dispatch
an inspector to examine the new units, "and if deserters . . . be
found in them, the authority to raise them revoked, and the officers and men placed in the regular service." Lee believed that
such "evil" units were mainly a means for deserters to white-
wash their crime to the army and then to take up freebooting in
the place of real war.[34]

If the cavalry service was such a threat—and such units
were at least ostensibly under the control of regular army commanders—how much worse were guerrilla units, who were self-
organized and altogether detached from the command
structure, off in remote parts of the border country doing what
they pleased, uninspected, acting as the very embodiment of
Lee's worst nightmares about unchristian warfare. Still, at
times, Lee had to admit that despite their built-in horrors, such

units might be useful at disrupting enemy communications and supplies, gathering information, and compelling the enemy to station thousands of troops in remote regions to combat them, thus weakening their main forces.

Throughout the hill country of the upper South, often behind enemy lines, Southern guerrilla units began to organize themselves early in the war, which the Confederacy recognized in the Partisan Ranger Act of April 1862. The guerrillas of which Lee was most aware were in northern Virginia, particularly the forces of Major John S. Mosby, who fought with considerable effect in Loudon County. Unlike other commanders, Mosby kept strict control of his men, and he coordinated his efforts with the Confederate officers of the regular army, notably Jeb Stuart. Lee appreciated his efforts, frequently singling him out for commendation after one or another action, with such phrases as "Mosby has covered himself with honors" and Mosby fights with "merit and continued success."[35]

And yet, in common with other commanders in the regular army, Lee had increasing doubts about such warfare. Unlike other soldiers, guerrillas lived in their own homes between raiding expeditions, making for lives that were rather more fun than the boring, disciplined ones spent in military camps and the terrifying episodes of major battles. Other troops were envious, often to the point of deserting and joining such bands, not least because the opportunities for loot were so much greater. In his angry mood after Gettysburg, as part of his critique of Stuart, Lee pressed his cousin to rein in Mosby, about whom he had been hearing too many negative stories to let pass any longer. "I greatly commend his boldness and good management," Lee wrote.

> I have heard that he has now with him a large number of men, yet his attention seems more directed to

the capture of suttler's wagons, &c., than to the injury of the enemy's communications and outposts. . . . I have heard of his men, among them officers, being in the rear of this army selling captured goods, suttler's stores, &c. It is also reported that many deserters of this army have joined him. . . . If this is true, I am sure it must be without the knowledge of Major Mosby, but I desire you to call his attention to this matter.[36]

Lee did not mention, if he knew it, that Mosby sometimes executed Union prisoners, a policy returned in kind by the Union general George A. Custer, his leading opponent.

If such abuses were true of Mosby, the best of the lot, what of the behavior of other, even less disciplined bands? Lee was doubtless aware of the horrors carried out by ostensibly Confederate but completely out of control and vicious guerrilla bands in Missouri and the hill country of Appalachia. He also received many reports about other bands in northern Virginia that used Mosby's methods without his redeeming discipline and effectiveness against the enemy army. Moreover, such units became an annoyance to the regular cavalry of the Confederacy operating in western Virginia. On January 11, 1864, Brigadier General Thomas L. Rosser, cavalry commander in the Shenandoah Valley, convinced Stuart, Lee, and the Confederate authorities to disband all such units, except Mosby's. "Without discipline, order, or organization, they roam broadcast over the country, a band of thieves, stealing, pillaging, plundering, and doing every manner of mischief and crime," Rosser told his superiors, knowing what they might loathe. "They are a terror to the citizens and an injury to the cause. They never fight; can't be made to fight . . . and have engaged in this business for the sake of gain. . . . They sleep in their houses and turn out in the cold only when [told] by their chief that they are to go upon a plundering expedition." Rosser, Stuart, and Lee excepted Mosby from this condemnation, and Lee then recommended that such units be disbanded. "The evils resulting from their organization more than counter balance the good they accomplish," Lee concluded. And he followed this up later by insisting that "it is almost impossible . . . to have discipline in these bands . . . or to prevent them from becoming an injury instead of a benefit to the service." This was a "system" of warfare that "gives license to many deserters & marauders, who . . . commit depredations on friend and foe alike" while undermining the morale of regular troops.[37]

The Confederate Congress repealed the Partisan Ranger Act forthwith but authorized the secretary of war to allow bands he thought were doing good service to continue: He then relicensed most of the units, which may have been a practical recognition on his part that they would continue to do battle their way no matter how the authorities might try to curtail them.

As for Lee, however deep his misgivings may have been, he not only continued to praise Mosby until the end of the war but saw some merit in the principle of self-organized guerrilla units operating behind Union lines. In the summer of 1864, the regular Confederate army could do nothing to protect the citizens of the "Northern Neck" of Virginia, between the Rappahannock and Potomac rivers, who were wide open to Union amphibious raids. Lee thus suggested to Davis, "I know of no way to afford them relief, except by their own energy and strength. If they will organize themselves under proper leaders, they can so punish these marauding [Union] bands as to drive them from their country." Writing to the secretary of war the same day, Lee was harder on the Northern Neck citizens long since caught behind the reach of Union troops. "I have always heard that there were a great many men in that country who should have been in this army. . . . I think the least they can do would be to turn out and defend their own homes [and] operate against the enemy as Mosby has done in the Piedmont country." Lee then wrote Mosby to see if he might operate in the Northern Neck, far from his own territory, to train the citizens to organize themselves. To do so, Mosby detached Captain Thomas W. Richards, one of his chief unit commanders, with some of his men. Lee insisted that Richards be prohibited from enrolling deserters but concluded that "I think such a command, well managed, will contribute greatly to the security of the people and their property."[38] Lee saw increased value in guerrilla warfare as the end of the war approached and alternative military methods faltered. In fact, he was reputed to have told Jefferson Davis as the siege at Petersburg neared its end that "with my army in the mountains of Virginia, I could carry on this war for twenty years longer."[39]

However, on April 9, immediately before riding off to the McLean House for his final meeting with Grant, Lee firmly rejected this alternative. Edward Porter Alexander, Lee's head artillerist and a reliable reporter, later wrote that he had presented Lee, in a forceful way, with the alternative of ordering his troops into the woods to fight on as guerrillas, a plan Alexander clearly had been discussing with other younger officers. "If I took your suggestion & ordered the army to disperse, how many do you suppose would get away?" Lee asked Alexander, who thought maybe two thirds. "We would scatter like rabbits & partridges in the woods, & they could not scatter so to catch us." That number would be "too insignificant to accomplish the least good," responded Lee, who understood that his surrender would mean the end of the Confederacy. "And as good Christian men . . . we must consider only the effect which our action will have upon the country at large."

Lee then painted a picture of the brutalities of guerrilla war. "The men would have no rations & they would be under no discipline. They are already demoralized by four years of war. They would have to plunder & rob to procure subsistence. The country would be full of lawless bands . . . and a state of society would ensue from which it would take the country years to recover. Then the enemy's cavalry would pursue . . . & wherever they went there would be fresh rapine & destruction." Whatever others might do, such war making would be beneath Lee's dignity. "As for myself, while you young men might afford to go to bushwhacking, the only proper & dignified course for me would be to surrender myself & take the consequences of my actions." Alexander, "ashamed" that he had proposed such a "wildcat" scheme to Lee, felt his own "little plan . . . vanish in thin air" during Lee's reply. Indeed, even before Richmond had fallen, Alexander himself had written, expressing values he shared with his commander, that "civilized armies cannot fight like savages without bases of supply. Should they try it, their fighting would at once degenerate even below the value of the fighting of savages." And, back in Richmond, on April 20, eleven days after his surrender, Lee wrote in his last wartime letter to Davis, who was in flight southward, "a partisan war may be continued, and hostilities protracted, causing individual suffering and the devastation of the country, but I see no prospect by that means of achieving a separate independence."[40]

Old and tired out by war, Lee simply could not conceive of becoming a guerrilla chieftain, preferring a hateful surrender. There could be no honor in such fighting, nor could he imagine that it might work as a strategy, even if it had been quite effective in the hands of men such as Mosby. Nor could he conceive that men without gentlemen officers and martial discipline would fight other than a barbarian war. In part, this feeling was grounded in Lee's much earlier experience fighting the Indians of Florida and Texas, who used such tactics, as had the Mexicans during the American conquest of their capital. Back then, Lee had written to John Mackay, "We were annoyed during the day by desultory shots from the house tops & corners of streets, but our men becoming impatient, turned to & after killing some 500 of the mob & deserters from the army, who had not the courage to fight us lawfully, the thing was put a stop to."[41] Now, while he could just barely imagine paternalistically controlling free black Confederate troops, the prospect of lower white orders fighting without genteel control and perhaps claiming political power later on was simply unthinkable. Given poor whites' natural propensities to lawless mayhem, if unleashed they would become like bands of Indians or Mexican mongrels.

Rejection of guerrilla warfare was consistent with Lee's antebellum sense of social hierarchy. He had always feared that the Northern disease of mobocracy—democracy run amok—would infiltrate and ruin the South, and guerrilla war was the military expression of that mentality, to which he would never capitulate. He refused to support an alternative that in his opinion would effectively surrender Southern moral distinctiveness and superiority. His sense of political taboo kept him from reconceptualizing the method of warfare the Confederacy might use, even though he had made a few tentative moves in that direction earlier on.

A mode of control of guerrilla bands might have been suggested by the strategy Lee had used when, after Gettysburg, he had attached an inspector from his staff to Jeb Stuart's cavalry, empowering this officer to discipline Stuart and report directly back to Lee. And Lee was sufficiently taken with John S. Mosby that he could ask one of Mosby's best lieutenants to go to a remote part of the Confederacy, well within the Union orbit of power, to set up a guerrilla operation. Moreover, guerrilla war was quite widespread during the Civil War, and many young men, even young gentlemen such as Edward Porter Alexander, were prepared to take to bushwhacking. There also was available to Lee the well-known precedent of the Spanish guerrilla war against the Napoleonic invaders, which, when coupled with Wellington's English army, had been enormously successful during the Peninsular War of the early nineteenth century.

Far closer to home and more to the point, during the American Revolution guerrilla forces often had been the main American combatants. During the war, George Washington, Lee's idealized father figure, was able to keep only a small regular force in the field and so learned to employ irregular bands of militia effectively, all the while proclaiming that, as a gentleman, he abhorred them. Much of the Revolutionary War was an essentially guerrilla conflict, with militia bands spying on British columns and raiding them as well as defending areas remote from the regular army. Although his later reputation rested on a very small number of engagements in which he used regular troops, Washington actually incorporated many more disjointed hit-and-run assaults than set-piece battles. Washington had enough imagination and flexibility to become quite masterful at using the sort of guerrilla tactics Lee avoided.[42]

By April 8, 1865, Lee was right that it was too late to sanction such warfare. But earlier he might have considered extending the legacy of Washington and the tactics of Mosby, whom he valued, into a vast network of guerrilla bands disciplined by trained cadres controlled in turn by a central military staff. Through these means, earlier and later victorious civil-war guerrilla armies have maintained considerable discipline even while dispersed. And Lee had some of the institutional sensibility to have walked farther down that road. He had considerable experience in using a strict system of discipline, as well as some practice in assigning officers from the center to the periphery, from where they would then exercise authority and report back to him. Yet because of social, political, and religious considerations, and a certain theoretical rigidity, as well as personal ill health and exhaustion, Lee would not fight just any war. Honor, decency, and conservatism meant that for Lee guerrilla war would be the war not fought. In this, Lee conformed with the gentlemen of station and honor who had wished to make a Christian commonwealth out of their new nation and who preferred death to what they considered disorder and dishonor.

CINCINNATUS

fter the conclusion of the Revolutionary War, and again following his eight years as founding president, George Washington gave up power and returned to his "farm" at Mount Vernon to resume the simple agrarian life. If Washington had consciously modeled himself on the noble Cincinnatus, a Roman military hero who had renounced dictatorship for rustication, Washington's stepgrandson-in-law wished to copy the first president. Lee spent the first two months following Appomattox in a rented home in Richmond, where he was surrounded by unwelcome urban bustle, Union troops, and altogether too many nosy visitors. While there, becoming aware of the possibility of his arrest and trial for treason, he longed to escape to the countryside where he might find bucolic repose. To an old friend, he wrote, "I am looking for some little, quiet home in the woods, where I can procure shelter and my daily bread, if permitted by the victor. I wish to get Mrs. Lee out of the city as soon as practical."[1] This arcadian fantasy became a leitmotif of Lee's postwar life—the wistful desire for escape from the dutiful life he believed he had to maintain until death.

As he scouted for a place of his own, Lee accepted the offer of an old friend to take up residence in a modest overseer's home on a plantation near Cartersville, fifty miles west of Richmond. He rode the countryside on his favorite horse, Traveler, looking for land suitable for wheat cultivation and livestock grazing, something more modest than the plantations of his gentry forebears. As soon as he could determine whether he would be free of the legal vise of the conquerors, he wrote his son Fitzhugh, "I shall endeavour to procure some humble, but quiet abode for your mother and sisters, where I hope they can be happy. . . . I want to get in some grass country, where the natural product of the land will do much for my subsistence."[2] Quite understandably after the horrors of four years of war, Lee desired personal peace and escape from the hurly-burly of men and politics.

Nevertheless, a scant few weeks later, when an offer arrived for the presidency of Washington College, in the quiet and lovely Blue Ridge town of Lexington, attractive because of its relative distance from Richmond and its constant reminders of the damages war had brought, Lee quickly returned to a life of social engagement and institutional leadership. By mid-September 1865, he rode off alone on Traveler to take up his new post, sending for Mary Lee several months later after he had established a residence. He stayed in educator's traces until the end of his life, five years later. Still, the fulfillment of his Cincinnatian destiny remained a comforting dream until the end of his days. Even as he had taken up his task, he had written to Fitzhugh, contrasting private desire with public duty: "I accepted the presidency of the college in the hopes that I might be of service to the country & the rising generation, & not from any preference of my own. I should have selected a more quiet life & . . . should have preferred a small farm where I could have earned my daily bread."[3] His head instructed Lee that he should choose complete retirement and isolation if he were to emulate his hero George Washington, but his heart and his sense of duty kept him in an active life, if in a little place.

Lee continued to articulate this dualism of duty and pleasure. In 1867, two years into his final posting, he wrote Fitzhugh, "It would be most pleasant to my feelings could I again . . . gather all around me, but I fear it will not be in this world. Let us all so live that we may be united in that world where there is no more separation, and where sorrow and pain never come. I think after next year I will have done all the good I can for the college, and I should then like . . . to move . . . east of the mountains" to that mythic little farm.[4] By locating his dream in more distant country—far from the coastal plantation lands of his ancestors, in a sort of imitation of Eden—Lee was mentally approaching that stress-free final place where he would reunify his family for eternity.

In his paternal roles within his own family, in society more generally, and as an educator, Lee actively engaged in life rather than retreated from it. He remained both head of his family and General Lee, commander of the Army of Northern Virginia. Within Lee, fantasies of escape and his normal austerity and reserve combined with a considerable sense of social commitment as he strove to help the next generation of young men make better lives. And yet there was a dark and mordant tone in all his words after the war that revealed the scars of that terrible experience and deepening pessimism. Continued effort was shot through with a sense of irretrievable loss, a retreat of a different sort.

Though Lee never took to farming, two of his sons, Fitzhugh and Rob, did, on Custis lands, and their father was full of sage agricultural advice for them, both practical and moral. Indeed, he filled a considerable portion of his postwar correspondence with his specialized knowledge, derived perhaps from his few unhappy years at the end of the 1850s when he had tried to turn a profit at Arlington. For example, on October 26, 1867, he wrote to Rob in the manner of an enlightened agricultural reformer, "the only way to improve your crop is to improve your land, which requires time, patience, and good cultivation. Lime, I think, is one of the chief instruments, and I advise you to apply that systematically and judiciously. I think, too, you had better purchase another pair of mules." Like Southern farmers everywhere after the Civil War, Rob was undercapitalized, and so his father freely offered him a loan to cover such expensive improvements. "I can help you in these items, and, if you need, can advance you $500. Then, as regards a house, I can help you in that too."

Lee coupled such advice and aid to moralistic conclusions of the relentless sort that had always been normal for him. Responding to Rob's tale of minks eating his hens, Lee preached, "a failure in crops will occur occasionally to every farmer, even the best, with favourable surroundings. It serves a good purpose, inculcates . . . energy and perseverance. . . . You are very young still, and if you are virtuous and laborious you will accomplish all the good you propose to yourself." The next spring, Lee commented again about these reverses: "You must . . . take a lesson from the last season. What you cultivate, do well. Improve and prepare the land in the best manner; your labour will be less, and your profits more."[5] Paternalism came in well-worn top-down language.

Rob seems to have taken his father's intense interest in all his affairs with both resentment and a grain of salt. Years later, when he was writing his memoirs, Rob recalled a visit from his father in 1868, when Rob was unmarried. "My father, always dignified and self-contained, rarely gave any evidence of being astonished or startled. His self-control was great and his emotions were not on the surface, but when he entered and looked around my bachelor quarters he appeared really much shocked [at my slovenliness]. However, he soon rallied and concealed his dismay by making kindly fun of my surroundings."[6] Lee toured the farm, discussing Rob's plans for improvement and, after he returned home, sent his son new sets of china and silver plate.

Lee's letters to Rob also contained admonitions about marrying well. "I am clear for your marrying, if you select a good wife; otherwise you had better remain as you are for a time. An imprudent or uncongenial woman is worse than *the minks.*" Lee did not leave off with such warnings, however. He actively hunted for a wife for Rob among the wide circle of his young women cousins and acquaintances, with many of whom he formed deep attachments of his own. After that visit to Rob in his distressingly unhomelike bachelor quarters, he wrote to Caroline Stuart, who had dropped by during his visit: "I have been looking for you and [your sister] Annette all the spring and I believe that it is the 'hope deferred' that made me sick. You ought not to disappoint me, Carrie, for I cannot stand broken promises like the young men. I enjoyed my visit to Robert very much and wished that you were there all the time. Everything would have gone well then. The leaky house . . . would not have been felt and his household would have been perfectly satisfactory." During his sojourn with Rob, Lee evidently had pressed his courtship of Carrie on Rob's behalf. "You have had such experience of the ill success of my 'courtships' that I hardly think you can expect any good results from them. How far has my suit with you prospered, or what encouragement do you suppose it has given me to undertake anything of the kind with another? None; nor have I attempted it."[7] It was as if Lee flirted on behalf of his sons, promising the lucky young woman an ardent father-in-law and by generational extension a suitable groom. In his lifetime, Lee never succeeded in marrying off Rob, although he certainly considered it his proper business.

Lee offered his daughters just as much instruction about the appropriate shapes of the domestic sphere, although he also smothered them with an intense and sentimental affection. This was especially true in the case of his youngest and favorite daughter, Mildred, his "Precious Life." Even during the war, he often paused to offer Mildred words of love and discipline. In February 1862, he wrote her from Savannah, "and are you really sweet sixteen? That is charming, and I want to see you more than ever. . . . I hope, after the war is over, we may again all be united, and I may have some pleasant years with my dear children." And then the father interrupted this reverie to interject his comprehension of the transitory nature of life for old and young. "Rob says he is told that you are a young woman. I have grown so old, and become so changed, that you would not know me. But I love you just as much as ever, and you know how great a love that is."[8]

This great love included admonitions that Mildred perform her womanly duties with exactitude. During the war, Lee repeatedly urged sacrifice on Mildred as the appropriate home-front accompaniment to the sacrifices the soldiers were making. As Lee was all too aware that his daughters were still buying clothes, attending parties, and traveling to visit other young women, there was a certain annoyance in his letters that they might be having too good a time of it as the Confederacy struggled. "You must study hard, gain knowledge, and learn your duty to God and your neighbor; that is the great object of life," Lee told Mildred in his Christmas letter to her in 1862. Two years later, as Lee was growing quietly desperate about the future of his nation, the advice intensified. "Habituate yourself to useful employment, regular improvement . . . diligence and study . . . and to the benefit of all those around you. . . . Never neglect the means of making yourself useful."[9]

After the war, as poverty and the depression of defeat blanketed the South, Lee continued to remind Mildred about the necessary practice of sacrifice for properly disciplined gentry women. "You must bear in mind that it will not be becoming in a Virginia girl now to be fine or fashionable, and that gentility as well as self-respect requires moderation in dress and gaiety," he wrote her in 1867. "While her people are suffering, she should practice self-denial and show her sympathy in their affliction." Lee's use of Stoicism, applicable to all noblewomen and noblemen, sometimes amounted to an extremist effort to control his daughter. He was quite liberal in giving instructions about Mildred's very body, as well as her clothes—he knew exactly how she should look and how much she should weigh.

> I am delighted at your increased bodily dimensions, and your diminished drapery. One hundred and twenty-eight pounds avoirdupois is approximately a proper standard. Seven more pounds will make you all right. But I fear before I see you the unnatural life, which I fear you will lead in Baltimore, will reduce you to skin and bone. Do not go out to many parties, preserve your simple tastes and manners, and you will enjoy more pleasure. Plainness and simplicity of dress, early hours, and rational amusements, I wish you to practice.[10]

Polonius Lee criticized the most private characteristics of his daughters, body and soul.

Lee also told Mildred that no other man would ever love her as strongly as he did. Indeed, one of the reasons he criticized her gallivanting and high living was that such practices took her away from him, which he resented even while he struggled to understand their appeal. "I want to see you very much, and miss you at every turn, yet am glad of this opportunity for you to be with those who, I know, will do all in their power to give you pleasure," he wrote when Mildred was away at Ashby plantation on the Eastern Shore of Maryland for Christmas in 1866. "I was much pleased, too, that, while enjoying the kindness of your friends, we were not forgotten. Experience will teach you that, notwithstanding all appearances to the contrary, you will never receive such a love as is felt for you by your father and mother. That lives through absence, difficulties, and time."[11]

Lee's fatherly jealousy and covetousness for his daughter's exclusive love, which lurked beneath such platitudes, was not lost on his children. Years after his father's death, Rob commented on how pleased his father had been when Fitzhugh finally had remarried, which he saw as a fulfillment of his courting exercises on his son's behalf among the appropriate gentry daughters of the Old Dominion. "He was an earnest advocate of matrimony, and was constantly urging his sons to take themselves wives." In contrast were the sentiments Mildred had received from her father, as Rob noted shrewdly. "With his daughters he was less pressing. Though apparently always willing to have another daughter, he did not seem to long for any more sons."[12]

While Lee's two younger sons married, none of his daughters ever did. In 1888, Mildred recorded with great sadness in her diary that she had been unable to find an appropriate husband to measure up to her father's standard. "To me he seems a Hero—& all other men small in comparison." And in 1905, at the very end of her life, she concluded about her retrospectively empty life of travel and housekeeping for others, "most women when they lose such a Father, replace it by husband & children —I have had nothing."[13] Mildred's eldest sister, Mary Custis Lee, led an even more deracinated life, roaming the world as a rich adventurer, lonely for her distant family and for a marriage she thought she might have contracted. And although Rob and Fitzhugh led relatively comfortable lives as plantation proprietors, and in Fitzhugh's case as a congressman late in the century, their elder brother, Custis, had an increasingly miserable time as titular president of the renamed Washington and Lee University, where he withdrew into his obsessively tidy home, plagued by his inherited rheumatoid arthritis, depressed, and perhaps alcoholic. He remained unmarried and may have been homosexual, referring as he did to his valet, William Price, as "my chamber maid, who is a man," who did everything for him. During his declining years, with extreme coldness, Custis and William Price squeezed Mildred out of her previous role as his hostess.[14] Such were some of the fruits of Robert E. Lee's demanding fathering.

Overbearing and hypercritical he might have been toward his children, but he was deeply loving at the same time, much more expressively with his daughters than with his sons. Typical of the Virginia gentry class in which he was bred, Lee had a sense of paternal connection that was not restricted to his own nuclear family but extended outward to his wide circle of kin and beyond them to all the young people of genteel standing with whom he came into contact. Essentially distant and correct with the boys, Lee allowed his emotions to flow far more freely with the girls. During and after the war, his most satisfying relationships clearly were with the belles of his social class.

As he did to his daughters during the war, Lee often rallied the young women of his acquaintance to the Confederate banner of discipline and duty, to a kind of feminine equivalent to soldiering. On the surface, such a role was crystal clear in Lee's mind. To his daughter-in-law Charlotte he wrote in 1863, "I want all the husbands in the field, and their wives at home encouraging them, loving them and praying for them." Spartan duty ought to include vigorous reproduction, especially during war. To an old friend whose wife was pregnant, he wrote in 1862, "tell Mrs. Maggie we want boys not girls now. Soldiers are the

word in time of war."[15] Actual war blurred gender distinctiveness as women often assumed "male" roles, but for men such as
Lee it was important to heighten those boundaries, the better to
foster a sense of duty for all.

Such attempts at role clarification were not, however, to
imply that appropriately womanly women were other than
tough. Indeed, in one letter written to his wife and daughters
late in 1863, Lee held up a stirring example to encourage them
to harden their feelings and bend their backs to the cause on
the domestic front. "I fear my daughters have not taken to the
spinning-wheel and loom, as I have recommended. I shall not be
able to recommend them to the brave soldiers for wives," he
scolded. Lee then offered the story just told him by a young
South Carolinian wife during a visit to her husband, a junior officer.

> She said she had not seen her husband for more than
> two years, and, as he had written to her for clothes,
> she herself thought she would bring them on. It was
> the first time she had traveled by railroad, but she got
> along very well by herself. She brought an entire suit
> of her own manufacture for her husband. She spun
> the yarn and made the clothes herself. She clad her
> three children in the same way, and had on a beautiful
> pair of gloves she had made for herself. Her children
> she had left with her sister. She said she had been
> here a week and could not go back without seeing me.
> Her husband accompanied her to my tent, in his nice
> gray suit. She was very pleasing in her manner, and
> was clad in a nice, new alpaca. . . . Ask Misses Agnes
> and [her frivolous friend] Sally Warwick what they
> think of that. They need not ask me for permission to
> get married until they can do likewise. She in fact was

an admirable woman. Said she was willing to give up everything she had in the world to attain our independence, and the only complaint she made of the conduct of our enemies was their arming of our servants against us. Her greatest difficulty was to procure shoes. She made them for herself and children of cloth with leather soles. She sat with me about ten minutes and took her leave—another mark of sense—and made no request for herself or husband.[16]

Such was Lee's womanly wartime beau ideal: uncomplaining, deferential, self-sufficient, duty bound, and withal lovely and feminine. Yet Lee also believed that most women were rather weaker than this paragon, and many of his attitudes were based on the belief that, even during war, women, lesser beings that they were, needed protecting and comforting. The heroic Carolinian had been a welcome exception.

In part, Lee was haunted by the rape of the Sabine women, an image he frequently invoked. "I fear . . . the yankees will bear off [our] pretty daughters," he wrote his daughter Annie, early in the war, when describing Yankee raiding practices among the coastal Carolina plantations. "I fear the enemy will capture you & bear you & your sweet sisters away," he wrote to his young cousin Jennie Washington, late in the war, as Union troops swept through the Virginia piedmont where she was living.[17]

Lee was less fearful of literal rape than of the loss of Southern women from his protection to that of the enemy and the threats to masculine and paternal honor this entailed. His larger concern was that, given their natural moral weakness and their eagerness to please men, captured Southern women might be seduced—again, on a symbolic rather than an actual plane—into giving out vital information to their enemies. In this vein, he wrote his wife in 1863 that he had given passes through the Southern lines to a Mrs. Murdock and her daughters. "I know the yankees will get out of them all they know. I hope they know nothing to injure us, but the yankees have a very coaxing & insidious manner, that our Southern women in their artlessness cannot resist, no matter how favourable they may be to our cause or how full of good works for our men."[18]

Enchanting women were also a danger because they could distract soldiers from their duties. On the other hand, the company of beautiful belles was a most significant compensation for the horrors of war. Throughout the conflict, especially when his army was encamped for prolonged periods, Lee actively sought the visits of lovely women, whose company remained his greatest source of relaxation and hope. They reminded him why war was worth fighting, dominance worth attaining. Quite conscious of these emotions, he wrote to his daughter Agnes during the long siege at Petersburg, "Miss Jennie Pegram is at present agitating the thoughts [of the soldiers]. I see her light face as she flashes it on her bearers—but in pity she turns it away from me, for it is most dazzling." Lee was a bit guilty when he admitted to Agnes just how attractive he found Pegram. And then he concluded about the intermissions characteristic of war making, "Cupid is always busy when Mars is quiet."[19]

Quite often, when flirting with young women, Lee displaced his own desires by expressing them to young women whom he saw as attached to his sons. Thus he wrote to Margaret Stuart in 1864, "a soldier's heart, you know, is divided between love and glory," going on to "warn" her that one soldier, his son Rob, "goes to Richmond today who has his share of both [love and glory]. You will probably see him. Elevate his desire for the latter but do not hearken to his words for the former."[20] This rather complex jest concerned desire that Lee expressed on behalf of his son to his son's sweetheart.

Margaret Stuart, and even more her sister Caroline, were special favorites of Lee during the war. When they visited the army, Lee offered them the freedom of his camp. "How are you this morning?" he wrote the day after they arrived, when he had failed to see them. "I hope well & bright. Tell me what you wish to do. If you want to go anywhere I will send up the wagon. . . . If you are not comfortable I can get you a room. . . . But I always have a tent for you. You would make my ungainly camp very bright & cheerful & we would hail your presence as the advent of angels."[21]

Following this visit, when Caroline sent the general a pair of underpants she had sewn for him, Lee was almost rapturous in his response. "Dear Carrie . . . your handiwork will impart to them I am sure some additional warmth. I examined them anxiously to see if I could discover any impression of your sweet self, but could not. I fear you did not look at them during your work."[22] Lee then told Carrie how much he wanted to see her again, as did other Confederate officers. What was he thinking when he wrote this letter? What had Carrie been thinking while sewing? Cupid was not so far from the surface of this task nor from the banter about angelic self and averted gaze.

Charlotte, the wife of his son Fitzhugh, was the recipient of Lee's most ardent missives. Shortly after he returned to Richmond from Savannah in the spring of 1862, he wrote her, "I want to see you very much & am always thinking of you. It is very hard I think for you to say you did not want to come to me [immediately]." Voicing his apprehension about the adorable weakness he attributed to most women, he wrote to Charlotte, his feminine pet, "You are such a little sieve you cannot retain anything. But there is no harm in you sweet child & I love you all the more for it & so does Fitzhugh."[23] By including his son—her husband—as another man who appreciated her innocent wiles, Lee partially censored too direct an expression of his manly love for her.

Later that year, in the middle of the Peninsula campaign, Lee took the time to answer a letter from Charlotte. "And now I must answer your inquiries about myself," he wrote her, and then painted a pen picture more personal and complete than he ever wrote to anyone else. "My habiliments are not as comfortable as yours. . . . My coat is of gray, of the regulation style and pattern, and my pants of dark blue . . . partly hid by long boots. I have the same handsome hat which surmounts my gray head . . . and shields my ugly face which is masked by a white beard as stiff and wiry as the teeth of a card." Lee then concluded with what can best be termed insincere self-deprecation, "In fact, an uglier person you have never seen, and so unattractive is it to our enemies that they shoot at it whenever visible to them, but though age with its snow has whitened my head, and its frosts have stiffened my limbs, my heart, you well know, is not frozen to you, and summer returns when I see you."[24] This rather lugubrious self-portrait concluded with the image of a still youthful heart overcoming an aging body in contemplation of a beautiful young woman. Charged with romance, this was also an appreciation of the life force for which young women stood in Lee's mind and heart.

This genre of writing was the most affirmative, indeed almost the sole positive form of expression for Lee both during and after the war; it was an urgent plea for joy written by a man who was deeply troubled by the catastrophe of war and usually deeply resigned to the fates, including often painful aging and fast-approaching death. Never totally free from the ritualist conventions in which they were expressed, Lee's desires humanized him, even as he would have blushed at the full contents of his thoughts, could he have acknowledged them to himself.

After the war, Lee's recreational life centered on long rides into the countryside on Traveler and extended visits to spas, in part to bring relief to Mary from her terrible rheumatoid arthritis and in part to socialize, with the gentlemen to be sure, but especially with Lee's wide circle of young female admirers. Many of his horseback rides led to visits with neighbors, often enough young women. One hot August day in 1865, Lee wrote to his old friend James H. Caskie to tell his daughter, Norvell, another favorite, "I rode over yesterday to see Miss Anna Logan—She looked killing and acted as bad. I took with me four beaux. They pretended to be overcome by the heat, but I knew from what they were suffering. . . . Her eyes were dark as India's sun & just as warm."[25] Again, Lee displaced his desire onto the suitable young bachelors.

Lee loved to gossip with his daughters, especially Agnes and Mildred, and to feel drawn into their circles of girlfriends. Indeed, when they traveled he asked them to extend invitations to his favorites to visit him in Lexington or at the spas. On March 28, 1868, he requested of Agnes, who was traveling among the plantations of the tidewater, "as to the young ladies [you are seeing] tell them that I want to see them very much & hope that they will come to the mountains this Summer, & not pass us by in Lexington. When you go to [the other plantations] do the same there for me & present me to all by name. Tell sweet Sallie Warwick I think she ought to come to Lexington if only to shew those babies; but in truth I want to see her more than them, so she may leave them with Major Poor if she chooses."[26]

When the young ladies—who must have been immensely flattered to have captured the attention of the South's most glorious hero, a man who remained attractive and charming— came to the mountains or the springs, Lee flirted with them gallantly. One cannot know much of the contents and limits of such happy hours, but it is clear from his letters that the company of these young women gave Lee considerable pleasure. On August 23, 1869, Lee wrote to Miss Bessie Johnston, who had just left White Sulphur Springs, "I send a stereoptic view of the Springs, the only one I could get. I hope it may serve to recall sometimes a spot to the insides of which you have given me so much pleasure. I also enclose a photographic picture of an old man who will think often of you, which I do not wish you to forget."[27] Whatever had passed in that private place—a glance, some words, an embrace—had been an exchange of intimacy that Lee sought to remember, even as he made Bessie Johnston aware that he knew he was not an appropriate young lover but a great and masculine (if aged) admirer nevertheless.

It is clear that many of the young women flirted right back. "Your own little friend Nettie," as she called herself, who had passed some time in the general's company, wrote to Lee in 1869, after receiving his photograph, as had so many other young women: "You have made me so happy. I cannot tell you in my little letter how much I prize your dear likeness. I will frame it with a glass over it, so that I can kiss it as often as I wish without wearing it away. I am glad my little violets obeyed me, but they could not tell dear Gen. Lee how much little Nettie loves him." Then, as if embarrassed by the intensity of the recollection of her pleasure, Nettie veered off into a discussion of seeing him again, if not in this world then "when we meet in the City with Golden streets and pearly gates, for I asked my Heavenly Father to let dear Gen. Lee live a long time, then to take him to the Home of the blest."[28] After coming quite close in flirtation, Nettie regained appropriate distance through piety, remembering for them both that heavenly love surpassed worldly love.

Quite often, Lee qualified his desire for a young woman and for himself by using his age in a rather distancing and self-protective manner. Less than a month after Appomattox, for example, he wrote to Belle Stuart from Richmond, "I am surprised Miss Belle that you should want the likeness of an old man when you can get that of so many young ones, but as Keith says such is the case, I send the last I have. I hope it may serve to recall sometimes one who will never forget you."[29] Beneath the modesty, Lee was pleased to have been asked; even right at the end of the horrific war he could summon up that old flirtatious gallantry. Indeed, such exchanges must have been therapeutic, as Lee sought to put the warrior role behind him and reintegrate himself into normal civilian life.

In a similar fashion during the postwar years, Lee often responded to the letters announcing the marriages or motherhood of women he remembered from earlier times and other places with fervid romantic nostalgia. Hearing from Julie Cheatham in 1866, Lee sent her his picture. "Do you recognize your old uncle? You will ever live in my memory as my 'beautiful Julie,' and I require nothing to recall you to my recollection. You stand before me now, as you then appeared in the broad sunlight of your youth & joy; undimmed by a single shadow of the intervening years." Then Lee continued with a peculiar although not unique burst of self-reproach, as if he was unworthy of the beautiful Julie of blessed memory. "I hesitate to darken the doors of those whom I regard, lest I should hang on them some disaster. But I hope some day that I may again see you, & that your little children may not learn to abhor me." Here Lee appeared to be taking blame for the loss of the war, expressing feelings of shame. Lee had just been to Washington to testify to Congress, which made him feel loathed. In this same frame of mind he wrote Markie Williams, "I saw . . . other friends, whose kind reception gave me much pleasure, yet I am considered now such a monster, that I hesitate to darken with my shadow the doors of those I love lest I should bring upon them misfortune." Lee had never pictured himself so negatively before the war. That he did so afterward was one more marker of his loss of faith in life.[30]*

Lee sometimes seemed to be acknowledging that he had lost his prewar sense of vivacity, his own "youth & joy." To himself he appeared to be something of an old warhorse, going through the romantic motions, still with a modicum of pleasure but with an accompanying sensibility that such passions were more of the past than the present and that death was not so far off. A letter from Laura Mason Chilton in 1869 led Lee to recall his days in the late 1850s when he had been a considerably more buoyant lieutenant colonel. "Your invitation to your wedding," he wrote her in reply, "has carried me back to the pleasant days when you were a little girl in Texas, when you and [your sister] Emmie gave me so much pleasure, the purest if not the greatest I enjoyed while there."[31] Remembering the lovely little girls had triggered memories of less pure pleasures with another, grown woman as well, Lee hinted.

Some revisitations of old loves were less positive, particularly with Lee's long-term, intense correspondent, his cousin Markie Williams, who had sat out the war in Philadelphia. In 1866, in hopes of making a match, Lee evidently encouraged Fitzhugh, his widowed son, to visit Markie, as part of the pattern of Lee's dealings with especially attractive young women. The voyage did not go well, and Lee later wrote Markie with unusual anger, "you did not behave with your usual charity towards your escort from Lexington. His devoted attraction entitled him to commendation, even if he seems unable to please. Did you fear he was a widower, Markie? You seem intuitively to recoil from

---

* Lee reconfigured this form of negativity about himself, which seized him from time to time until the end of his life, such as when he was thinking about a visit to his nephew Edward Lee Childe and Childe's sister, who lived in Paris. "I should . . . be nothing but a trouble & inconvenience wherever I went & I am afraid that my niece would be ashamed of her uncle, who would be a kind of wild man from the woods, in the midst of her gay & polished circle." It is hard to imagine Lee in buckskins, and this passage is comic, and yet it evokes something darker (Lee to Edward L. Childe, February 19, 1870, SH).

their fascinations, though your eventual escape is so impossible."[32] Markie deeply loved the father and resented that he had sent his son as emissary and potential substitute, but in return Lee at least affected to have been too dense to understand why this eligible young woman rejected such a fine marriage possibility as his Fitzhugh.

Markie continued to pour out her feelings in her letters, and usually Lee offered a sympathetic ear. In 1868, he wrote her, "You must not let your . . . perplexities weigh upon you, but take them cheerfully, until you find a way to dispose of them. Our cares multiply upon us as we progress in the world & we must strive to lighten them by prudence & resignation." Over the long term, Markie's complaining put Lee off, and in her case at least Lee retreated into formality and his distancing old-man ritual to express his frustration with her. When, in 1869, she wrote that he had been ignoring her, he wrote, "I am sure that a lady of your good manners need not be at a loss for the reason why you have not heard from me for some time. It is not customary for an old man to write to young ladies unless there is sufficient cause to justify it, & it is generally considered that a letter or other initiative is necessary to authorize the liberty."[33]

Markie intruded too much upon Lee's present and claimed so much of his attention that he put her down as presumptuous. But in her heart he remained ever dominant. When he died, Markie was disconsolate. She wrote to Agnes from Philadelphia that whereas Agnes had around her "so many sympathizing & grieving hearts," she herself was "in a distant country as it were—in a strange boarding house & mourning without one responsive heart."[34] Markie envied most of all Agnes's proximity to Lee in his last years, while she had banished herself to Yankeedom, unable to rekindle their intimate connection.

If Markie flunked the transformation to dearly loved

daughter-in-law for Fitzhugh, the glamorous and far younger Richmond belle Charlotte Haxall, whom Lee called Lottie, took Markie's place well before she became engaged to Rob in 1870. During the protracted courtship before that event, Lee relished Lottie's visits, to which he responded with ardent courtship letters on Rob's behalf, which quite vividly revealed his own reactions to her allures. After one such occasion, in the fall of 1867, Lee wrote her, "your letter has given me the only consolation I have experienced since your departure. You must have felt how much I thought of you, & how truly I regretted your absence. . . . You need not fear anyone taking your place in my affections. You were firmly fixed there when you were a sweet little school girl, & will remain there forever. . . . Come back to us then & fill to overflowing the measure of my gratitude in the way that you know."35*

Isolation, separation, and a great sadness suffused these letters to young women, which stood in the place of missives Lee once had written with playful and energetic erotic force. Such young women and such letters now triggered memories of times long past. Lee deeply felt his aging and the imminence of his end even while he repeated the rituals of flirtation, the erotic inferences of which he often projected onto younger men of actual eligibility. Even if in shadow form, young women were still absolutely central to his emotional life, as if in compensation for heartbreak. They were youthful, even childlike waifs, ignorant of war and hard usage, culturally constructed innocents in whom he could delight even while he knew that they could not

---

* Although she clearly had stormed the heights of the Lee family hierarchy, not all the Lees were as taken with Lottie as was the general. In 1867, Fitzhugh commented to his second wife, Tabb, "She is certainly attractive and stylish in her appearance but she does not care particularly for me." Lottie seems to have aroused Fitzhugh's envy and jealousy for his father's attentions, perhaps in part on his wife's behalf, because Lee was more smitten with Lottie than with Tabb—indeed, in this letter to Tabb, Fitzhugh called Lottie "the Monster" (Fitzhugh to Mary Tabb Bolling Lee, White House, July 27, 1867, VHS).

really lift his heavy spirits for long. He knew that in this life, whatever his longings, he could never return to Eden, nor bite again the golden apple of sensual awakening. Neither was there a remote and perfect little farm beyond the Blue Ridge available for his escape from the trials of the world.

Chapter 12

BARBARIANS IN THE GARDEN

*E*xpressive and indulgent (if also controlling) toward the young women who encircled him, Lee was far harder on young men. Indeed, they became his vocation when, after the briefest exercise in pastoral retreat in the summer of 1865, he accepted the presidency of Washington College. This choice was not such an occupational stretch for Lee, who had been a successful superintendent of West Point in the early 1850s and who was nothing if not used to the command of young men. Lee's new career also was therapeutic for him, partial compensation for all those dead young Confederates of his army. He would not, of course, indulge the survivors and their younger brothers but would shape them for the challenges of the South to come. Lee stated the matter quite clearly: "I have a self-imposed task, which I must accomplish. I have led the young men of the South in battle; I have seen many of them fall under my standard. I shall devote all my life now to training young men to do their duty in life."

For Lee, education essentially meant moral education, with the development of skills and intellectual exploration as servants to building sterling character. Thus, his educational philosophy could be stated in a few clear and simple maxims, accessible to all young men. "Obedience to lawful authority is the foundation of manly character" was one of his favorites. "My only object is to endeavour to make them see their true interest, to teach them to labour diligently for their improvement, and to prepare themselves for the great work of life" was another. In a theologically inconsistent but morally earnest manner, Lee believed that each student had the capacity to master evil and discover and implement the universal moral code. In this premise he was something of a progressive educator, who insisted on teaching by moral suasion rather than by the physical force favored by traditionalist, Calvinist-tinged educators. Indeed, he consciously departed from military discipline. "As a general principle," he told one of the young professors he had hired, "you should not force young men to do their duty, but let them do it voluntarily and thereby develop their characters. The great mistake of my life was in taking a military education." Lee's disciplinary system at Washington College grew from this faith in the potential for individual moral capacity and responsibility. At its core was the unwritten but clear honor code: Students pledged not to cheat and to report on themselves if they realized they had cheated. Yet when students did transgress, Lee was a strict disciplinarian. "Make no needless rules," he instructed his faculty, as well as "we must never make rules that we cannot enforce," from which it followed that when enforcement came, it would be precise and unflinching.[1]

"We have but one rule here, and that is that every student must be a gentleman," Lee wrote an incoming student, distilling his beliefs down to what he regarded as the cardinal point. Although he was not clear whether he meant each student ought to be a gentleman in order to be admitted or that he expected him to behave like a gentleman while enrolled, Lee did not imply that every young man had this potential. He ran his college for the young men of the gentry class from which he had sprung. That this was the pool from which he sought to draw his students Lee made perfectly clear in a letter he wrote late in 1865 to John B. Baldwin, Speaker of the Virginia House of Delegates, in which he discussed access to education at the University of Virginia in a way that could apply to his aspiring institution as well. Young gentlemen of the best sort ought to study the

> most elevated branches of science and literature. But this character of instruction is required by the few; men of high capacity, great industry, devoted to certain arts and professions; not for the many; nor is it needed for the industrial classes, who have neither the time nor opportunity for acquiring it. In this way, by raising the tone of society, the character of the people, that standard of education at the colleges of the country, would perform its part.[2]

Although young men of great merit from the industrial classes might be granted entry in exceptional circumstances, the student body, like the junior officer cadre of the Army of Northern Virginia, was designed for young gentlemen of Lee's class. Properly educated, they would refine, elevate, and lead the New South.

And such gentlemen were to be Christian gentlemen of Protestant persuasions. Although Washington College was nondenominational, Lee believed that Christianity was indispensable to character formation. When he was hired, he made it clear that he would restrict himself to administrative duties and would not teach the capstone class in moral philosophy and science customarily offered by college presidents, but he knew exactly what such a course ought to contain. Attempting to recruit the Reverend Churchill L. Gibson to the Chair of Moral Philoso-

phy—such colleges nearly always hired clergymen for that position—Lee spelled out what was needed: "The occupant should
be properly a man of true piety, learning & science; [who can]
make His Holy religion attractive to the young, to impress it
upon their hearts, & to make them humble Christians. . . . He
should not only be free from bigotry, but clear of sectarianism,
& not a participator in controversy."[3] In a sense, in one small
place, Washington College was to be another expression of the
kind of ecumenical, institutionalized Protestant piety that Lee
had sought to apply to his army and to the Confederacy as a
whole. To serve that end, and to set an unswerving example to
his students, at 7:45 each morning Lee sat in the left front pew
at the college chapel, where various Protestant clergymen of the
town took turns preaching, and he was an active vestryman of
the local Grace Episcopal Church and also attended state Episcopalian conferences.

A whole range of self-controlling behaviors ought to charac-
terize his students, Lee believed, as steps toward that lifelong
self-discipline that would be the best possible result of college
education. Thus, in 1869, the minute he heard of the formation
of a "Friends of Temperance" society among the students, he
wrote in warm support to them,

> my experience through life has convinced me that,
> while moderation and temperance in all things are
> commendable and beneficial, abstinence from spiri-
> tuous liquors is the best safeguard to morals and
> health. . . . I cannot too earnestly exhort you to prac-
> tice habitual temperance, so that you may form the
> habit in youth, and not feel the inclination, or tempta-
> tion, to depart from it in manhood. By so doing your
> health will be maintained, your morals elevated, and
> your success in life promoted.[4]

Such exhortation was identical to Lee's advice to his sons when they had been of college age—boys were boys, for whom universal and timeless truths ought always to be urged by the father-president. On the subject of temperance, he had written to Fitzhugh in 1858, "I hope you will always be distinguished for your avoidance of the 'universal balm,' whiskey, and every immorality. Nor need you fear to be ruled out of society that indulges it, for you will rather acquire their esteem and respect, as all venerate if they do not practice virtue." Clearly, Lee had followed the advice he offered his son and had been willing to pay whatever social price—which in his case was evidently small—that the pursuit of purity had cost in terms of remoteness from more morally relaxed men. In an allied context, Lee scolded Fitzhugh, "I was sorry to see . . . that you smoke occasionally. . . . You have in store so much better employment for your mouth. Reserve it . . . for its legitimate purposes." And in the sexual sphere, he added, "hold on to your purity and virtue."[5]

That was a fairly comprehensive list of personal sins to be avoided if one was to become a gentleman to Lee's standards. Beyond his sons and the sons of his college, Lee had thousands of namesakes all over the South after the war, and the parents of many of them felt the need to ask the general for advice about raising them, which the general provided with patient repetitions of the eternal verities. About Robert E. Lee French, he wrote the parents in 1866, "It is not so important that he should become 'handsome' or 'mischievous,' though a fair portion of both is not amiss, as that he should be . . . a good and useful man. . . . He should at once learn obedience, perfect & cheerful obedience to his parents, masters & spiritual teachers. . . . Other virtues will follow [on] to pure & true religion."[6] Although Lee included the point that the little facsimile Lee ought to be lively and fun, the overall import of his list concerned repression and duty as the nearly exclusive basis of good conduct. Such stoic gentlemanliness derived from what Lee had attempted to make of himself, but it was less egotism writ large than an expression of Lee's lifelong attempt to measure up to the very best and most old-fashioned moral values of his time, place, and class, an acknowledgment that conformity superseded individual expression, that all appropriate manly effort contributed to the struggle to serve the eternal code. Character not personality, duty not independence, were the goals under the gentleman's rules of life and in obedience to Christ.

To serve these ideals and practices, Lee scrutinized his charges in methodical detail. Washington College professors working under Lee gave daily marks for each student after each class and, at the close of each month, prepared a chart enumerating the grade and relative standing of each student in each course to submit to President Lee, who would then take any necessary measures.

If there was a decline in academic performance or some irregularity of conduct, Lee called the student to his office for a little chat, which most of them evidently found mortifying. One supposes such meetings often worked quite well, but Lee's records revealed, of course, the failures. If a student did not mend his ways after several visits to the president, Lee contacted the student's parents, urging them to intervene with their son. To one parent, Lee wrote, "I have endeavoured in my interviews with him to ascertain the cause of his inattention, but his reply is that he cannot study." Lee found no evidence of the boy's "indulging in bad habits," so he was a bit stumped. The boy had promised Lee that he "is going to turn over a new leaf, and will study faithfully till the end of the session." Lee thought this good, if unhappy, boy was homesick, and thus he suggested to the mother, who had been in correspondence with her son already, "if you could promise him a visit before commencement, I think . . . you would cause him to be so happy as to cause him to forget his troubles. . . . It is true as you say that an education cannot be forced on a boy; but I think every boy can be persuaded & led to do what is right by an affectionate mother."[7] Lee took a great deal of time and offered considerable kindness to a boy he thought was depressed rather than wicked.

If a student was systematically negligent, even after a series of chats, Lee was tougher on him. "I have in a very friendly way, called [John Lapsley's] attention to his apparent neglect of his studies," Lee wrote Lapsley's parents in 1866. Far from being rude or surly, Lapsley had taken the advice "in the same spirit in which it was given and at the time was no doubt in earnest" in promises for reform. However, Lapsley had not learned how to spend his time more profitably, and therefore, unless he improved, Lee recommended that his parents withdraw him from the college. "I do not think it would be to his advantage to continue here without reaping an adequate return for the expenditure of time and money."[8] The next step Lee took, "for systematic neglect of duties," as he put it to one parent, was to urge that a student voluntarily withdraw, with the possibility left open for a later return.[9] And even if such a case proved hopeless, Lee wrote a kind letter to the parents suggesting that their son's forced departure from college had been a temporary setback for a still promising lad.

Lee sometimes tempered his gravitas during his little chats with the delinquents with a hint of light spirits. One former student, years later, told the story of how he had been called in to see the president.

> I was a frolicsome chap at college, and, having been absent from class an unreasonable number of times, was finally summoned to the General's office. Abject terror took possession of me in the presence of such wise and quiet dignity. . . . In reply to General Lee's

grave but perfectly polite questions, I stammered out
a story about a violent illness, and then, conscious
that I was at that moment the picture of health, I hastened on with something about leaving my shoes at
the cobbler's, when General Lee interrupted me: . . .
"Stop Sir! One good reason is enough." But I could not
be mistaken about the twinkle in the old hero's eyes.[10]

If Lee was understanding, kind, and forgiving with students
who failed to live up to the intellectual rigors of the Washington
College program, he was extremely curt and decisive with those
whose failings he believed to have been due to bad attitude and
rude behavior. Sins of character were simply inexcusable. On
March 8, 1867, in the middle of a semester, Lee expelled E. J. Parsons, the son of former governor Lewis E. Parsons of Alabama,
probably for repeated public drunkenness. "In consequence of
his frank acknowledgment and written promise of good behav-
iour, his misconduct on a former occasion was overlooked by
the Faculty, and he was restored to his classes," Lee wrote Governor Parsons, "but he has been unable to keep the pledge then
given; and even if he could be permitted, he is unwilling to remain under the circumstances." Under direct questioning from
President Lee, Master Parsons had thrown in the towel, perhaps
resigning rather than waiting to be expelled. "I have therefore
authorized him to return home, & his connection with the college is dissolved." There was no appeal. "I hope this severe lesson will teach him the self-command he so much needs, and
enable him to refrain from the indulgence of a vice, which, if it
becomes a habit, may prove his ruin," the strict temperance man
Lee wrote. It was not that he considered young Parsons an altogether hardened character, Lee added: "He is a youth of good capacity, candor & truth. These qualities have endeared him to
members of the Faculty, & I trust his future course will reinstate

him in their good opinion, & in the confidence of his comrades."[11] It is difficult to see how young Parsons could have redeemed himself at a college from which Lee had just barred him, and it is clear that a major sin, rendered into a bad habit, was sufficient for expulsion, but still Lee wrote more in sadness than in anger.

Similarly, on January 7, 1870, Lee wrote to the Reverend B. B. Blair, of Point Pleasant, West Virginia, explaining the expulsion of three of his wards, the brothers James and Jules Menager and Charles McCulloch. All boarded with "one of the most worthy gentlemen of the city," and for the first two months had done fine. But toward the end of December, they had increasingly neglected their studies. "I have from week to week . . . called their attention to this course," Lee wrote, but after three or four such sessions they had not returned to classes, McCulloch claiming illness as the cause, "which of course I gave credit to," Lee reported, always taking a gentleman at his word. However, intelligence sources had disclosed "that the neglect of their studies by these young gentlemen . . . has been caused by their frequenting the public billiard room in Lexington where they wasted much of their time and money."[12] McCulloch was worse for having lied to Lee's face, of course, but the Menager brothers had somewhat more indirectly broken the code of honor of Washington College. Once more, Lee controlled his temper but acted with great clarity: The boys knew the rules that they had flouted, rules based on universal and comprehensible definitions of good and bad character.

If lawbreaking was involved, or if Lee believed that his authority was being threatened, his response could be quite ruthless. Many nineteenth-century colleges had student rebellions and riots, as Lee surely knew, and he was not about to put up with any shenanigans, to whatever degree they might spin out of control. At Washington College prior to Lee's arrival, students

had received a week's vacation at Christmas, but in 1866, following the practice at the University of Virginia, the standards
of which Lee wished to emulate, Lee limited the break to one
day. When they heard the news, the young gentlemen held a
mass meeting and then posted a petition threatening to boycott
classes during the accustomed holiday period. Lee evidently
told a professor, in a voice loud enough to be heard by a group of
students, "every man that signs that paper will be summarily
dismissed. If all sign it, I shall lock up the college and put the
keys in my pocket." The petition disappeared almost immediately, as none of the students wanted to risk calling the bluff of
the hero of Chancellorsville. In his good time—three years after
the showdown—Lee increased the vacation to three days. This
was something of a compromise but offered freely by the old
commander just in time for seniors to explain some history to
the underclassmen.[13]

Though Lee threatened mass expulsion over a peaceful collective petition, he had far more explosive problems to deal with
arising from Reconstruction. In common with his students,
many of whom were Confederate veterans or their brothers, Lee
was deeply opposed to the continued Northern military occupation of the South, as well as to the policies of the federal government concerning civil rights and suffrage for blacks. However,
when clashes over such issues spilled into the streets of Lexington, which they did frequently in the late 1860s, Lee believed
that he was morally charged with defending law and order, even
if that meant cooperating with what he considered to be occupying forces. Lee was also aware that if such events blew up, the
whole North would target him and the college for special disap-
probation, he being who he was. In this fear, Lee was quite right.
The peace of the community held enormous political stakes for
him and his college.

Major outbursts occurred from late November 1866 through

their most intense phase in the late winter and through 1867 and into the spring of 1868, the period of the bitterly divisive presidency of Andrew Johnson and the rise of Radical Republicanism in Congress. For two nights late in November 1866, after tense exchanges with the local military garrison, Washington College students marched loudly and nearly riotously through the town, and Lee then issued one of his addresses to the community, which the students called, quite aptly, his "General Orders." Lee appealed to the young gentlemen's "honor and self-respect" to suspend future marches, "trusting that their sense of what is due to themselves, their parents, and the institution to which they belong, will be . . . effectual in teaching them what is right and manly." Lee also pointed out to the students that during "disorderly proceedings," others in the town might take the occasion "to commit outrages for which you will have to bear the blame."[14] In this instance, matters cooled down.

On the evening of January 16, 1867, to break up a Unionist political meeting, several Washington College students from the Deep South attacked a schoolhouse for blacks run by the Freedman's Bureau, and one of them pistol-whipped a black man who tried to intervene. Soon after the young men were arrested, nearly the entire student body marched on the jail, preparing to storm it to free their comrades. A former Confederate captain, now a student, then stood up, reportedly calling out, "Steady men! . . . Remember General Lee! No violence. Remember General Lee. Let the law take its course. You must do what General Lee would wish." The crowd dispersed. Later, after their release from jail, four of the boys were summoned to Lee's office. When one volunteered that he had done the violence, Lee dismissed him on the spot, and he put the others on probation and placed formal letters of reprimand in their files.[15]

The following February, a similar incident spilled into the national press, Lee's worst fear. Erastus Johnston, a Union veteran who taught black children under the aegis of the American Missionary Association and who ran a store for blacks, had become a scapegoat for white Lexington. While ice-skating one cold winter afternoon, Johnston was harassed once again by several townspeople and students. Finally, when a twelve-year-old boy called him a son of a bitch, Johnston drew a pistol and swore he would shoot him. A crowd soon gathered, threatening Johnston while throwing sticks and stones as well. Later that night, a mob tried to break into his store, yelling, "Come out here, you damned Yankee son of a bitch! We want to kill you!" Johnston recognized many in the mob and, failing to get local justice, went to the military authorities, who spoke to Lee. After conducting his own investigation, the general quickly expelled three students.[16]

Lee was very angry with these shabby characters, and not just out of concern for the reputation of the college. In his letter to the guardian of one of the boys, J. G. Gordon, Lee indicated that Gordon had been in any event a no-account student: "He has made no progress in his course, & indeed had not attended his classes." But his arrest was the cause of immediate dismissal, and the best hope Lee could offer was that perhaps no further legal action would be taken against Gordon. One of the other students, Henry Platt, was an even nastier type. Before the Johnston incident, Lee had written Platt's father that Henry's conduct toward the family with whom he boarded had been "very objectionable and even offensive," so that they could no longer keep him. Clearly, Lee believed that only men of degraded character could commit such violent political crimes, and the other forms of bad behavior he found in this lot of boys confirmed his opinion.[17]

The Washington College students' treatment of Erastus Johnston was not an isolated event. After Johnston wrote to several Northern newspapers, more editorials and stories soon appeared, including the testimony in the New York *Independent* of Miss Julia Anne Shearman, a Northerner teaching in a Lexington school for blacks, who wrote that "never did I walk the streets of Lexington without rudeness" affronting her, especially from the "boys of the aristocratic school of the place," one of whom habitually greeted her as that "damned Yankee bitch of a school teacher."[18] Such adverse publicity cut the ground out from under the previously promising fund-raising efforts of Washington College in the North, particularly in New York City.

Feelings ran high for several months, the Southern gentlemen of the college frequently threatening to take to the streets to crush blacks asserting their rights and to drive away their white supporters. In late March, Lee had managed to quell another threatened procession through the town with another "General Order," but in early May a young black man, Caesar Griffen, was nearly lynched by a mob of students after he had shot the son of the rector of the university, who had pushed him off a sidewalk into the street. Yet another former Confederate captain, Assistant Professor Harry Estill, walked into this mob and ordered the students in the name of General Lee to turn their captive over to the authorities, which they did. During the subsequent unrest, which included pistol fire in the dead of several nights, Lee wrote one more "General Order," in the form of an open letter to the president of the campus YMCA, concerning the potential meanings of a lynching. Lee wrote that he chose not to believe that Washington College students would carry through with such an act, whatever threatening words they spoke: "I feel convinced than none would countenance such outrage against law & order, but that all will cheerfully submit to the administration of justice by the legal authorities."[19] Without another round of expulsions, this outburst was calmed.

However, the pattern of violence by Washington College students continued until the end of Lee's presidency and beyond.

In November 1868, Lee wrote to Colonel John W. Jordan, commander of the local federal garrison, that he was doing all in his power to prevent his students from disrupting an upcoming political meeting of Lexington's black community. And on January 29, 1869, Lee expelled Harry Neel of Saint Louis for shooting and wounding a black man on the streets of the town and then fleeing the college without permission.[20]

There was a considerable distance between Lee's ideal of the self-restrained Christian gentleman student and many of the rather barbaric young Southern intransigents at Washington College—the "hot little Southerners," Lee's wife, Mary Custis Lee, called them with approval.[21] Whatever the turmoil, however, Lee continued to appeal to the better angels of Southern manly nature. Given what he knew of the human propensity to sin, however hopeful an educator he tried to remain, he was not, of course, surprised by what he confronted, but neither did he give in to it. Opposed to Reconstruction himself, nevertheless, as far as Washington College was concerned, he never submitted to the cries for lynching that abounded in the South. No charges of his would be permitted to carry out such cowardly acts—at his college at least, law and order would prevail, even if that meant cooperating with the hated Yankee military rule, which he did, against Southern sentiment.

Far from a rustic retreat or a calm little Christian commonwealth training young gentlemen for noble leadership, Washington College proved to be a training ground in violence, where many students taught themselves to use any means necessary to destroy Reconstruction. The kind but stern leader of young men could only try, in his bailiwick, to limit a far wider Southern white set of political sentiments and practices. However, he did not speak out publicly against lynching as it spread across the South, and so, despite the fact that he clamped down on such abuses of power at his college, or perhaps in part because he did, he was used as the noblest symbol of the white South by men, many of whom were far more willing than he to countenance and sponsor widespread violence elsewhere. As a great symbol, he was swept into the construction of Southern nationalism and white supremacy, in which he too believed, even while he opposed the violent means commonly used to achieve those ends, a means he could barely suppress among his band of young bloods.

Chapter 13

SOUTHERN NATIONALIST

On February 17, 1866, Robert E. Lee was called before the Joint Committee on Reconstruction in Washington to discuss issues of race and politics. A reluctant witness, Lee nevertheless was quite forthright in his defense both of the 1861 secession of the South and of the current efforts of Southern white elites to wrest back control of their domain from the threats posed by empowerment of blacks.

On the surface, it continued to be important for Lee to claim that he was above partisanship and discord. He asserted at the onset of his testimony that he was not well acquainted with current political issues. "I have been living very retired, and have had but little communication with politicians," he testified, rather disingenuously, since he had been in constant communication with such men. The maintenance of an Olympian persona for public consumption was a major component of Lee's postwar Southern nationalism: He would be the true conservative statesman above the fray, a position that both increased his value to other Southern white leaders and heightened the esteem he had gained in the South during the war, which was of great importance to him. The naive prewar engineer who could not think politically without getting headaches had been politicized by the secession crisis and the war, and afterward Lee was quite aware that his suprapolitical status was especially helpful when synchronized with those of his comrades who sought to roll back Reconstruction.

By the time Lee testified to Congress, Andrew Johnson had begun to come into conflict with congressional Republicans over how far to push change in the defeated South. While the Republicans wanted to punish the leaders of the Confederacy and pass laws and constitutional amendments to guarantee civil rights for blacks, protect their rights as free workers, and offer them suffrage, Johnson opposed all such uses of federal authority, supporting Southern white men and Northern Democrats who were organizing to abort all such political and social changes and to return the former Confederacy to the Union with whites firmly in control of blacks.

Lee was well positioned to take up Johnson's proffered handshake. He testified to the congressional committee that the former secessionists "are for cooperating with President Johnson in his policy. . . . Persons with whom I have conversed," Lee stated (almost immediately refuting his position that he had been living very retired), "express great confidence in the wisdom of his policy of restoration, and they seem to look forward to it as a hope of restoration."

As nearly as possible, Lee argued, restoration should be a return to the status quo ante, the reinstitution of slavery excepted. As part of his position, Lee stoutly defended the legality of secession. Citizens of Southern states such as Virginia had not committed treason in 1861; "they considered the act of the State[s] as legitimate," under the Tenth Amendment, "merely using the reserved right which they had a right to do. . . . The act of Virginia, in withdrawing herself from the United States, carried me along as a citizen of Virginia . . . her laws and her acts were binding upon me."

Besides, Lee said, secession had been brought about by a blundering generation of national politicians. "The position of the two sections which they held to each other was brought about by the politicians of the country; that the great masses of the people, if they understood the real question, would have avoided." In that sense, demagogic politicians backed by gullible lower-class white voters had "wheedled" the nation, Lee stated. He was seeking to narrow the meanings of secession (and even the war) in the name of an essential constitutional continuity, the better to sharply limit new forms of federal intervention during Reconstruction. Along these lines, he was even in favor of Southern states repaying Confederate debts contracted during the war against the Union rather than repudiating them, as the Republicans were insisting—debts held by ex-Confederates such as himself.

Much of Lee's testimony concerned his opinions toward blacks. On the most general level, Lee said that "every one with whom I associate expresses kind feelings towards the freedmen. They wish to see them get on in the world, and particularly to take up some occupation for a living, and to turn their hands to some work." Lee also expressed his "willingness that blacks should be educated, and . . . that it would be better for the blacks and for the whites." Although he did not believe that blacks had the same intellectual capacities as whites, he was "acquainted with those who have learned the common rudiments of education."

Guarded and rather condescending by implication during the rest of his testimony, Lee never questioned his belief in the inferiority of blacks as a race, often pairing an attribute he found endearing with results he found irritating. "Wherever I have been they have been quiet and orderly," he told the congressmen, "not disposed to work, or rather not disposed to any continuous engagement to work, but just very short jobs, to provide them with the immediate means of subsistence." Asked whether the black race had as great a drive to accumulate money and property as whites, Lee answered, "I do not think it has. The blacks with whom I am acquainted look more to the present time than the future. . . . They are an amiable, social race. They like their ease and comfort, and, I think, look more to their present than their future."

There he was in Lee's mind's eye: the stereotypical slave, now free but still lazy, irresponsible, and undisciplined, if charming and amusing. What white people such as Lee could not understand was that after their emancipation, many blacks strove mightily to remove themselves from white surveillance and to work on their own toward subsistence and as much economic security as they could garner from short-term employment. Such efforts to gain independence and increase their distance from their former masters appeared to men such as Lee to be a lack of effort that proved black racial inferiority.

Lee was certain that the well-bred Southern whites he knew were kind to these childlike folks. But responding to the possibility of the political elevation of blacks, of the sort that many radicals in Congress were then proposing, Lee's feelings immediately were shown to be less benign. As for white Northerners who came south to aid the freedmen, Lee conceded that proper gentlemen "would avoid them . . . not select them as associates . . . not admit them into their social circles." If Congress were to pass an amendment giving suffrage to blacks, men of his class "would object. . . . I think it would excite unfriendly feelings between the two races. I cannot pretend to say to what extent it would go, but that would be the result." Lee threatened nothing in the way of violence, but he feared that general white opinion could turn that way. Indeed, even given the incentive of increased Southern representation in the House of Representatives should blacks be given the franchise, Lee concluded that white Virginia "would accept the smaller representation." For the foreseeable future, black suffrage would open the door to political and social catastrophe. "My own opinion is that, at this time, they cannot vote intelligently, and that giving them the [vote] would lead to a great deal of demagogism, and lead to embarrassments in various ways." Just as he had believed before the war that God would end slavery some distant day, Lee could admit the possibility of black suffrage only after some infinitely long process of labor and educational improvement (unlikely for blacks, under his definition of their intrinsically limited intellectual potential). "What the future may prove, how intelligent they may become, with what eyes they may look upon the interests of the State in which they may reside, I cannot say more than you."

Bland and calm until then, at the end of his testimony, Lee was drawn out by a series of direct questions into expressing his underlying antipathy for the notion of renegotiating race relations in order to promote a biracial social and political modus vivendi. Asked "Do you not think that Virginia would be better off if the colored population were to go to Alabama, Louisiana," and other Deep South states, Lee replied, "I think it would be better for Virginia if she could get rid of them. . . . I think that everyone there would be willing to aid it." Yes, he thought Virginia was absolutely injured and its future would be impaired by the presence of blacks; yes, with its great natural resources, once rid of blacks, Virginia would attract white immigration. And Lee argued "that is no new opinion with me. I have always thought so, and have always been in favor of emancipation— gradual emancipation." Lee harkened back to the colonizationist stance of his wife and mother-in-law, a position he had never actually adopted but that might serve him rather well before Congress. The best possible result for race relations in Virginia, he maintained, would be the gradual disappearance of blacks, a curious reworking of the meaning of gradual emancipation and colonization. Failing that, Lee could accept blacks only in the most marginal fashion.[1]

Such were Lee's opinions when he was at his most reserved, in the sort of public forum he usually sought to avoid. Writing privately, Lee was even more candid about his postwar racial views. In common with most Southerners of the master class, Lee had had relatively little to say about blacks during slavery days, when he had been a confident paternalist who believed that he could manage the servants. Indeed, near the end of the war, he had expressed less concern about black soldiers under direct white control than about guerrilla soldiers drawn from the poor white population. But when, with emancipation, the racial order in fact had been undermined, Lee could maintain paternalist equilibrium only when he saw blacks as clearly subordinate—any move toward political or social equality was deeply upsetting to him.

Rarely one to use hot language, Lee nevertheless expressed considerable distaste for blacks. Particularly was this true for blacks immediately around him, which meant those servants he and Mary Lee sought to employ after the war. As contracted labor, these free blacks presented a new phenomenon: blacks bargaining over wages and conditions of employment. After Lee began to set up housekeeping in Lexington in the fall of 1865, he addressed the servant problem in several letters to Mary, who was to follow him to the college. "You had better bring up Miss Skipworth's woman. I fear we shall not be able to procure white servants. . . . Servants of some kind (black) I have no doubt can be obtained." But Lee clearly expressed his belief that blacks ought to be the employees of last resort. Freed blacks proved hard to obtain, whatever Lee's distaste, and they did not seem willing to settle down under the control of former masters. On October 29, Lee wrote Mary, "as regards servants, I cannot speak

positively till the time comes for employing them. They are leaving their homes here as elsewhere, but there seems to be enough
& some have offered their services. If any good ones offer, I advise their engagement. Indifferent ones I think can be had here.
We shall want but one man." Lee then ran through the names of
their ex-slaves, finding one named Jimmy to be the least incompetent. The next day, he commented about hiring a man whom
one might think Lee would have put in the indifferent category:
"I have engaged a man for the balance of the year who professes
to know everything. He can at least make up the fires & go on er-
rands & attend to the yard & table."[2] Uncharacteristic sarcasm
revealed Lee's reaction to a man who had been altogether too
uppity for a black servant when Lee had interviewed him. Lee
chafed at such new relationships between the races, where
blacks did not instantaneously display the appropriate deference but asserted themselves above their stations. Racial unrest
characterized everyday exchanges as well as politics of a more
public and dramatic sort.

As late as 1869, Lee wrote his son Rob about his ex-slave
Jimmy, resident on Rob's plantation, with whom Lee had shared
bonds he considered proper before the war. Even with the prospect of hiring Jimmy, however, Lee was now tentative. "I forgot
to speak for Jimmy," Lee wrote Rob. "If he wishes to come to me
& is sufficiently acquainted with gardening to undertake the
garden, & will attend to the stable & all outdoor matters—send
him up. I will give him $10 per month, as long as he suits me &
I suit him."[3] The new order was certainly not the best of all possible worlds.

Immediately after the war, Lee began expressing a contempt
for blacks that he had never uttered before, including that desire
to get freedmen out of his sight by literally pushing them out of
Virginia. Early in June 1865, he urged Colonel Thomas H. Carter
to discharge his ex-slaves and replace them with whites. Carter

replied that such a desire would be utopian in his neighbor-hood, as he could get only black labor to do the drudge work. "I have always observed," Lee then insisted, "that wherever you find the Negro, everything is going down around him, and wherever you find the white man, you see everything around him improving."[4]

Lee understood Colonel Carter's point—there were simply no whites willing to compete with blacks at the bottom of the labor barrel—but still he wished that black removal could be ef-fected. That October, Lee wrote to Fitzhugh about improving Fitzhugh's land, "I fear that you will be able to do but little with black labour, & until you can put up some buildings, you will not be able to attract white." And a year later, Lee wrote to Rob, his other plantation-owning son, "The mill dam I know is a trou-blesome work, but I hope you will accomplish it, & I fear you will have to execute it with negro labour. I presume at present there is none other to be had. You might get aid from the Vir-ginia Emigration Co.; which now has an agent in Europe en-deavoring to procure emigrants."[5]

Lee had become an active supporter of the Virginia Immi-gration Society, as part of his notion of how his state ought to both modernize and whiten. In 1869, he wrote to Colonel Joseph H. Ellis, director of the society, that he believed that the "agricul-turist" as much as the industrialist had need for "regular & con-stant work" that "can only be served by the introduction of a respectable class of labourers from Europe" to replace blacks. Other sources of nonwhite labor would not work well, such as those that had been introduced in California, the Caribbean, and Latin America, "for although temporary benefit might be derived from importation of Chinese or Japanese, it would re-sult I think in eventual injury to the country, & her institutions. We not only want reliable labourers but good citizens whose in-terests & feelings would be in unison with ours." Whole families of white Europeans, such as the folks flooding the North, were what was wanted. "I have been & still am an advocate for European immigration."[6] Lee's view of a labor force appropriate for modernization resembled the one he saw developing in the North, but white immigrants voted with their feet not to compete with black labor in the war-scarred, impoverished South. In 1868, for example, of 213,000 overwhelmingly northern and western European immigrants, only 713 settled in Virginia.[7]

Lee's interest in European immigration to replace black labor—a desire quite widespread in the upper South—contained considerable bitterness about the incapacity and perfidy of blacks. In 1868, Lee wrote Rob that he had recently had a visit from a Dr. Oliver of Scotland, who was examining lands for immigrants from his country. "From his account, I do not think the Scots and English would suit your part of the country," which would be too hot and hilly to please them. "I think you will have to look to the Germans; perhaps the Hollanders, as a class, would be more useful." Lee was also active among those pushing for a railroad into the Shenandoah Valley of Virginia from the eastern seaboard, for "then I think there will be no difficulty in getting whites among you." In the meantime, white Southerners would have to bend their backs to the plow, unaccustomed though they were to hard physical labor. "People have got to work now. It is creditable to them to do work; their bodies and their minds are benefited by it, and those who can and will work will be advanced by it." Lee was fully aware that for white Southerners manual labor was degraded by its association with blacks. Nevertheless, he insisted that, however irreplaceable it was likely to be, black labor was now fundamentally antagonistic to white interests: "You will never prosper with the blacks, and it is abhorrent to a reflecting mind to be supporting and cherishing those who are plotting and working for your injury, and all of whose sympathies and associations are antagonistic to yours." Catching his pen in an unaccustomedly overt expression of that racist anger resident in the dark side of paternalism, Lee quickly corrected himself. "I wish them no evil in the world—on the contrary, will do them every good in my power, and know that they are misled by those to whom they have given their confidence." Yet right after paternalistically sympathizing with Virginia's black innocents who had been misled by Northern carpetbagging politicians, Lee went back to the racial divide: "Our material, social, and political interests are naturally with the whites."[8]

In Lee's mind, as in those of most of his countrymen, North as well as South, the racial hierarchy was clear. English and Scots were above Germans and Hollanders, who were much better than Chinese and Japanese, all of whom were superior to blacks. To the English journalist W. H. Nettleton, who was about to return home, Lee wrote in 1866, "Your visit to America must have impressed upon you the fact that, though climate, government, and circumstances have produced changes in the character of the people, yet in all essential qualities they resemble the races from which they are sprung; and that to no race are we more indebted for the virtues which constitute a great people than to the Anglo-Saxon. You will carry back with you to England my best wishes." When, in 1870, Mrs. Emily Hay forwarded a pamphlet written by the Anglo-Canadian immigration propagandist Professor Goldwin Smith, Lee responded that he was gratified by Smith's interest in Virginia "& wish that the tide of emigration from England could be turned toward the State. Englishmen need not fear the exhibition of hostility against them in Virginia. They would be cordially welcomed . . . agriculturists especially."[9] To his son Rob, Lee had expressed his doubts that significant numbers of Englishmen would settle in Virginia, but if they did, as fellow Anglo-Saxons, they would be the most welcome of white newcomers: In Lee's essentialist racial categorization, they were bone of his bone, blood of his blood. Such attitudes were quite in line with the cutting edge of contemporary racialist thought.

Mary Custis Lee was more vituperative on the issue of race than her husband, although he did not really disagree with the underlying sentiments she expressed. To take but one of many examples, on May 20, 1866, she wrote from Lexington to her old friend Emily Mason, "We are all here dreadfully plundered by the lazy idle negroes who are lounging about the streets doing nothing but looking what they may plunder during the night. We have been raided on twice already. . . . But all thro' the country the people are robbed nearly as much as they were during the war. . . . When we get rid of the Freedman's bureau & can take the law in our hands we may perhaps do better. If they would only take all their pets north it would be happy riddance to all."[10]

It must be added that in other moods, when he was not feeling threatened and betrayed, Lee continued to express a kinder paternalism toward this less fortunate race. In this vein, he wrote to a Northern Presbyterian clergyman who was seeking to find suitable genteel Southern white men to distribute Northern educational funds earmarked for the freedmen, "I entirely agree with you . . . that the education and advancement of the colored people at the South can be better attended to by those who are acquainted with their characters and wants than by those who are ignorant of both." Lee recommended Drs. Hoge and Brown in Richmond as useful contacts, while begging off from becoming the distribution agent for Lexington—"I could not attend to it on account of other duties . . . nor do I know any colored preacher competent"—but he then assured this preacher, rather disingenuously, because privately he fumed against black behavior, that "the colored people in this vicinity are doing very well, are progressing favorably, and, as far as I know, are not in want. There is an abundance of work for them, and the whites with whom they are associated retain for them the kindest feelings."[11] This calmer part of Lee lived in considerable disjuncture with the Anglo-Saxonist who was so angry at the local blacks, which is not to suggest that both sides may not have coexisted.

Lee placed his postwar racial views in the larger framework of Southern white political nationalism, both as an observer and as a most often covert participant. He read many Southern newspapers with keen interest and clipped numerous articles to which he referred in his wide-ranging correspondence on historical and contemporary political matters. His every statement was carefully digested and rebroadcast within the Southern white nationalist camp, particularly in the Virginia cadre as it strategized an early return to political dominance.[12] Lee was a close associate of Alexander H. H. Stuart and John B. Baldwin, both from nearby Staunton, who were key organizers of the so-called Conservative Party—an alliance of antebellum Democrats and Whigs, many of the latter of whom had been reluctant secessionists transformed into ardent Confederates during the war. Within this emerging coalition, Lee developed a presentation of serene disengagement from everyday politics, though he maintained a strong defense of Southern principles as part of a tenacious larger strategy in which he encouraged others. Privately, he could be quite the vitriolic anti-Yankee in his defense of the Southern cause, even while in public he sought to burnish his image as heroic senior statesman. He was always well aware of the already legendary stature attributed to him, and of its long-term political usefulness to the larger cause he continued to serve.

Calmness and rationality ought to be the Southern tone of defense, Lee urged his fellow ex-Confederates, many of whom became angry controversialists confronting Northern authority. Right after the war, he constructed his credo, which he repeated in numerous ways: "It should be the object of all," he wrote to a magazine publisher on September 4, 1865, "to avoid controversy, to allay passion, give full scope to reason and to every kindly feeling. By doing this and encouraging our citizens to engage in the duties of life with all their heart and mind, with a determination not to be turned aside by thoughts of the past and fears of the future, our country will not only be restored in material prosperity, but will be advanced in science, in virtue and in religion."[13]

At the very first, Lee partially conceded that the victors had a certain right to dictate terms to the vanquished South. In August 1865, he had written to the governor of Virginia, "the questions which for years were in dispute between the State and General Government, and which unhappily were not decided by the dictates of reason, but referred to the decision of war, having been decided against us, it is the part of wisdom to acquiesce in the result, and of candor to recognize the fact."[14] Yet even when at his most conciliatory right after the war, Lee's knee bent only a little, and his position contained more resistance than compliance. He never conceded that reason had prevailed in the war nor that the outcome was just. Even when Lee was first voicing it, conciliation became a public tactic rather than an end in itself. He believed that lowering the rhetoric would lead to Southern white control over the South more quickly than would stridency and violence.

Along these lines, in private correspondence Lee tried to quiet such zealots as Jefferson Davis and Jubal Early, who responded angrily to every Northern insult. In public arguments, he told Early in 1866, one ought to "omit all epithets or remarks calculated to excite bitterness or animosity" in the North. To the inveterately pugnacious Davis, he wrote the same year, "I have thought, from the time of the cessation of hostilities, that silence and patience on the part of the South was the true course. . . . Controversy of all kinds will . . . only serve to continue excitement and passion, and will prevent the public mind from the acceptance of the truth. These considerations have kept me from replying to accusations made against myself, and induced me to recommend the same to others."[15] Lee failed to dissuade either Early or Davis. And it was clear that he disagreed not with the contents of their arguments—conviction of *"the truth"*—which he in fact shared with them, but only with their tone and potential effectiveness.

While most of this reticence was personal, some was due to Lee's reading of the state of politics. In 1867, he turned down suggestions to run for the nomination for the governorship of Virginia—a post he likely would have won by acclamation—in part because "I believe my election would be injurious to Virginia." Such an election would have indeed been provocative, for Lee had not had his civil rights restored by the national government, which in fact was one of the causes of Lee's quietness on national political questions. Lee was attempting to regain his rights and his property at Arlington through petitions to Andrew Johnson, to the dismay of more hard-core ex-Confederates, who considered Lee's actions a tacit admission of having committed treason. But Lee had concluded that as for himself, "it [would be] better even now to proceed quietly . . . & to exercise as much patience as possible."[16] The quietist stance suited Lee's personality, his sense of politics, and his self-interest.

However calmly he put his public positions, Lee was anything but escapist, retreatist, or apologetic about his political beliefs. Religiosity helped. Lee would bow to no man but only to the will of God. As he wrote to Markie Williams from Richmond on June 20, 1865, two months after surrender, "I can do but little but am resigned to what is ordered by our Merciful God, who

will I know do all that is good for us." A few months later, he reiterated that he would "bow in humble submission to His will,
who never . . . punishes us without a merciful purpose. His will
be done! I have endeavoured to do what is right, & in his eyes, it
can never be made wrong." Piety reinforced resistance to the
Northern Caesar; no man or group of men could declare Lee's
right actions wrong. As he said to Markie in his June letter, "I am
aware of having done nothing wrong & cannot flee."[17] He was
inwardly prepared to take his stand.

Unwilling to reconcile themselves with living in the United
States under the heel of the conquerors, a significant number of
prominent ex-Confederates refused to sign the loyalty oath required of them and fled to slaveholding Brazil and Cuba, to
Britain, France, Canada, and most numerously to Mexico. When
they wrote Lee to gain his approval of their actions, he replied
that although he understood their choices, he thought they were
wrong. For example, naval Captain Matthew Fontaine Maury, a
Virginia blue blood, wrote to Lee from Mexico City on August 8,
1865, that Emperor Maximilian (a pro-Confederate French pup-
pet soon to be destroyed by Mexican nationalists) was "most
anxious to introduce the immigration" of former Confederates.
"To my mind the demonstration is complete and our Republican form of Government is a failure," Maury insisted. "The best
thing for us now is to aid in building up here in Mexico a good
and stable Empire which in times that are coming may serve
both as a light and a beacon to our noble state."[18] Maury was
proposing to reconstruct a Confederate vanguard to help launch
the second round of the Civil War when the time was propi-
tious.

From his country retreat near Cartersville, Lee replied to
Maury that "the thought of abandoning the country and all that
must be left in it is abhorrent to my feelings, and I prefer to

struggle for its restoration and share its fate, rather than to give up all as lost." Lee professed great admiration for the beauty and charms of Mexico but then wrote, "I still look with delight upon the mountains of my native State." As for despair of American republicanism, Lee reasoned, "We certainly have not found our form of government all that was anticipated by its original founders; but that may be partly our fault in expecting too much and partly in the absence of virtue in the people. As long as virtue was dominant in the Republic so long was the happiness of the people secure." Lee remained something of an old Federalist here, suspicious of the rabid democracy that had displaced the disinterested rule of the elite Founding Fathers; he read the Civil War as caused by a subsequent surfeit of democracy. Yet he continued to Maury, "I cannot, however, despair of [the republic] yet. I look forward to better days and trust that time and experience, the great teachers of men under . . . God, may save us from destruction and restore us to the right hopes and prospects of the past." Invited to resettle in England as the permanent guest of a wealthy nobleman, one of several such offers to move abroad, Lee responded more simply, "I cannot desert my native state in the hour of her adversity. I must abide in her fortunes and share her fate."[19]

Calmed by his inner spiritual resources as well as by his sense of place, Lee dug in for the long haul. As early as June 17, 1865, he had written to Walter Herron Taylor, his old adjutant general, about the new veterans, "Virginia wants all aid, all support & the presence of all her sons, to sustain & recuperate her. They must . . . take part in her government, & not be deterred by obstacles. . . . There is much to be done which only they can do." Lee recognized that it was unlikely that he would assume a leading role at the national level but insisted in 1867 that "in what relates to our families & states, we can diligently labour, & . . .

earn success. . . . If we can sustain our State governments & maintain our elevated standard of morals, religion, & literary culture, we cannot lose much." Washington College was Lee's local showcase of elevated standards and Southern commitments: In what he controlled in his own hands, however modest, he would seek to create a purified little republic that later might be copied in larger ways. Hints of that muted Christian Confederate utopianism remained until the end of his life, even though the test case in Lexington failed to fulfill his desires.[20]

In many respects, the South, for Lee, remained Virginia writ large, and what he urged for Virginia in his mind applied to the entire region. For the first time in his life, Lee developed a considerable interest in questions of constitutionalism, of the sort that provided the backbone of Southern ideology for the next ninety years. Hardly an original constitutional thinker, Lee adopted in his letters a set of simple ideological maxims through which he made sense of the political issues of the day. Despite his professed retreat from public life and not precisely against his will, many of these letters encouraged other Southern elite white men to continue to fight collectively against national authority and to reverse defeat over the long haul.

Lee argued that collectively maintaining bedrock constitutional principles had been the chief Southern motivation all along. "The reputation of individuals is of minor importance to the opinion which posterity may form of the motives which governed the South in their late struggle for the maintenance of the principles of the Constitution," Lee wrote his cousin Cassius in 1866. Those principles, enshrined in Philadelphia in 1787, had always defined Southerners; indeed, it was Northerners who had departed from fundamental constitutional values. Lee told a conservative Northern politician in 1866, "All the South has ever desired was that the Union, as established by our forefathers, should be preserved; and that the Government, as originally organized, should be administered in purity and truth." Now it was for the North to rejoin the South in a rebirth of virtue on a national scale of a sort for which the South had been the steadfast sectional preservationist. "If such is the desire of the North, there can be no contention between the two sections; and all true patriots will unite in advocating that policy which will soonest restore the country to tranquillity and order, and serve to perpetuate true republicanism."[21]

As proof of Southern steadfastness, Lee quite often used slippery historical reconstructions: He wrote to another Confederate general in 1869, "I was not in favor of secession & was opposed to it. In fact I was for the Constitution & the Union established by our forefathers. No one is more in favour of that Union & that Constitution, & as far as I know it is that for which the South has all along contended, & if restored . . . there will be no truer supporters of that Union."[22] The South had been consistent; it was the North that had seceded from the ideal and therefore must return to the earlier "true" Union.

One of the great virtues of this position for Lee was that it allowed him to believe he was off the hook of treason. After all, he had been consistent in his underlying true unionism all along. Here, as so often, George Washington was Lee's guide. "I need not tell you," Lee wrote to General P. G. T. Beauregard in October 1865,

> that true patriotism sometimes requires of men to act exactly contrary, at one period, to that which it does at another, and the motive which impels them—the desire to do right—is precisely the same. . . . Washington himself is an example. At one time he fought against the French under Braddock, in the service of

the [British] King; at another he fought with the French at Yorktown, under the orders of the Continental Congress of America, against him. He has not been branded by the world with reproach for this; but his course has been applauded.[23]

Lee neglected to say that if the British had won, Washington's position would have been rather different, just as he omitted to note that he himself had taken up arms against the nation that Washington had helped found, his nation. Using the "desire to do right" as his guide, Lee made, in effect, a higher-law argument against constitutionalism in the name of constitutionalism. Men such as he had embodied the true Constitution, which Republicans had destroyed; secessionists had been patriots and Unionists traitors to "right." This rather brazen Southern assertion, presented quietly here, long served the postwar white South in good stead.

The most basic principle of this Dixie version of constitutionalism was "states' rights," a term sacred to Southerners that Lee defined as early as 1866, when he wrote an old friend from his Saint Louis years who was then living in Illinois, "I had no other guide, nor had I any other object than the defense of those principles of American liberty upon which the constitutions of the several States were originally founded, and unless they are strictly observed, I fear there will be an end to republican government in this country."[24]

The culprit undermining true states' rights republicanism remained, as it had been in 1861, the Republican Party. In a famous 1866 letter to Lord Acton that became one of the basic documents of Southern states' rights advocates for many decades after his death, Lee argued that "Virginia to the last made great efforts to save the union" in 1861, "and the only difficulty in the way of an amicable adjustment was with the Republican

Party. Who then is responsible for the war?" Victorious, these emboldened Republican conquerors now threatened the permanent destruction of true republicanism.

> I yet believe that the maintenance of the rights and authority reserved to the states and to the people not only essential to the adjustment of the general system, but the safeguard to the continuance of a free government. I consider it as the chief source of stability to our political system, whereas the consolidation of the states into one vast republic, sure to be aggressive abroad and despotic at home, will be the certain precursor of that ruin which has overwhelmed all those who have preceded it.

Indispensable to the "perfect equality of the rights of all the states" under the correctly constructed Constitution had been "the right of each state to prescribe for itself the qualifications of the suffrage." Underlying this set of constitutional assertions, and always central to it, was the desire to keep blacks away from political office and the ballot box and to restore white home rule. That was the fundamental purpose of the states' rights partisans.[25]

Lee wrote to Lord Acton of state resistance to despotic centralization in the context of congressional debates over military Reconstruction. When Virginia became Military District Number 1 and Virginians under this regime began to organize a constitutional convention that would accommodate radical Republican demands, many in the state urged boycott and underground resistance, including, at least implicitly, violence. Lee, however, who was giving practical politics a great deal of his attention, urged that "all persons entitled to vote should attend the polls & endeavour to elect the best available men to represent them in the convention, to whose decision every one should submit." In several other letters to prominent Virginians, Lee argued that although the convention's decisions "may not be considered at the time the most advantageous, it should be recollected that it can be improved as opportunity offers, and in the end I trust all things will work together for our good."[26]

In all political campaigns during the late 1860s, Lee offered similar advice. In 1869, he urged that right-minded men should vote for "the most conservative eligible candidates," who would vote for "the excision of the most obnoxious clauses," which was to say ex-Confederate disfranchisement. By this means, as he wrote in 1867, a strong dissent at the least could be registered: If they stayed out of the debate, the Virginia Republican white leadership "would be very well pleased . . . if the business were left to them and the Negroes."[27] In the not so long term, Lee anticipated a return to traditional white rule.

At one level, this expectation was a sort of quasi-religious faith. "The dominant party cannot reign forever, and truth and justice will at last prevail," Lee wrote Fitzhugh in 1867. "If we all unite in doing our duty, and earnestly work to extract what good we can out of the evil that now hangs over our dear land, the time is not distant when the angry cloud will be lifted from our horizon, and the sun in his pristine brightness again shine forth."[28] Lee rarely reached florid metaphorical heights; perhaps one of the reasons he did so here was that he was actually quite fearful about what might happen, the better to calm himself by remembering that in the darkest days hope can defend against despair.

During the turmoil of late 1867, learning of his old commander's attitude about the necessity of participation in political events sponsored by Northern Republicans, James Longstreet, who was living in Louisiana, sensed that he might woo Robert E. Lee to join him in his migration to the Republican Party—an act for which Longstreet was reviled by his fellow Southerners for the rest of his life and long beyond. Lee responded that he did indeed believe that it was "the part of wisdom as well as of duty . . . to conform to existing circumstances. . . . But, while I think we should act under the law and according to the law imposed upon us, I cannot think the course pursued by the dominant political party the best for the interests of the country, and therefore cannot say so or give it my approval." Lee was unwilling to reconcile with postwar Northern opinion through such a mode of sectional compromise.[29]

Longstreet represented a moderate white alternative to what was becoming the accepted rejection of Reconstruction by Southern white elites. Right in Virginia, by 1867, William Mahone, an ex-Confederate general, had positioned himself as a "conservative Republican," willing to make an alliance with both blacks and moderate white Democrats as a means to create an accommodationist resolution to Reconstruction. Mahone's "New Departure" formed the more moderate minority faction of the Conservative Party—actually a coalition—that accepted black suffrage, citizenship, and legal rights but not black leadership. Mahone, Alexander H. H. Stuart, and others worked through Horace Greeley to convince President U. S. Grant to accept the 1870 election of the Conservative Party as the means to end Reconstruction in Virginia, by accepting black suffrage in exchange for reenfranchising ex-Confederates (which would guarantee unchallenged white domination of the state government). To accommodate Mahone and Grant, Stuart and his majority Conservative faction, Lee's closest allies, also rejected the gubernatorial candidacy of ex-Confederate colonel Robert E. Withers, who wanted to play the race card with brutal clarity right away.

Men like Lee went along with the Mahone coalition only because they believed its biracialist tendencies soon would be rejected for truly conservative white rule. Once back in power, the

Democratic Party of Virginia did indeed squeeze Mahone and his followers from their ranks. In 1877, seven years after Lee's death, arousing the voters over the massive state debts run up for railroad bonds, Mahone's Readjuster Party, composed of black and white Republicans, won a sweeping gubernatorial and legislative victory. While not sharing power with blacks, Mahone abolished the poll tax and the use of whipping posts for them and, as part of his proeducation program, founded a normal school for blacks. This was the sort of Southern moderate alternative to which Lee never truly subscribed.[30]

Far from accepting genuine black political participation or the other tenets of Republicanism, even as rephrased by Mahone, Lee wanted to build the broadest and most legitimate conservative white base so as to reclaim unadulterated power. Lee believed that, given the caste structure of the South, the outside imposition or internal election of any sort of racial democracy could not last long. As early as the spring of 1866, in an interview he gave to the marquess of Lorne, Lee argued that "the blacks must always here be the weaker; the whites are so much stronger that there is no chance for the blacks, if the Radical party passes the laws it wants against us."[31] Thinking about power politics in this way was new to Lee—a real marker of his political emergence from stoic resignation. Lee had developed senses of strategy and tactics in the political realm.

As well as being drawn into a role as éminence grise within the Old Dominion, Lee actively and publicly supported the national Democratic Party during the 1868 campaign, which the Democrats waged on a virulently racist anti-Reconstruction platform. Shortly after the Democratic convention of 1868, William S. Rosecrans, the former Union general, came down to White Sulphur Springs, Virginia (where Lee was vacationing in the company of many other elite ex-Confederates), with the express purpose of extracting active support from the usually

reticent Lee for the Democratic position. In a rather major departure from his rule of political noninvolvement, Lee agreed to
make a public statement and asked his ally Alexander H. H. Stuart to draft a letter that Lee then signed, as did thirty-two of the
other senior men at the Springs, responding to what they called
Rosecrans's "patriotic motives" and claiming to speak "on behalf
of the Southern people, and the officers and soldiers of the late
Confederate Army."

Rosecrans's partisan point was that the most conservative
possible group of older Southern leaders could be trusted with
the restoration of power to them as the means to ending tensions and violence in the South. To this end, Stuart and Lee returned to the language of beneficent white paternalism toward
blacks. "The idea that the Southern people are hostile to the Negroes and would oppress them, if it were in their power to do so,
is entirely unfounded. They have grown up in our midst, and we
have been accustomed from childhood to look upon them with
kindness." On a practical level as well, whites needed black
labor, which made Southern farms productive while providing
black employment. "Self-interest, if there were no higher motive, would therefore prompt the whites" to protect the blacks.
Such paternalism could be based, of course, only on white domination—the position that conjoined the Democrats and Lee's
men. "It is true that the people of the South, in common with a
large majority of the people of the North and West, are, for obvious reasons, inflexibly opposed to any system of laws that
would place the political power of the country in the hands of
the negro race." However, such opposition sprang not from any
"enmity"—race hatred—but from a "deep-seated conviction"
that blacks lacked the "intelligence . . . necessary to make them
safe depositories of political power. They would inevitably become the victims of demagogues, who, for selfish purposes,
would mislead them into the serious injury of the public."

Southern whites desired peace and the restoration of the
Union, Stuart and Lee continued, and "relief from oppressive
misrule." They wanted a return to the "birth-right of every American," by whom they meant every white male, "the right of self-
government." After such a restoration, with blacks once more
placed firmly in a subordinate position, Stuart and Lee
promised that the natural Southern white ruling class, acting
within the law, would "treat the negro populations with kindness and humanity."[32] This proposal—white restoration, black
subordination, white paternalism as a free grant from above
rather than stemming from power sharing with blacks—was
the formula upon which Reconstruction was to end in 1876,
when the Republicans agreed to this position, first staked out by
the Democrats in 1868 with a big public boost from Lee, the
South's most august white figure.

Taking an active interest in politics, including participating
in Democratic partisan sloganeering, marked a great change in
Lee's public persona, although he still tried most of the time to
maintain the image of the disinterested and austere gentleman.
In parallel fashion, after the war, the private Lee often gave way
to expressions of considerable political anger, which he almost
never had allowed himself to utter previously, perhaps even in
private. Similarly, Lee allowed himself to articulate feelings of
shame for the first time, as when he wrote women friends that
he realized he was considered such a monster that he hesitated
to darken their doors, lest he bring misfortune on them. Perhaps
shame triggered anger, while powerlessness elicited deep resentment, all tumbling beyond Lee's impressive self-control.
Much of this negativity concerned blacks, although he also vili-
fied the national government and the Republican Party. The private Lee said and wrote in a vituperative vein that many other
Southern nationalists expressed in public. More cautious in the
tone of his public utterances, Lee took the high road of the

Southern white project while privately understanding and even replicating something of the spirit of the violent agenda others were practicing.

To be sure, Lee also continued to express considerable magnanimity toward the conquerors, of the sort he repeated to a clergyman on June 20, 1865, when he reportedly said, "I have fought against the people of the North because I believed they were seeking to wrest from the South her dearest rights. But I have never cherished toward them bitter or vindictive feelings, and have never seen the day when I did not pray for them."[33] Such Christian feelings never faded entirely, but Lee often expressed bitterness and vindictiveness within his innermost circle.

Late in 1866, Markie Williams wrote a letter to Lee that provoked, he told her, memories of his "own grief" about one searing incident in the war—when Markie's brother Orton was captured and executed as a Confederate spy after a Union drumhead court-martial in 1863. The recollection was as clear to him now "as on the day of its occurrence, & my blood boils at the thought of the atrocious outrage, against every manly & Christian sentiment which the Great God alone is able to forgive. I cannot trust my pen or tongue to utter my feelings."[34] Lee did not articulate fully the anger he felt toward Union authorities, but neither could he bring himself to practice Christian forgiveness toward them as he knew he ought.

Most often, Lee's expressions of alarm and anger concerned federal Reconstruction policy, when he often used stronger words than in his more public pronouncements. To his cousin Annette Carter, Lee wrote in 1866 that the Southern states must unite "not only for their protection, but for the destruction of this grand scheme of centralization of power . . . to the ruin of all others, & the annihilation of the Constitution, the liberty of the people & of the country." If the Republicans were not reversed,

Lee anticipated the "end of republicanism on this continent." And to General E. G. W. Butler, Lee wrote that although Americans were forever proclaiming "our boastful aspersions to the world . . . that our government was based on the consent of the people," in fact "it rests upon force, as much as any government that ever existed."[35] Lee hated naked American power, of which he felt the South was a passive victim.

Edward Lee Childe, Lee's Parisian nephew and a particular favorite to whom Lee sometimes referred as "my little brother," was the recipient of a whole string of letters during the last four years of Lee's life that contained explicit anger toward Reconstruction policy. Expanding on the theme of tyranny in Washington and coupling it to an excess of both democracy at home and imperialism abroad, Lee wrote in 1867, "The tendency seems to be one vast Government, sure to become aggressive abroad & despotic at home; & I fear it will follow that road which history tells us such Republics have trod, might is believed to be right, & the popular clamor the voice of God." In another letter that month, Lee emphasized vehemently that the constitutional form of federalism for which the South had seceded was the only defense against encroaching central tyranny and that the war against the South had not ended. "The greatest danger . . . is the subversion of the old form of government & the substitution in its place of a great consolidated central power, which wielded by the will of the majority Party, will soon disregard every constitutional check, trample upon the reserved rights of the states & in time annihilate the Constitution."

After the passage of the Fourteenth Amendment and the active enrollment of black voters in the South, Lee wrote to Childe, "the party in power are determined to retain its position even at the risk of destroying the country & of putting an end to republican government." Lee was certain he knew the linchpin of this Northern strategy: "The South is to be placed under the domination of the negroes." Lee believed this plan was a radical Republican conspiracy. "The purpose for which the north went to war has been perverted by the radical party. Had their secret policy been then announced I cannot believe it would have been tolerated by the country." In this argument, Lee overlooked the electoral victory of the radicals in 1866 and the continuous evolution of politics, especially during dramatic times such as these, but even if he had acknowledged an awareness of the ongoing process, he could then have fallen back on the position that the tyrannical majority was imposing its authority by force against the reserved rights of states, conspiracy or no conspiracy. But the idea of a conspiracy was stronger and more emotional: Here as elsewhere Lee violated his own proscription of heated language.

As he sensed he was nearing death, Lee felt considerable despair, at least in the near term, for the future of the United States. He still believed in republicanism in principle but felt that the American people—by which he meant the Northern, Republican majority—had been too base to defend it properly. "It was not the form of government that was at fault, but its administration: not the constitution but the people. The former was too pure for the latter. It requires a virtuous people to support a republican government & the world has not yet reached the proper standard for morality & integrity to live under the rule of religion & reason." Lee's emerging political anger was tied here to his traditional, stoic, and antidemocratic conservatism, such as he had expressed in 1856 when discussing the distant expiration of the necessary evil of slavery. Until a second coming of religion and reason—some time when Christ might will a fundamental social rebirth in the two-thousand-year-long wink of his eye, fallen man could not be expected to do right, and ordinary men would not govern with justice and morality. Yet Lee, as always, reasserted his optimistic belief in the eventuality of God's granting the right—in the faith through which he knew that heaven would soon be his. "But the time I believe will come, though I shall never see it," when reason and true religion would reign.

Reporting in 1870 on his last trip, through Georgia, North Carolina, and Florida, on which he was lionized and on which he went to see the tombs of his father and his beloved daughter Annie, the old general wrote to his nephew that the "disasters . . . the ravages . . . of war," terrible as they were, "were not equal to the depredation & stagnation [these states have] undergone since from the legislation of Congress," but nowhere else was the "desolation equal to that felt by Virginia." He had not seen his native state recover, in spirit or in materiality. "The energy and wisdom of the inhabitants will I hope restore all things in time & the good sense of the American people will bring things back to the principles of the old Constitution."[36] Angry about the current state of affairs, Lee looked back to an older social order—taken as a kind of golden age—as a precursor of an eventual return to just rule.

If Robert E. Lee could often subdue his anger toward the North and assertive blacks, Mary Custis Lee never could. The vituperation contained in her letters must have been present in the table talk at the Lee household as well.

More of a United States nationalist than her husband as secession had approached, Mary Custis Lee also had converted to Southern nationalism more quickly and emphatically. The sufferings of neighbors and friends at Yankee hands horrified her nearly as much as did the confiscation of Arlington and its use as a military cemetery for Union war dead. This was utter pollution of those things that she held most dear. To take one of many such letters on the subject, Mary wrote to Eliza Stiles that the "thievish villains" in the Union army had robbed every stitch of clothing and every household item, and had turned out the slaves to wander the world. "Sooner than be reunited to such a people again, would I live under the despotic rule of Russia."[37] Mary Custis Lee never again considered herself an American—her nation, she insisted, was the South.[38]

Such hatred seemed to feed her. On March 10, 1867, she referred to the radical leaders of Congress as "malignant enemies . . . cowards and base men. . . . The country that allows such scum to rule them must be fast going to destruction & we shall care little if we are not involved in the crash—God only knows what our future may be." In dozens of letters she railed against these "savages" who would "debase & desecrate" her fair Arlington. As for blacks, in addition to her fury that the lazy and idle Lexington blacks who surrounded her were always plundering the white folks, she was equally exercised when they were placed on juries and given the vote. In the midst of an anti-Yankee tirade in 1867, she added, "What a farce the proceedings of the Washington Congress are. We have almost ceased to read them, & feel as if we had no part or lot in them, & should think soon all decent white people would be forced to retire from that city & give place to the dominant race."[39] Here Mary Custis Lee was clearly reflecting discussions she had had with her family and closest friends.

It was not uncommon for Southern women to be more outspoken in their bitterness than Southern men—Lee, for example, had often remarked, as he repeated to his son Fitzhugh in 1869, "We are all as usual—the women of the family very fierce, and the men very mild"—and it was clear that the men listened to the women.[40] In the Lee case, Mary had always been better read and more politically aware than her husband, who looked to her for support and guidance in those realms as well as in religion, where he deeply admired her piety and conviction. In these respects, the Lees always maintained a deep and abiding companionship. With her support, he became a committed

Southern nationalist by his actions during the war and by his political reformation during the continuing war against Reconstruction. Ever the self-controlled gentleman in his self-conception, Lee had become far more politically engaged and emotionally charged. The old-fashioned Virginia gentleman-Roman of Stoic and Christian resignation was displaced significantly by the participant in continuous political struggle in this world. He consciously became part of that larger Southern white project that found great use for him after his death as in his life, a man for all ages very much tailored—with his cooperation—to his time, his place, his class, his race.

EPILOGUE

HANNIBAL'S GHOST

*A*lways interested in cultivating his heroic image, which others carved into shining white marble after his death, Robert E. Lee also was aware of some of the dangers of martial glory, whether embodied in himself or in the militarization of society. He wanted to be remembered as the true servant of Christ, not Mars. After his war was over, he refused to celebrate it or defend it as a mode of resolving social problems. Indeed, as he aged he became increasingly antiwar. Yet after he died, others immediately seized his image, turning it toward a defense of the Confederate war effort, placing it in the center of the Lost Cause, as that of the general of all generals, the one who had done no wrong while he had fought with audacity, tenacity, and Christian purity. Beyond that Southern use, as memory of the Confederacy faded by the time the United States entered the imperial twentieth century, Lee was nationalized alongside Washington as one of the two most esteemed American men of war.

During the late 1860s, Lee watched the rise of the heavily militarized and centralized German Empire with appalled interest, as did many other retired Civil War generals. Commenting on that continent-shattering string of conflicts through which Otto von Bismarck forged his nation, Lee found it difficult to believe that the Europeans, so much less democratic and more mature than their American cousins, would resort to nationalist demagoguery and brutal war-making. After Prussia attacked Austria in 1866, Lee wrote Edward Lee Childe, "I had hoped that in this age, Europe with all her experience, would have found some other mode of deciding a question of right than with the sword, & not have followed young America, & listened to the clamour of interest & passion rather than to the calm voice of reason & justice." Lee found it disillusioning that the Europeans had not evolved at least one step toward that more hallowed future in which he urgently wanted to believe. "It is astonishing how prone all nations are to resort to that arbitrament of war, when might so often decides against right; in which reason has no influence & success is the only criterion of merit."[1] In this analysis, Lee of course referred back to the American Civil War, where Northern might won success, defeating Southern right and merit. But even if he implied that had the South won justice and reason would have triumphed, at a more general level he was also condemning the irrationality and injustice of all war.

As the Prussian hobnailed boots kept marching, Lee grew ever more disgusted with German armed imperialism. During the Franco-Prussian War, Markie Williams wrote Lee, asking if he was not "glad that the Prussians are succeeding." Lee replied with some heat, identifying with the downtrodden French, that the Prussians "are prompted by ambition & thirst for power. The French are defending their homes & country. May God help the suffering & avert misery from the poor."[2] Clearly, the Confederacy was to France as the North was to the Prussians in this argument by implicit analogy, but it was the visitation of war on ordinary civilians that was most disturbing to Lee.

Lee's thinking on warfare had evolved over the late 1860s: Clearly, he had given alternative modes of international conflict resolution, including a sort of world court, considerable reflection. He wrote Edward Lee Childe on August 22, 1870,

> I wish [the Prussians and the French] had submitted their differences to the arbitration of friendly powers, according to the articles of the Treaty of Paris of 1856. It would have been such a grand moral victory in the eyes of the present & future generations, that it could not help but have been followed by other nations. It would have been however almost expecting too much from present civilization, had it been done. We are not yet ready for such an elevated act, & must butcher & slaughter each other I fear for years to come.

Lee never wrote more eloquently of the ravages of war, never more fully revealed the depths to which the Civil War had revolted him, and not just because the Confederates had lost but also because of the destruction all warfare caused. In this instance, as the Prussians closed in on Paris, he was also concerned for the safety of his sister's family. "I hope you will get out of it in time to escape even witnessing the horrors of war," Lee wrote his nephew. "Without going into the merits of the question at issue I cannot help deploring the result & lament the misfortunes that seem to threaten a gallant people, who in their contests just or unjust have borne themselves nobly in the field."[3]

Lee went back and forth between the particular and the universal in his condemnation of this and any war. He felt sympathy for the French not because they were right, which he may or may not have thought, but because they were suffering. Along

similar lines, Lee could not bring himself to read the military
histories of the American Civil War that began to appear almost
immediately after Appomattox, not even those that glorified his
own role. Although a few months after the war ended he had
begun collecting materials to compose a book of his own concerning the Army of Northern Virginia, he never wrote a word:
Indeed, the offer of the presidency of Washington College freed
him from making a serious attempt at the task. In a very telling
letter of January 24, 1867, to Edward A. Pollard, editor of the
Richmond *Examiner* and a bitterly unreconciled ex-Confederate
who was author of the 752-page tribute to Lee entitled *The Lost
Cause: A Southern History of the War of the Confederation,* Lee
wrote in response to Pollard's request for a publisher's blurb, "I
have felt so little desire to recall the events of the war since the
cessation of hostilities that I have not read a single work that
has been published on the subject." He was not about to make
an exception for Pollard. Unlike most retired generals, who
enjoy refighting their wars in printed polemics, Lee did not desire to bring up terrible memories, nor to convert them into
postwar fantasies of past glories.[4]

Neither was Lee remotely interested in continuing to read
advanced texts analyzing war. In 1866, Childe sent Lee a copy of
Colonel Edward B. Hamley's analysis of modern warfare, *The
Operations of War.* Hamley, on the British general staff college
faculty, discussed logistics, strategy, and tactics in order to help
his students and readers begin to catch up to the professional-
ization of Prussian military training through systematic study
of what he called military science. Whatever Lee's feelings
about the Prussian threat, in 1868 he replied to his nephew, "the
subject is one in which I have had some experience & hope
never again to have need of recurring to & therefore I have
never read the book."[5] Such statements reflected not merely a

lack of interest but a refusal to venture back into the military's emotional iron teeth, even in retrospective reading.

Most tellingly, Lee was put off by the developing passion for constructing monuments to the Civil War and its fallen soldiers. When the founders of the Gettysburg Battlefield Memorial Association wrote Lee in 1869, as he paraphrased their invitation, "to attend a meeting of the officers engaged in that battle . . . for the purpose of marking upon the ground by enduring memorials of granite the position and movement of the armies in the field," Lee replied in a withering fashion considerably less polite than was his habit: "My engagements will not permit me to be present, and I believe if there I could not add anything material to the information existing on the subject. I think it wiser moreover not to keep open the sores of war, but to follow the examples of those nations who endeavoured to obliterate the marks of civil strife and to commit to oblivion the feelings it engendered."[6]

While Lee was quite prepared to use the past in a rather nostalgic manner when it came to old Southern constitutional principles and paternalist racial reassurances, he refused even to contemplate using the war as any sort of precedent or value in itself. Lee would have plowed the battlefields over rather than convert them into the shrines others would make of them. After his battles were over, he thought with increasing intensity that all war was colossally stupid and that the Civil War had been so disastrous—and not only because the wrong side had won— that no one should make monuments to it.

Neither did Lee think he had been a perfect Southern hero, nor did he delude himself into a belief that the South had triumphed in the war. Although he never would have stooped to discuss what would now be called his "image," Mary Custis Lee did. In 1867, she wrote a cousin that "the appreciation of my

husband's efforts in the noble cause in which we have lost all
but honour, is particularly gratifying to me, especially as it was a
failure & success is usually the test of military ability—but who
can value either the applause or jeers of the 'vulgar crowd' when
they are led by [Radical Republican congressmen such as Ben]
Butler or [Thaddeus] Stevens & many others." Clearly, the Lees
keenly felt the defeat of the Confederacy and the domination of
the North, a feeling Lee himself had expressed when he wrote
those Northern friends in considerable shame that he would not
darken their doors, monster that he knew he was considered to
be in the victorious part of the nation. A month after Lee died,
his widow wrote an old friend, "Had he been successful instead
of the Hero of the Lost Cause he could not have been more
beloved and honored," an interestingly defensive form of veneration.[7] Despite his tenacious political self-re-creation following
his utterly committed military career, Lee was still well aware of
the words he had uttered about his imperiled honor when he
had joined the Confederate cause, and, along with his wife, he
believed when he died that he had indeed lost everything else.
Many decades after the death of his father, Lee also continued to
remember the Lee family's classical inheritance—ties to George
Washington, of course, but behind him, returning all the way
back to the ancients, were bonds with that hero who had also
lost everything save honor, the figure the Romans had crushed
two thousand years earlier, and with whom Light Horse Harry
had identified his destiny—Hannibal's ghost.

For later didactic purposes, even Lee's death needed to be
heroic, and so was it rewritten. According to a thorough and incisive modern analysis by a team of physicians headed by two
distinguished neurologists, Lee, who had long suffered from
angina and from atherosclerosis, died of a stroke on October 12,

1870. In the two weeks prior to death, he had exhibited the syndrome of abulia—absence of will—in which a stroke victim is incapable of producing sustained speech. And yet generations of Southern schoolchildren were raised on stories, which these doctors consider "preposterous," that the day before his death Lee had said, in reference to his wartime lieutenant A. P. Hill, "Tell Hill he *must* come up!" and that at the moment of his death he said, "Strike the tent." In fact, as several family members and physicians noted at the time, Lee had not been capable of uttering more than very occasional monosyllables for days. It was in 1875 that Colonel William Preston Johnston, son of General Albert Sidney Johnston and professor of history and modern literature at Washington College, a melodramatist who was present during much of the deathwatch, created these memorable phrases, writing in his florid memoir, "a Southern poet has celebrated in song those last significant words, 'Strike the tent;' and a thousand voices were raised to give meaning to the uncertain sound, when the dying man said, with emphasis, 'Tell Hill he *must* come up!' " Douglas Southall Freeman, Lee's hagiographer—the grandest codifier of the Lee cult—uncritically used this dubious source, repeating that with Lee's last breath, " 'Strike the tent,' he said, and spoke no more." Even if it was a physiological impossibility, for Lee worshipers the dying hero had to have uttered the perfect epitaph.[8]

Immediately after Lee died, former colleagues swooped in to transform Robert E. Lee into the chief Confederate monument. Whatever his personal humility and revulsion for war, whatever his complex sense of struggle and ultimate failure, they needed him to be their political and cultural epitome, and so they reconstructed him to serve their view of history. As Thomas L. Connelly put it in his brilliant analysis of the building and sustaining of the Lee cult, "the ultimate rationale of this pure nation was the character of Lee. The Lost Cause argument stated that any society which produced a man of such splendid character must be right."[9] After death, Lee's nation—the white South— needed him not as a human but as an unblemished paragon, and so was he remade.

Twelve days after the death of their leader, the veteran offi- cers of the Army of Northern Virginia were called to a memorial meeting at Lynchburg by ex-general Jubal Early, a mediocre commander, whom Lee in fact had cashiered—if halfheart- edly—from his independent command late in the war, but a brilliant if vitriolic postwar polemicist. Early spelled out the nec- essary first step to Lee's canonization in his opening remarks. "Comrades," he said,

> his fame belongs to the world and to history, and
> . . . sacred duty devolves upon those whom, in defense
> of a cause he believed to be just, and to which he re-
> mained true to the latest moment of his life, and led
> so often to battle . . . we owe it to our fallen comrades,
> to ourselves, and to posterity, by some suitable and
> lasting memorial, to manifest to the world, for all
> time to come, that we were not unworthy to be led by
> our immortal chief, and [are] not now ashamed of the
> principles for which Lee fought.[10]

Early did not consider whether the veterans owed it to *Lee* to construct his memorial; rather, Early planned to serve the ends of Jubal Early, the slain soldiers, their survivors, and their chil- dren by converting the dead Lee into the most ubiquitous Con- federate war memorial. His organization and many other similar ones erected hundreds of statues of Lee, many depicting him astride Traveler, on courthouse lawns across the South. In 1883, with such support, Edward V. Valentine carved for the

Washington and Lee University chapel—the nearly papist Lee shrine of shrines, holy of holies—the white, white marble statue of Lee asleep on the field of battle but ready to awaken and take up his arms once more for the South.

Speaking to the same convention, Jefferson Davis articulated some of the key character indicators that were echoed by generations of cult makers. Even more important than Lee's military capacities, Davis said, were "his moral qualities [which] rose to the height of his genius. Self-denial—always intent upon the one idea of duty—self-control. . . . This good citizen, this gallant soldier, this great general, this true patriot, had yet a higher praise than this . . . he was a true Christian."[11] And it was indeed stainless Christian character that lay at the very heart of the legend: Generations of Southerners remade Lee into a Protestant saint, the sum of all good in their culture. To paraphrase Connelly, the Virginia gentleman Lee who was heir to Washington, who supposedly hated slavery and secession and yet followed dutifully when Virginia left the Union, this military genius who made no mistakes, losing battles only due to the faults of his tarnished subordinates, who was never overwhelmed on the battlefield but only by Northern material superiority grinding him down, this man who refused to countenance nihilistic guerrilla warfare at the end of the war, this self-sacrificing college president who refused to capitalize financially on the war, this Christ of humility and nobility, was constructed almost immediately after his death and remained enshrined well into the twentieth century as a justification for the aspirations and values of many white Southerners.[12]

Much of Southern white domination was so dark—not just the beatings and rapes and lynchings but the nasty undertone of many everyday exchanges and forms of discrimination—that so long as this system survived, which it did well into the 1950s,

Southerners had a continuously urgent need for Saint Robert, the shining exemplar of all that was caring and pure and Christian about their rule. Focusing on the noble in the Southern white code cloaked the ignoble. Abstracting Lee from human weakness and sin was intrinsic to the encoding so necessary for white Southerners to rationalize and deny the deepest contradictions of their rule.

By the beginning of the twentieth century, this legend was fully nationalized by making Lee into the second George Washington, bled of most of his essentially sectional meanings. Lee was reconstructed to represent the restrained and gallant gentleman, admirable in the North as well as the South. He became the most valiant American warrior fighting nobly for freedom, transcending the Civil War divide. This transformation was made possible in part because Northern society had come to accept the wisdom of segregation in the South, to share the belief in the inferiority of the black "race."

The nationalizing of Lee had begun in part with the return of the Democratic Party to the White House. When Grover Cleveland finally ended the Republican presidential monopoly in 1884, elected to a considerable degree by his solid Southern base, he gave numerous ex-Confederates cabinet offices, major diplomatic postings, Supreme Court appointments, and other patronage plums. It behooved him as well to return captured Confederate battle flags to the South, both to pay political debts and to reconcile the sections.

In a very real sense, Cleveland put a federal imprimatur on the return of the South to national governmental power, and this was one culmination of the wider process by which Southerners won the propaganda and political battles over the legacy of the Civil War. National reconciliation had a *Southern* base. In 1876, Republicans had agreed to the abandonment of blacks to Southern politicians, and in the subsequent decades the segregation system deepened while violence against blacks spread cancerously, a process that gained increasing Northern acquiescence—indeed, among many, active support—and that gained national constitutional approval in 1896, when the Supreme Court upheld legalized segregation in the *Plessy v. Ferguson* decision.

This nationalized white supremacism matched the new forms of systemic racism growing in Europe as it conquered most of the nonwhite world and helped prepare the groundwork for the American imperialist war of 1898, an event celebrated widely at the time as the military reconciliation of officers from both Civil War armies and militia units from both parts of the nation, joined together through letting the blood of the off-white Spaniard. All white men learned to rally to one national flag, as if all had been good Americans in the Civil War, regardless of the insignificant distinction of which side they had served, the better to compete in the modern world of imperialist expansion.

The Lost Cause argument and the national beatification of Robert E. Lee were central to the wider political meanings of this nationalist transformation. The chief Southern stake was to justify continuing white social, economic, and political power over blacks within a politically reunited nation. With Saint Robert E. Lee at the symbolic helm, this deeper Southern cause always had been right, and white power always had been protective and just toward blacks.

Under the reluctantly Confederate surface beat the heart of the true American who stood for Christlike peace and reconciliation. The truly disinterested hero served a cause that lost on the material plane, only to be rescued through the symbolic process of heavenly resurrection. In this legendary reconfiguration of Lee and the Civil War, white Southerners in fact won the contest by providing the whole nation with the sacrificial hero who was taken to define the deepest moral legacy of that conflict, with racial justice shunted aside by national white consensus.

If Lee himself, in private, during his last years, walked a considerable distance along the dark side of the white supremacist road, most Southerners have never wanted to hear that news, any more than they willingly dwelled on the degree to which white supremacy was the dominant Southern white value for decades after the war. More generally, so intent have so many been on taking Lee as hero that it remains difficult to this day for a historian to attempt to rescue the human from the Marble Man of his posthumous construction. Yet Lee's star is fading, along with the passing of segregation, and fewer Americans, even in the Deep South, still venerate Lee uncritically, although pockets of neo-Confederates continue to worship him as the deity of Southern "tradition" or "heritage," the code words by which they mean the old white supremacist order, based, whether consciously or not, on a belief in the natural superiority not merely of the "white race" but of a hereditary ruling class such as the Virginia gentry.

Moreover, the picture of masculinity Lee was said to have represented has also begun to pass. Unquestioning obedience to duty, deep emotional repression in the name of self-control and self-denial, endless discipline, and the attempt to enact moral purity, taken as a package, now seem rather less than humble and psychologically realistic and even can appear to amount to an invitation to hypocrisy. Lee was certainly capable of moral grandiosity, but he was also, despite his frequent moralizing pronouncements, characterized by his relentless awareness of his human faults and failures as well as his moral striving. Although most still would agree that Lee had many admirable qualities, the abstracted Marble Man does not continue to serve for the majority of women and men in America as the paragon of all that is unquestionably good in the realm of masculine identity.

Lee was a human of whom legends were made. During much of his life he tried to live up to an ideal construction of the Virginia gentry leader, something he learned from the culture in which he participated and did not transcend. He was indeed duty bound, self-controlled, and deeply pious—that was his goal and his persona, which others took as the whole story, inflating him into sainthood, thus oversimplifying and dehumanizing him in the cause of sanctifying his name. Lee had set himself to a superhuman standard by his aspirations, and in this sense he contributed to his own canonization. But he never believed he had arrived, only that he had struggled and, like all sinners, failed. In this sense, he was a Marble Man manqué. After his death, he could do nothing to prevent others from bleeding him of his humanity and elevating him into the pantheon for their social and political uses.

To use less grandiose imagery—and Lee himself was humble as well as self-important—one could see him as an ambitious man of the perfectionist type. He controlled and drove others, and he pushed himself to attempt to conform to a certain cultural vision of heroic manhood. But of course perfectionists are brittle and deeply anxious, often about the very qualities that make them vulnerable humans, of which they are often ashamed or unaware. Seen this way, as revealed by his own words, Lee actually walked the earth with conflicts and tensions, aspirations and fears. And he walked not above but within all the contradictions of a specific society; he represented Southern white male gentry values, not universal ones. He was a citizen of a particular time and place, not some sort of eternal masculine verity above mortality for all time. He was a leader in the Southern rebellion, in which so many fought so nobly for such a bad cause. This makes him far more interesting than some boring marble representation of the supposedly unitary and perfect saint. To accept Saint Robert would be to accept the code of the white South at face value, to deny the reality of terrible historical questions by embracing the willful self-blinding of hero worship. How much more compelling is it to grapple with a natural man who lived a vivid and significant life during terrible times, a person as complicated and contradictory as are we all.

ACKNOWLEDGMENTS

*I*t gives me great pleasure to thank, however inadequately, those who have softened the rigors of writing this book. Each institution and person involved strengthened my scholarship, my writing, and, most important, my spirits.

Throughout the gestation of this project, Dean John Pierce and President Jack Blaney of Simon Fraser University responded to my material needs with great generosity. A major grant from the Social Sciences and Humanities Research Council of Canada eased my ability to conduct extensive archival research over a three-year period, and the National Endowment for the Humanities provided for a fellowship at the Huntington Library, which provided a home away from home to enable me to write in peace. Special thanks to Roy Ritchie, research director of the Huntington. Archivists in many places aided my quest, most notably Lee Shepard, Frances Pollard, and Vaughan Stanley. Will Dickeson and Alex Long were excellent research assistants.

Several friends and colleagues took time away from their own work to bless me with astute and challenging readings of the very rough first draft of this book: Lesley J. Gordon, Christopher Morris, Mike Parrish, Mark M. Smith, Daniel E. Sutherland, Tatiana van Riemsdijk, and my once and always mentor, Robert H. Wiebe. Special thanks to my reassuring agent, Bella Pomer. At Random House, my editor, Robert D. Loomis, pushed me with toughness, encouragement, and considerable persistence toward greater intellectual and literary clarity, and Timothy Mennel copyedited my work with great skill. And finally, this book could not have been written without the companionship and sharp critical abilities of my dear wife, Santa Aloi, who is always there for me when the chips are down.

Abbreviations

D&M	Clifford Dowdey and Louis H. Manarin, *The Wartime Papers of Robert E. Lee* (Boston: Little, Brown, 1961)
DU	William G. Perkins Library, Duke University, Durham, North Carolina
GHS	Georgia State Historical Society, Savannah
HL	Huntington Library, San Marino, California
L&L	J. William Jones, *Life and Letters of Robert Edward Lee, Soldier and Man* (Washington, D.C.: Neale, 1906)
LC	Library of Congress, Washington, D.C.
LV	Library of Virginia, Richmond
MC	Eleanor S. Brockenbrough Library, Museum of the Confederacy, Richmond
MHS	Missouri Historical Society, Saint Louis
ML	Morgan Library, New York City
OR	*The War of the Rebellion: A Compilation of the Official Records of the Union and Confederate Armies,* 127 vols. (Washington, D.C.: Government Printing Office, 1880–1901)
SH	Jesse Ball Dupont Library, Stratford Hall, Stratford, Virginia
UVA	Alderman Library, University of Virginia, Charlottesville
VHS	Virginia Historical Society, Richmond
W&L	Leyburn Library, Washington and Lee University, Lexington

NOTES

INTRODUCTION–STRUGGLING FOR SELF-MASTERY

1. Marcus Aurelius, *Meditations,* trans. Maxwell Staniforth (London: Penguin Books, 1964), 139. The following two passages also served as guides for Lee and many men like him:

   > Be careful not to affect the monarch too much, or to be too deeply dyed with the purple; for this can well happen. Keep yourself simple, good, pure, serious and unassuming; the friend of justice and godliness; kindly, affectionate, and resolute in your devotion to duty. . . . Reverence the gods, succour your fellow-mortals. Life is short, and this earthly existence has but a single fruit to yield—holiness within, and selfless action without. (97)

   > O soul of mine, will you never be sincere, all one, all open, visible to the beholder, more clearly than even your encompassing body of flesh? Will you never taste the sweetness of a loving and affectionate heart? Will you never be full and unwanting; craving nothing, yearning for no creature or thing to minister to your pleasures, no prolongation of days to enjoy them, no place or country or pleasant clime or sweet human company? (151)

2. Lee to Professor J. B. Minor, January 17, 1867, UVA.
3. On Lee's two tattered books, see Richard B. McCaslin, *Child of the Revolution: Robert E. Lee and the Confederacy* (Baton Rouge: Louisiana State University Press, forthcoming). I am much indebted to Professor McCaslin for sharing his manuscript with me. Late in life, Lee edited a book written decades earlier by his father, which included a long discussion of the *Meditations* in a letter Light Horse Harry wrote to Robert E. Lee's elder brother, the then-teenage Carter. Lee Senior quoted a long passage of Marcus Aurelius's thoughts on education and concluded, "You will agree that a boy thus reared must turn out good when a man, and you will, I hope, hold before your eyes as a model, Marcus Aurelius." Henry Lee to my dear Carter, Nassau, New Providence, December 1, 1816, quoted in Henry Lee, *Memoirs of the War in the Southern Depart-*

ment of the United States (1812), ed. Robert E. Lee (New York: University Publishing, 1869), 60–61.

4. See Thomas L. Connelly, *The Marble Man: Robert E. Lee and His Image in American Society* (Baton Rouge: Louisiana State University Press, 1977). As early as his West Point days, Lee is reputed to have borne this nickname, given him by another cadet who saw him ride by.

5. See Maxwell Staniforth, "Introduction," in Aurelius, *Meditations*, 21. Useful analyses of stoicism in the American South, mainly concerning literature, include Duane J. MacMillan, ed., *The Stoic Strain in American Literature: Essays in Honour of Marston LaFrance* (Toronto: University of Toronto Press, 1977), particularly the essay by Peter Buitenhuis, "The Stoic Strain in American Literature," 3–16; John Mayfield, " 'The Soul of a Man!': William Gilmore Simms and the Myths of Southern Manhood," *Journal of the Early Republic* 15 (fall 1995): 477–500; and two essays on Will Percy and his son Walker: Edward J. Dupuy, "The Dispossessed Garden of William Alexander Percy," *Southern Quarterly* 29 (winter 1991): 31–41; and Lewis A. Lawson, "Walker Percy's Southern Stoic," *Southern Literary Journal* 3 (fall 1970): 5–31. Stoicism is sometimes treated independently and sometimes as a synonym for honor in Bertram Wyatt Brown's always stimulating book, *Southern Honor: Ethics and Behavior in the Old South* (New York: Oxford University Press, 1982).

6. Lee to John Mackay, Fort Hamilton, N.Y., January 30, 1846, ML.

7. For an astute analysis of the contradictions between passivity and the drive to power among Southern gentry males, see Kenneth S. Greenberg, *Masters and Statesmen: The Political Culture of American Slavery* (Baltimore: Johns Hopkins University Press, 1985).

1–Patrimony Recaptured

1. Lee to Cassius Lee, Saint Louis, August 28, 1838, SH; Lee to Carter Lee, Saint Louis, January 7, 1839, UVA.

2. Edmund Jennings Lee, *Lee of Virginia, 1642–1892* (Baltimore: Genealogical Publishing, 1974); Florence Tyler Carlton, *A Genealogy of the Known Descendants of Robert Carter of Corotoman* (Irvingtown, Va.: Foundation for Historic Christ Church, 1982); John McGill, *The Beverley Family of Virginia* (Columbia, S.C.: R. L. Bryan, 1956); Robert Isham Randolph, *The Randolphs of Virginia* (Chicago: privately published, 1936). In his Pulitzer

Prize–winning hagiography of Lee, Douglas Southall Freeman of Richmond wrote:

> For five generations, at least, the ancestors of Robert E. Lee had sustained their social position or had bettered it by advantageous marriages. For in those instances where the younger son inherited comparatively small property he increased it by winning the hand of some wealthy heiress. No misalliance marred the strain of Robert E. Lee's blood or lowered his inherited station as a gentleman. Eugenically, his career is perhaps, above all, a lesson in the cumulative effect of generations of wise marriages. Along with gentle blood, Lee inherited a tradition of public service and of leadership.

Freeman grafted "Modern Science" onto traditional notions of class, and although this passage is to say the least embarrassing, it reveals some of the meanings the gentry class still held as late as 1934, when Freeman wrote this passage. Douglas Southall Freeman, *Robert E. Lee: A Biography*, 4 vols. (New York: Charles Scribner's, 1934–1935), 1: 164.

3. David Hackett Fischer, *Albion's Seed: Four British Folkways in America* (New York: Oxford University Press, 1989), 274–75. Of the many fine analyses of seventeenth- and eighteenth-century Virginia gentry society, Fischer, 207–418, and Daniel Blake Smith, *Inside the Great House: Planter Family Life in Eighteenth-Century Chesapeake Society* (Ithaca: Cornell University Press, 1980), are among the most helpful. There are few such comprehensive studies of the Virginia gentry class after 1800, although three recent monographs grapple with major issues: Diana Hochstedt Butler, *Standing Against the Whirlwind: Evangelical Episcopalians in Nineteenth-Century America* (New York: Oxford University Press, 1985); Daniel W. Crofts, *Old Southampton: Politics and Society in a Virginia County, 1834–1869* (Charlottesville: University Press of Virginia, 1992); and William G. Shade, *Democratizing the Old Dominion: Virginia and the Second Party System, 1824–1861* (Charlottesville: University Press of Virginia, 1996). For comparative purposes, see David Cannadine, *The Decline and Fall of the British Aristocracy* (New Haven: Yale University Press, 1990).

4. *The Life of the Rev. Devereux Jarratt, Rector of Bath Parish, Dinwiddie County, Virginia, Written by Himself* (Baltimore: Warner and Hannah, 1806), 39, quoted in Fischer, 384–85.

5. Rhys Isaac, *The Transformation of Virginia, 1740–1790* (Chapel Hill: University of North Carolina Press, 1982).

6. Smith, 136, 160; on the definition of patriarchy, North and South, see Fischer, 280.

7. For a recent, spirited argument that eighteenth-century Americans had never been deferential and that the American Revolution therefore did not present a special assault on supposed deference, see Michael Zuckerman, "Tocqueville, Turner and Turds: Four Stories of Manners in Early America," *Journal of American History* 85 (June 1998): 13–52. I believe there was always a good deal of rebelliousness but that it took place within social hierarchies that, if never unchallenged, did exist in the political and social spheres.

8. John Bell Hood, *Advance and Retreat: Personal Experiences in the United States and Confederate States Army* (New Orleans: G. T. Beauregard, 1880), 7–8.

9. Undated fragment, almost certainly written during wartime, VHS. This fragment has been quoted widely, including *L&L,* 444, and Emory Thomas, *Robert E. Lee: A Biography* (New York: W. W. Norton, 1995), 397.

10. The fullest and most incisive analyses of the scandals of Light Horse Harry and Black Horse Harry can be found in Paul C. Nagel, *The Lees of Virginia: Seven Generations of an American Family* (New York: Oxford University Press, 1990). On Robert's father, see also Charles Royster, *Light-Horse Harry Lee and the Legacy of the American Revolution* (New York: Alfred A. Knopf, 1981).

11. Thomas, 34–37.

12. "An Old Dragoon," *Lexington (Virginia) Gazetteer,* July 24, 1867, and Joseph E. Johnston, both quoted in Freeman, 1:68, 74.

13. Freeman, 1:81–82.

14. *L&L,* 112. Connelly (172) reads this letter as indicating Lee's insecurities about personal shortcomings; I believe it also can be interpreted more widely.

15. W. H. Fitzhugh to John C. Calhoun, Ravensworth, February 7, 1824, quoted in Freeman, 1:39.

16. Lee to Charles Carter Lee, Louisville, May 10, 1855, UVA.

17. Freeman, 3:236. McCaslin describes the Washingtonian inheritance as central to Lee's life and military career.

18. Lee's indifference to visiting his father's grave site became the subject of a curious historical controversy in 1994. John Morgan Dederer argued that Lee did go there three times, expressing appropriate veneration, while J. Anderson Thompson, Jr., and

Michael Santos argued that he made only two perfunctory visits, a lack of interest they used to demonstrate that he, the son of a man with a classic narcissistic personality disorder including a sadistic streak, became something of a psychological cripple as an adult. In reply to this essay, Gary W. Gallagher nicely points out the absence of any direct evidence on which to base such theoretical considerations. *Virginia Magazine of History and Biography* 102 (January 1994): 73–88, and (January 1995): 75–123.

19. Lee, *Memoirs of the War,* 39–40, 50–53, 57, 60, 65–66, 73, 78.

2–Marriage, Eros, and Self

1. Lee to "Mon Ami," Turtle Island, Mich., July 31, 1835, VHS. For a witty and incisive piece of historical sleuthing, which includes the full text of this letter, see John L. Gignilliat, "A Historian's Dilemma: A Posthumous Footnote for Freeman's *R. E. Lee,*" *Journal of Southern History* 43 (May 1977): 217–36. Freeman became aware of this letter and bought it from an autograph dealer only after the final volume of his Pulitzer Prize–winning biography had appeared. Freeman's ensuing dilemma stemmed from the fact that he was of the school of historians who believed in writing "total history," and this letter, which he read literally rather than as a lighthearted satire, did not conform to his picture of the perfectly self-controlled gentleman warrior who never experienced as base an emotion as the blood lust that this letter seemed to indicate. For a subsequent edition of the biography, Freeman added a footnote so vague and ambiguous as to amount to a burying of the apparent contradiction.

2. For an insightful analysis of Victorian-era romantic correspondence, including its erotic content, see Karen Lystra, *Searching the Heart: Women, Men, and Romantic Love in Nineteenth-Century America* (New York: Oxford University Press, 1990).

3. Lee to Delectable Jack, Fort Monroe, Va., June 26, 1834, ML; Lee to my dearest Jack, Saint Louis, October 22, 1837, GHS; Lee to Henry Kayser, Fort Hamilton, N.Y., June 16, 1845, MHS, quoted in Freeman 1:198.

4. Lee to my dear Mary, Old Point, April 17, 1832, HL; reprinted in Norma B. Cuthbert, ed., "To Molly: Five Early Letters from Robert E. Lee to His Wife, 1832–1835," *Huntington Library Quarterly* 15 (May 1952): 257–76, at 260.

5. Lee to my dearest brother [Carter], Cockspur Island, May 8, 1830, UVA.

6. Lee to Andrew Talcott, Ravensworth, July 13, 1831, VHS. On the onset of sickliness, see Lee to Carter, Old Point, October 12, 1831, UVA.

7. Lee expressed this pride to other men, as when he wrote in 1845, "There are only six of them yet, though I dare say in time they will equal the days of the week," which they soon did. Lee to Henry Kayser, Fort Hamilton, N.Y., October 15, 1845, MHS.

8. Lee to my dear brother [Carter], Warrenton Springs, August 2, 1836, UVA.

9. Lee to Andrew Talcott, Fort Monroe, Va., April 10, 1834, VHS.

10. Lee to my dearest Mary, Fort Monroe, Va., November 27, 1853, quoted in Cuthbert, 268.

11. Lee to dearest Mary, Detroit, August 21, 1835, quoted in Cuthbert, 271–73. Emphasis in original.

12. Lee to Markie Williams, Baltimore, May 10, 1851, in *"To Markie": The Letters of Robert E. Lee to Martha Custis Williams,* ed. Avery Craven (Cambridge, Mass.: Harvard University Press, 1933), 27.

13. Lee to my dear Mary, Saint Louis, October 16, 1837, VHS.

14. Lee to my dear Carter, Cockspur Island, January 4, 1831, UVA.

15. Lee to Jack [Mackay], Fort Monroe, Va., November 28, 1833, SH; Lee to Mary Custis Lee, White Sulphur Springs, August 31, 1840, VHS; Lee to Bettie and Mattie Mason, Saint Louis, August 31, 1840, VHS, quoted in Thomas, 98–99. Gaines was actually sixty-three at the time.

16. Lee to Mary Lee, Saint Louis, August 5, 1837, VHS. Emphasis in original.

17. Lee to Markie Williams, Fort Hamilton, N.Y., September 2, 1844, and September 17, 1845, *"To Markie,"* 4, 13.

18. Lee to my beautiful Tasy, Fort Hamilton, N.Y., March 11, 1843, Ethel Arms Collection, LC; Lee to Tasy, March 13, 1843, VHS; the poem is quoted in Thomas, 106.

19. Lystra, 4, 23.

20. Lee to Eliza Mackay Stiles, Cockspur Island, Wednesday, [month unknown] 13 [1831?]; n.p., Saturday night [November 3, 1831?]; Arlington, January 4, 1832, typescripts in F. R. Mackay Papers, GHS.

21. Lee to Robert E. Lee, Jr., Arlington, December 28, 1851, VHS; Lee to Andrew Talcott [ca. March 1847], in Margaret Sanborn, *Robert E. Lee: A Portrait,* 2 vols. (Philadelphia: J. B. Lippincott, 1966–1967), 1:91. Sanborn, a very reliable scholar, noted that she read this letter in the Library of Virginia a bit more than thirty years ago. I have not been able to find the letter and believe that it has been silently withdrawn from the collection.

3–Fatherhood and Salvation

1. Lee to Mary, Mexico, June 2, 1847, UVA.
2. Lee to Jack Mackay, Saint Louis, October 22, 1837, GHS.
3. Lee to his mother[-in-law], Baltimore [March 24, 1838], VHS.
4. Lee to my dearest mother[-in-law], Fort Monroe, Va., May 20, 1833, VHS. Emphasis in original.
5. Lee Diary, 1855–1861, VHS, quoted in Connelly, 179; Lee to Mary Lee, Louisville, June 5, 1839, quoted in J. William Jones, *Personal Reminiscences of General Robert E. Lee* (1875) (Baton Rouge: Louisiana State University Press, 1994), 369. (Hereafter cited as *Reminiscences.*)
6. Lee to my dearest Mary, Fort Monroe, Va., November 27, 1833, HL, quoted in Cuthbert, 269.
7. Lee to my dear mother[-in-law], Fort Hamilton, N.Y., October 31, 1843, VHS. Emphasis in original.
8. Lee to dearest Mary, Fort Brown, Tex., December 20, 1856, VHS.
9. Lee to Carter, January 7, 1839, UVA; Lee to Henry Kayser, Fort Hamilton, N.Y., October 15, 1845, MHS.
10. Lee to Custis, Arlington, April 5, 1852, VHS.
11. Ibid., Baltimore, May 4, 1851, in *L&L,* 71–74.
12. Ibid., Arlington, December 28, 1851, in *L&L,* 77; also, Baltimore, February 1, 1852, quoted in Freeman, 1:312.
13. Ibid., Baltimore, April 13, 1852, VHS. Emphasis in original.
14. Ibid., Baltimore, March 28, 1852, VHS. Emphasis in original.
15. A series of letters between Robert and Mary Lee, concerning Rooney in the 1850s, is in Thomas, 169, 429.
16. Lee to Custis, Fort Hamilton, N.Y., December 18, 1845, facsimile copy in W&L.
17. Lee to Fitzhugh, Fort Hamilton, N.Y., March 31, 1846, in *L&L,* 39–40.
18. Ibid., Arlington, May 30, 1858, VHS.
19. Robert E. Lee, Jr., *Recollections and Letters of General Robert E. Lee* (1904) (New York: Konecky and Konecky, n.d.), 9–10. (Hereafter cited as *Recollections.*)
20. Lee to my dear little Agnes, City of Mexico, February 12, 1848, VHS. Emphasis in original.
21. Lee to my precious Agnes, San Antonio, September 5, 1857, Manuscripts Department, Tulane University Libraries, New Orleans.
22. Lee to my precious Annie, West Point, February 25, 1853, in *L&L,* 67.
23. Lee to his mother-in-law, Baltimore, March 17, 1852, VHS.

24. See Butler, 28.
25. Lee to Mary, July 8 [1849], VHS. There is no year noted on the let-
    ter, by which to date this manuscript fragment, but the Virginia
    Historical Society has placed it at 1849. Lee was in Baltimore from
    1849 until late 1852.
26. Lee to Mary, West Point, May 2, 1853, VHS. For the remainder of
    these quotations and a narrative of these events, see Sanborn,
    1:225–26.
27. Lee to Mary C. Lee, Camp Cooper, Tex., May 18, 1857, VHS. Also
    see Mary P. Coulling, *The Lee Girls* (John F. Blair: Winston-Salem,
    N.C., 1987), 63.

4–Race and Slavery

1. See Thomas's thorough chapter, "They Wanted a Skillful Engineer
   . . . and Sent Me," 86–100.
2. Lee to my dear mother[-in-law], Saint Louis, November 7, 1839,
   VHS; Lee to Hill Carter, January 25, 1840, quoted in Freeman,
   1:177. Emphasis in originals.
3. Lee to Mary, White Sulphur Springs, August 4, 1840, VHS. At the
   end of the Civil War, Mary Lee wrote to Emily Mason, "I do not expect to be in my home in Richmond again my dear Miss Em. It is
   entirely broken up now & inhabited by Jews . . . who have desecrated it" (September 10, 1865, MC). Lee's anti-Semitism was
   milder and less discriminatory than that of, for example, Ulysses
   S. Grant and William T. Sherman, who acted on such prejudices
   during the war by issuing orders, which Abraham Lincoln over-
   ruled, to expel Jews from portions of the conquered South.
4. Lee to Mary Lee, Mexico City, February 13, 1848; Lee to John
   Mackay, City of Mexico, October 2, 1847; Lee to Mary Lee, San Antonio, September 25, 1846, and Monelora, November 4, 1846, all
   in VHS; Lee to Major D[elafield], Ship *Massachusetts*, off Lobos,
   February 28, 1847, W&L. Also see Gary W. Gallagher, " 'We Are
   Our Own Trumpeters': Robert E. Lee Describes Winfield Scott's
   Campaign to Mexico City," *Virginia Magazine of History and Biography* 95 (July 1987): 363–75.
5. Lee to my dearest Mary, South Bend of Lake Michigan, September
   2, 1835, in Cuthbert, 275. Emphasis in original.
6. Lee to Mary, Des Moines Rapids, September 10, 1837, VHS. Emphasis in original.
7. Lee to Eliza Mackay Stiles, Arlington, January 23, 1836, SH.
8. Ibid., Camp on the clear fork of the Brazos, May 24, 1856, SH; Lee

to Mary, Camp Cooper, Tex., April 12, 1856, VHS; Lee to Mary, n.p., August 25, 1856, in *L&L*, 80.

9. Lee to Mary, Fort Brown, Tex., January 24, 1857, DU; Lee to Major Earl Van Dorn, San Antonio, July 3, 1860, Custis-Lee Family Papers, LC.

10. Lee to Carter, Old Point, August 17, 1832, UVA. Emphasis in original.

11. Lee to Mary Lee, Old Point, April 17, 1831, in Cuthbert, 262. Emphasis in original.

12. Lee to Hill Carter, Fort Hunter, February 24, 1843, VHS. Lee to James E. Everett, Baltimore, August 1, 1852, SH. Everett was a slave agent in Washington, D.C., to whom Lee assigned his slave Philip Minday; Lee to Mary Lee, Baltimore, September 25, 1849, VHS. This last document is partially destroyed.

13. Barbara Jeanne Fields, *Slavery and Freedom on the Middle Ground: Maryland during the Nineteenth Century* (New Haven: Yale University Press, 1985), 2, 62. Fields ascribes the decay of slavery both to ideological shifts—libertarian and evangelical—on the part of slaveholders and to economic changes, from labor-intensive tobacco planting to wheat production, which needed only seasonal labor, for which slave labor was not sufficiently productive. Baltimore was a typical American port town, with the trades of stevedoring, shipbuilding, and tobacco manufacturing all hungry for cheap but flexible free-black and immigrant labor.

14. Lee to Edward C. Turner, Arlington, February 13, 1858, UVA.

15. Lee to Fitzhugh, Arlington, May 30, 1858, and San Antonio, September 7, 1860, VHS; Lee to William Overton Winston, Alexandria, July 8, 1858, William Overton Winston Papers, VHS; Lee to Winston, July 12, 1858, MC. In the second letter to Winston, Lee mentioned Reuben, Edward, and Parks by name as belonging to the Custis estate.

16. Lee to G. W. Custis Lee, Arlington, July 2, 1859, in *L&L*, 102.

17. The full text of the letters to the New York *Tribune* are reprinted in Freeman, 1:390–92. Also see Lee to Custis, Arlington, July 2, 1859, in *L&L*, 100–102; Lee to George K. Fox, Lexington, April 13, 1866; and Lee to E. S. Quirk, Lexington, March 1, 1866, VHS.

18. Mary to her mother, n.p., April 11 [1834], VHS. For a thoughtful analysis of colonization among Virginia Evangelical Episcopalians, notably Mary Custis Lee and Bishop William Meade, see Tatiana van Riemsdijk, "'Time and Property from Heaven': Wealth, Religion, and Reform in Chesapeake Society, 1790–1832" (Ph.D. diss., University of California, San Diego, 1999), chap. 5.

19. Diary of Mary Lee, entries for June 1853 and January 1860, VHS.
20. Journal of Agnes Lee, Arlington, entry for July 16, 1854, in Mary Custis Lee deButts, ed., *Growing Up in the 1850s: The Journal of Agnes Lee* (Chapel Hill: University of North Carolina Press, 1984), 40. I am indebted to Frances Pollard for this citation. For a full discussion of the tiny slaveholder vanguard pushing for slave literacy, see Eugene D. Genovese, *A Consuming Fire: The Fall of the Confederacy in the Mind of the White Christian South* (Athens: University of Georgia Press, 1998), 23–30, and van Riemsdijk, chap. 4.
21. Lee to Mary Lee, Fort Hamilton, N.Y., April 18, 1841, UVA.
22. Mary Lee to my dear Abby, Arlington, February 10, 1859, MC.
23. Mary Lee to W. G. Webster, Arlington, February 17, 1858, LV. Emphasis in original.
24. Mary Lee to Annie [Canada, 1860], VHS.
25. For the full text of this letter of Lee to Mary Lee, from Fort Brown, Tex., on December 27, 1856, see Freeman, 1:371–73.
26. Lee to Mary Lee, Baltimore, July 8 [1849], VHS.

5–Politics and Secession

1. Lee to Henry Kayser, Fort Hamilton, N.Y., May 19, 1844, and December 23, 1843, MHS.
2. Lee to John Mackay, Saint Louis, June 27, 1838, ML. On West Point cliquishness, see James L. Morrison, Jr., *"The Best School in the World": West Point, the Pre–Civil War Years, 1833–1866* (Kent, Ohio: Kent State University Press, 1986).
3. Lee to Robert E. Lee, Jr., Baltimore, January 12, 1852, VHS. See Donald S. Spencer, *Louis Kossuth and Young America: A Study of Sectionalism and Foreign Policy* (Columbia: University of Missouri Press, 1977).
4. An entry in Lee's commonplace book, n.p., n.d., Robert E. Lee Headquarters Papers, VHS.
5. Lee to Carter, City of Mexico, February 13, 1846, UVA.
6. Lee to Mary Lee, Fort Brown, Tex., December 27, 1856, quoted in Freeman, 1:371–73.
7. Lee to Custis, San Antonio, December 14, 1860, in *L&L*, 119.
8. Lee to Major Earl Van Dorn, San Antonio, July 3, 1860, Custis-Lee Papers, LC.
9. Lee to Edward V. Childe, Fort Brown, Tex., January 9, 1857, VHS. Emphasis in original.

10. Lee to Custis, San Antonio, December 14, 1860, in *L&L,* 119. Also see Lee to Agnes Lee, Fort Mason, Tex., January 29, 1860, VHS.

11. Lee to Fitzhugh, San Antonio, December 3, 1860, VHS. Emphasis added.

12. Lee to Annette Carter, Fort Mason, Tex., January 16, 1861, W&L; Lee to Markie Williams, Fort Mason, Tex., January 22, 1861, *"To Markie,"* 58; Lee to Fitzhugh, Fort Mason, Tex., January 29, 1861, VHS; Lee to General Winfield Scott, Arlington, April 20, 1861, in D&M, 9.

13. Lee to Ann Marshall, Arlington, April 20, 1861, in D&M, 10. Emphasis added.

14. Mary Lee to Eliza Mackay Stiles, Arlington, February 9, 1861, GHS; Mary Lee to Mildred, Arlington, [February] 19 and 24, VHS. Emphasis in original.

15. Mary Lee to Rev. Ralph R. Gurley, n.p. [ca. April 25, 1861], UVA. Emphasis in original.

16. Lee to Mary Lee, Fort Mason, Tex., February 23, 1861, VHS, misdated and reprinted in part in Freeman, 1:420, and in *L&L,* 120–21; Lee to Markie Williams, January 22, 1861, *"To Markie,"* 58–59.

17. Lee to Fitzhugh, Fort Mason, Tex., January 29, 1861, VHS; Lee to Custis, Fort Mason, Tex., January 30, 1861, DU.

18. Lee to Fitzhugh, Fort Mason, Tex., January 29, 1861, VHS.

19. Lee to Agnes, Fort Mason, Tex., January 29, 1861, VHS.

20. James May to Cassius Lee, Alexandria, April 22, 1861; Cassius Lee to Robert E. Lee, Alexandria, April 23, 1861; and Robert E. Lee to Cassius Lee, Richmond, April 25, 1861, SH.

6–The Trials of War

1. Scott quoted in J. F. C. Fuller, *Grant and Lee* (1933) (Bloomington: Indiana University Press, 1957), 107; A. M. Lea to Sam Houston, February 23, 1860, Sam Houston Papers, Texas Historical Collection, University of Texas Library, Austin; *Richmond Dispatch,* April 22 and May 1, 1861, quoted in Freeman, 1:469. The first two quotations are cited in Albert Castel, "The Historian and the General: Thomas L. Connelly versus Robert E. Lee," in Gary W. Gallagher, ed., *Lee the Soldier* (Lincoln: University of Nebraska Press, 1996), 210, 220 n. 7. This excellent collection—which reprints primary sources and both early and contemporary scholarship and includes an excellent selective, annotated bibliography—is the

best single source for the general reader who wishes to begin to explore Lee as a military figure. As the war began, Albert Sidney Johnston was also held in high esteem across the South; certainly among Virginians, never modest about the leading qualities of their state, Lee reigned supreme.

2. Lee to Mary Lee, October 7, 1861, quoted in Freeman, 1:598; Lee to my dearest Mary, Camp at Valley Mountain, September 9, 1861, in D&M, 71.

3. Thomas, 225; Freeman, 1:602; Richmond *Enquirer,* June 20, 1862, quoted in Gallagher, "Another Look at the Generalship of Robert E. Lee," in *Lee the Soldier,* 284.

4. Mary Lee to Colonel [Edward S.] Sanford, n.p., May 30, 1861; and Mary Lee to Mrs. Richardson, Lexington, April 8 [ca. 1868], MC. Emphasis in originals.

5. Lee to my dear daughter, Coosawhatchie, S.C., December 25, 1861, in *Reminiscences,* 385–86; Lee to Mary Lee, Richmond, May 11, 1861, in D&M, 26; Lee to Custis, Coosawhatchie, S.C., January 19, 1862, in D&M, 105–6.

6. D&M, 106; Lee to J. P. Benjamin, Coosawhatchie, S.C., December 20, 1861, *OR*, 1:6; Special Orders, Valley Mountain, September 8, 1861, VHS.

7. Lee to Mary Lee, Huntersville, Va., August 4, 1861, in D&M, 62.

8. Ibid., Headquarters, June 22, 1862, quoted in Freeman, 2:257.

9. Lee to my dear Mary, Richmond, May 16, 1861, in D&M, 31. The text of Meade's sermon was Genesis 47:8–9, in the King James Version of the Bible.

10. Lee to Mary Lee, Richmond, May 25 and June 11 and 24, 1861, in D&M, 37, 48, 54.

11. Lee to Mary Lee, Coosawhatchie, S.C., December 25, 1861, in D&M, 95–97; Lee to my darling daughters, Savannah, November 22, 1861, in D&M, 88–89.

12. See the discussion of the Civil War religious views of Presbyterian clergyman George Armstrong and Methodist bishop George Foster Pierce in Eugene D. Genovese and Elizabeth Fox-Genovese, "The Social Thought of Antebellum Southern Theologians," in Wilfred B. Moore, Jr., and Joseph F. Tripp, eds., *Looking South: Chapters in the Study of an American Region* (New York: Greenwood Press, 1989), 37–40.

13. Lee to my precious Markie, West Point, June 29, 1854, *"To Markie,"* 48.

14. Lee to Carter Lee, City of Mexico, March 18, 1848, UVA.

15. Lee to Mary Lee, Richmond, June 24, 1861, in D&M, 53.

16. Lee to Colonel George H. Terrett, Richmond, May 10, 1861, in D&M, 24; Lee to Mary Custis Lee, Valley Mountain, Va., September 17, 1861, in D&M, 73; Lee to General Milledge L. Bonham, Richmond, May 24, 1861, in D&M, 33. Lee's argument for removing troops from towns resembled the argument frequently made by plantation owners about isolating slaves when breaking them to work discipline.

17. Lee to Philip St. George Cocke, Richmond, May 13, 1861, UVA. Cocke regained his brigadiership prior to his suicide on December 26, 1861; whether or not he killed himself on a matter of honor is not known.

18. G. B. Cosby to Captain Payton, Yorktown, Va., August 19, 1861, enclosing a copy of General Lee's order, in *OR*, 1:4, 635. Lee's lesser cordiality to Payton was also due to Payton's far more junior rank, and it is also possible that Payton was not as wellborn as Cocke.

19. Lee to Mary Lee, Richmond, July 2, 1861, in D&M, 55–56; Lee [to Mildred Lee], Savannah, February 26, 1862, UVA.

20. Lee to Mary Lee, Coosawhatchie, S.C., December 22, 1861, VHS.

21. Lee to Custis, Valley Mountain, Va., September 3, 1861, in D&M, 70.

22. Lee to my precious daughter [Mildred], Charleston, S.C., November 15, 1861, in D&M, 86.

23. Lee to dear Mary, Coosawhatchie, S.C., January 28, 1862, in D&M, 107.

24. Lee to General Samuel Cooper, Savannah, January 8, 1862; Lee to General Roswell S. Ripley, Savannah, February 19, 1862; and Lee to Mary Lee, Savannah, February 23, 1862, in D&M, 101–2, 116, 118–19.

25. Lee to my precious Annie, Savannah, March 2, 1862, in D&M, 121. Late in 1861, in an interestingly parallel circumstance, William T. Sherman experienced a clinical depression. For an analysis of Sherman's case, which demonstrates the depths to which Lee never quite descended, see Michael Fellman, *Citizen Sherman: A Life of William Tecumseh Sherman* (New York: Random House, 1995), 84–109.

26. Lee to Andrew Magrath, Coosawhatchie, S.C., December 24, 1861, in D&M, 93. Also on this subject, see Lee to Judah P. Benjamin, Coosawhatchie, S.C., December 3, 1861, in *OR*, 1:6, 335.

27. Lee to Custis, Savannah, February 23, 1862, MC; Lee to Mary Lee, February 23, 1862, in D&M, 118–19; Lee to Custis, Coosawhatchie, S.C., December 29, 1861, in D&M, 98.

28. For an insightful discussion about the fears of the Confederate

leadership concerning the corrupting, individualist qualities of laissez-faire capitalism, see Drew Faust, *The Creation of Southern Nationalism: Ideology and Identity in the Civil War South* (Baton Rouge: Louisiana State University Press, 1988), 41–57.

29. Lee to my darling daughters, Savannah, November 22, 1861, SH; Lee to Mary Lee, Savannah, February 8, 1862, in D&M, 111–12.

30. Lee to my dear Carter, Richmond, March 14, 1862, W&L. Emphasis added.

31. Mary Lee to Eliza Stiles, White House Plantation, March 8, 1862, SH.

7–Audacity

1. Gary W. Gallagher, ed., *Fighting for the Confederacy: The Personal Recollections of General Edward Porter Alexander* (Chapel Hill: University of North Carolina Press, 1989), 91. (Hereafter cited as *Alexander*). For this edition, Gallagher uncovered an unexpurgated memoir Alexander drafted in preparation for his book about the war. Unlike almost all Lee's men after the war, who adulated him, albeit often for their own personal and political reasons, Alexander was skeptical, professional, and quite insightful about Lee's strengths and weaknesses.

2. Quoted in Freeman, 4:172.

3. *Alexander*, 222, 358; also see Freeman, 3:316–21. Half of the Texans in that brigade died during the subsequent attack. From time to time, there was something approaching the suicidal in Lee's battle lust.

4. *Alexander*, 213, 389–91, 421, 479–83. Alexander also observed that Lee frequently manifested profound "hostility" when he received messages he did not like—whether at the messenger or the message Alexander could never clearly discern.

5. Walter H. Taylor to Eli Barrot, May 13, 1861, in Walter H. Taylor, *Four Years with General Lee, 1861–65, with Personal Reminiscences* (Norfolk: Ausbaum, 1906), 5, 6.

6. Taylor to Bettie Saunders, August 8, November 15, December 5, 1863; January 24, 28, February 21, March 4, 8, 20, 25, August 7, 15, November 7, 27, December 18, 26, 1864; February 5, 20, and March 21, 1865, all quoted from the superb edition edited by R. Lockwood Tower, *Lee's Adjutant: The Wartime Letters of Colonel Walter Herron Taylor* (Columbia: University of South Carolina Press, 1995). Emphasis added.

7. Francis Lawley, "General Lee," *Blackwood's Edinburgh Magazine* 111 (March 1782): 356–57, quoted in Connelly, 208.

8. Quoted in Connelly, 207.

9. Freeman, 2:462. On the deep appeal of battle, see J. Glenn Gray, *The Warriors: Reflections on Men in Battle* (New York: Harcourt, Brace, 1959); and Michael Fellman, *Inside War: The Guerrilla Conflict in Missouri during the American Civil War* (New York: Oxford University Press, 1989), 176–92. To take another example, when Sherman was marching his men into battle at Kenesaw Mountain, he paused, prior to ordering an attack in which three thousand of his men were to be killed or wounded within an hour, to reflect on the sight of the Confederate army felling logs, digging ditches, and crowning the hills with batteries, remarking that the scene was "enchanting, too beautiful," almost, for words: Fellman, *Citizen Sherman,* 179.

10. Lee to Davis, near Richmond, June 5, 1862, in D&M, 184.

11. Lee to Major General Lafayette McLaws, Headquarters, July 25, 1862, in *OR,* 1:11 (3), 653.

12. Lee to Longstreet, Headquarters, August 1, 1862, in *OR,* 1:11 (3), 659.

13. Lee to Davis, September 7, 1862, in *OR,* 1:19 (2), 597. On feigning illness, see especially Lee to James A. Seddon, Headquarters, February 21, 1863, in *OR,* 1:25 (2), 638–39.

14. Lee to Davis, Camp on the Opequon, September 23, 1862; and Lee to Longstreet, Headquarters, October 28, 1862, in *OR,* 1:19 (2), 622, 686.

15. Lee to Davis, Camp near Fredericksburg, March 21, 1863, in *Lee's Dispatches,* 81–83; also see Lee to Davis, two miles from Fredericktown, Md., September 7, 1862; and Lee to Davis, Camp on the Opequon, September 22, 1862, in *OR,* 1:19 (2), 597, 617–18.

16. Lee to Major General A. P. Hill, Headquarters, January 12, 1863, in *OR,* 1:19 (2), 732.

17. General Orders, October 1864, Walter H. Taylor Papers, SH.

18. Lee, "Battle Report on the Seven Days," Headquarters, March 3, 1863, in D&M, 211–22, at 219, 221.

19. General Orders, no. 138, Headquarters, Army of Northern Virginia, December 31, 1862, in *OR,* 1:21, 549–50. On the growing nationalist sentiment within the Army of Northern Virginia, which in many respects had come to embody the Confederate cause, see Gary W. Gallagher, *The Confederate War* (Cambridge, Mass.: Harvard University Press, 1997), 61–111.

20. Lee, "Report on the Battle of Chancellorsville," September 23, 1863, in *OR*, 1:25 (1), 795–805, at 803. For a lively and insightful analysis of this stretch of the war, see Daniel E. Sutherland, *Fredericksburg and Chancellorsville: The Dare Mark Campaign* (Lincoln: University of Nebraska Press, 1998).

21. Lee to my precious life [Mildred], Headquarters, near Richmond, July 28, 1862, in D&M, 240.

22. Lee to Mary Lee, Fredericksburg, November 22 and December 16, 1862, in D&M, 343, 365; Lee, "Battle Report of Fredericksburg Campaign," Headquarters, April 10, 1863, in D&M, 366–78, at 373; Lee to my darling little daughter [Mildred], Fredericksburg, December 25, 1862, in D&M, 381.

23. Lee to Agnes Lee, Fredericksburg, February 6, 1863, in D&M, 400; Lee to Charlotte Wickham Lee, Fredericksburg, March 3, 1863, VHS; Lee to Mary Lee, Fredericksburg, April 24, 1863, in D&M, 439.

24. Lee to Mary Lee, Fredericksburg, April 19, 1863, in D&M, 438.

25. Lee to James A. Seddon, Headquarters, January 10, 1863, in D&M, 388–90.

26. Freeman, 4:59, quoting Isaac R. Trimble, who wrote a memoir of these events in the mid-1880s.

27. Lee to Davis, Headquarters, June 10, 1863, in D&M, 508.

28. General Orders, no. 73, Chambersburg, Pa., June 27, 1863, in D&M, 534.

8–Defeat at Gettysburg

1. Lt. Col. Arthur J. L. Fremantle, *Three Months in the Southern States: April–June 1863* (1863) (Lincoln: University of Nebraska Press, 1991), 268–69. Emphasis in original.

2. Lee to Davis, near Gettysburg, July 4, 1863, in D&M, 539.

3. Ibid., Hagerstown, July 7, 1863, in D&M, 540–41; Lee to Mary Lee, Williamsport, July 7, 1863, in D&M, 542.

4. Lee to Davis, Hagerstown, July 8 and 10, 1863, in D&M, 544–45; General Orders, no. 76, in *OR*, 1:27 (2), 301.

5. Lee to Mary Lee, Camp, near Hagerstown, July 12, 1863, in D&M, 547.

6. Ibid., Bunker Hill, July 15, 1863, in D&M, 551.

7. Lee to Mary Lee and Lee to Margaret Stuart, Camp Culpepper, July 26, 1863, in D&M, 559–61.

8. Lee to Davis, Headquarters, July 29, 1863, in D&M, 563.

9. Lee to Inspector General Samuel Cooper, Headquarters, July 31, 1863, in *OR*, 1:27 (2), 305–11, at 308–9.

10. Lee to Davis, Camp Culpepper, July 31, 1863, in D&M, 565.

11. Charleston *Mercury*, July 30, 1863, quoted in Thomas, 306; the comments of Wade Hampton, Robert G. H. Kean, Randolph H. McKim, and James Longstreet are all quoted in Gallagher, " 'If the Enemy Is There, We Must Attack Him': R. E. Lee and the Second Day at Gettysburg," in *Lee the Soldier*, 498–99, 516 nn. 2–4. Emphasis in original.

12. Lee to Davis, Camp Orange, August 8, 1863, in D&M, 589.

13. Ibid.; Lee to Mary Lee, Fredericksburg, March 19, 1863, in D&M, 413; Lee to Longstreet, Camp Rappahannock, October 26, 1863, in *OR*, 1:52 (2), 549–50.

14. Lee to Davis, Headquarters, Orange Court House, August 22, 1863, in D&M, 593.

15. On the Confederate uses of days of prayer and the Redeemer Nation tradition, see Faust, *Creation of Southern Nationalism*, and also Mitchell Snay, *Gospel of Disunion: Religion and Separatism in the Antebellum South* (New York: Cambridge University Press, 1993).

16. Headquarters, August 13, 1863, in *Recollections*, 105–6.

17. Lee to Stuart, Headquarters, November 14, 1862, and May 23, 1863, HL. Also see ibid., April 17, 1863, in *OR*, 1:25 (2), 731.

18. Ibid., August 5 and 7, 1863, HL.

19. Ibid., August 15 and 18, 1863, in *OR*, 1:29 (2), 648, 652.

20. Ibid., September 23, 1863, in *OR*, 1:29 (2), 743.

21. Ibid., October 30, 1863, HL; and November 2 and 4, 1863, in *OR*, 1:29 (2), 816, 821; Emory M. Thomas, *Bold Dragoon: The Life of J. E. B. Stuart* (New York: Harper and Row, 1986), 272–73.

22. Lee to General Samuel Cooper, "Battle Report of Gettysburg Campaign," Headquarters, January 20, 1864, in D&M, 569–85.

23. Lee to General George E. Pickett [ca. August 4, 1863], in *OR*, 1:27 (3), 1075. Also see Lesley J. Gordon, *General George E. Pickett in Life and Legend* (Chapel Hill: University of North Carolina Press, 1998).

24. Return of Casualties in the Army of Northern Virginia, at the Battle of Gettysburg, July 1–3, in *OR*, 1:27 (2), 338–46. James McPherson estimates "at least 24,000" casualties in *Ordeal by Fire*, 2d ed. (New York: McGraw-Hill, 1992), 329, while Emory Thomas estimates "perhaps 28,000," 304.

25. Lee to William M. McDonald, Lexington, April 15, 1868, VHS.

26. For an excellent analysis of the postwar blaming of Longstreet, see William Garrett Piston, *Lee's Tarnished Lieutenant: James Longstreet and His Place in Southern History* (Athens: University of Georgia Press, 1987). One of several recent accounts emphasizing Lee's strategic poverty at Sharpsburg and Gettysburg is Michael A. Palmer, *Lee Moves North: Robert E. Lee on the Offensive* (New York: John Wiley, 1998).

9–To the Lost Cause

1. Lee to Mrs. E. A. Stiles, Camp Rapidan, November 25, 1863, SH.
2. General Orders, no. 7, Headquarters, January 22, 1864, in *OR*, 1:33, 1117.
3. Lee to General Ambrose P. Hill, Headquarters, June [1], 1864, in D&M, 759–60.
4. Lee to Davis, Petersburg, June 21, 1864, in Douglas Southall Freeman, *Lee's Dispatches* (1915) (Baton Rouge: Louisiana State University Press, 1957), 254–55. (Hereafter cited as *Lee's Dispatches.*)
5. Both quotes in Freeman, 3:499.
6. For a thorough and insightful analysis of the experiences and attitudes of Lee's soldiers during the terrible last year of the war, see J. Tracy Power's fine book, *Lee's Miserables: Life in the Army of Northern Virginia from the Wilderness to Appomattox* (Chapel Hill: University of North Carolina Press, 1998).
7. Lee to Davis, Headquarters, August 9, 1864, in *Lee's Dispatches*, 288–89; Lee to Col. L. B. Northrop, Headquarters, January 5, 1864, in *OR*, 1:33, 1064–65; Lee to Brigadier General A. R. Lawton, Headquarters, January 18, 1864, in *OR*, 1:33, 1094; Lee to——, Headquarters, January 25, 1865, in *OR*, 1:46 (2), 1134–35; Lee to secretary of war, Headquarters, January 19, 1865, in *OR*, 1:46 (2), 1099; Lee to Brigadier General I. M. St. John, Headquarters, February 21, 1865, in *OR*, 1:46 (2), 1246.
8. Lee to Z. B. Vance, Headquarters, December 14, 1864, SH; Lee to Jefferson Davis, Headquarters, January 18, 1865, in *Lee's Dispatches*, 318–22. On overly avid participation in the marketplace, evaluated by preachers and others as a leading Southern sin, see Faust, " 'Sliding into the World': The Sin of Extortion and the Dynamic of Confederate Identity," in *Creation of Southern Nationalism*, 41–77.
9. Lee to secretary of war, August 23, 1864, in *OR*, 1:42 (2), 1199–1200.

10. Lee to Davis, Orange Court House, January 27, 1864, in D&M, 662–63.
11. Ibid., Headquarters, August 13, 1863, in *Lee's Dispatches,* 369.
12. Lee, Circular and General Order Number 4, Petersburg, February 22, 1865, in *OR,* 1:46 (2), 1246–50.
13. Lee to Davis, Headquarters, August 17, 1863, in D&M, 591; Lee to James A. Seddon, Headquarters, October 30, 1863, in *OR,* 1:29 (2), 805–6.
14. Lee to Davis, Headquarters, April 7 and 13, 1864, in *Lee's Dispatches,* 154–58.
15. Lee to secretary of war, Headquarters, January 27, 1865, in *OR,* 1:46 (2), 1143.
16. Ibid., December 1, 1864, and February 24, 1865, in *OR,* 1:42 (3), 1249, and in D&M, 910.
17. Ibid., November 18, 1864, in *OR,* 1:42 (3), 1213.
18. Lee to Davis, Petersburg, February 8, 1865, in D&M, 892–93; General Order Number 2, Headquarters, February 11, 1865, in *OR,* 1:46 (2), 1229–30.
19. Lee to J. C. Breckinridge, Petersburg, February 24 and 28, 1865, in *OR,* 1:46 (2), 1254, 1265.
20. See William W. Bennett, *A Narrative of the Great Revivals Which Prevailed in the Southern Army* (Philadelphia: Claxon, Demsen, and Haffelfinger, 1877); Drew Faust, "Christian Soldiers: The Meaning of Revivalism in the Southern Army," *Journal of Southern History* 53 (February 1987): 63–90.
21. Lee to my precious Annie, Coosawhatchie, S.C., December 8, 1861, in *Recollections,* 56; General Order Number 15, Headquarters, February 7, 1864, in D&M, 668–69.
22. General Order Number 14, Headquarters, February 3, 1864, in *OR,* 1:33, 1145; Lee to secretary of war, Headquarters, May 6, [ca. 8], and 10, 1864, in *OR,* 1:36 (1), 1029, and 1:38 (2), 960, 974; Lee to Davis, Headquarters, June 14, 1864, in D&M, 777–78, and Petersburg, December 14, 1864, in *OR,* 1:42 (3), 1272.
23. Lee to Mary Lee, Chaffins [Va.], October 9, 1864, VHS.
24. Lee to Dr. Orlando Fairfax, Fredericksburg, December 28, 1862, in *L&L,* 473; Lee to General H. Cobb, Fredericksburg, December 13, 1862, and Lee to His Excellency Francis W. Pickens, Fredericksburg, December 18, 1862, in *OR,* 1:21, 1067–68.
25. General Order Number 44, Headquarters, May 20, 1864, in *OR,* 1:36 (3), 800; General Order Number 61, Headquarters, May 11, 1863, in *OR,* 1:25 (2), 793; Lee to Carter Lee, n.p., n.d., quoted in Freeman, 3:2.

26. Lee to Wade Hampton, Chaffins [Va.], October 29, 1864, Hampton Family Papers, 55.

27. Lee to Charlotte Wickham Lee, Camp Culpepper, July 26, 1863, in *L&L*, 278.

28. Lee to Edward Lee Childe, Ringgold Barracks, Tex., November 1, 1856, January 7 and 9, 1857, SH; Lee to Markie Williams, West Point, June 23, 1853, *"To Markie,"* 31.

29. Lee to Eliza Stiles, Camp Culpepper, July 25, 1863, SH; Lee to Mary Lee, Richmond, June 10, 1862, and December 27, 1863, in D&M, 189, 345; Lee to Mrs. Fitzhugh Lee, Fredericksburg, December 10, 1862, in D&M, 357.

30. Lee to Mary Lee, Camp near Winchester, October 26, 1862, and Lee to my precious daughter [Mildred], Richmond, November 3, and Culpepper Court House, November 10, 1862, and Lexington, March 21 and 22, 1870, all in VHS. Annie's fatal illness and its impact on the Lee family is discussed in Coulling, 106–12.

31. Lee to my dear cousin Ellen——, n.p., April 20, 1863, MHS. For analysis of the mourning processes of another Civil War general, see Fellman, *Citizen Sherman*, 192–212.

32. 1 Corinthians 15:55–56, King James Version.

33. Lee to Mary Lee, Petersburg, November 12, 1864, LV.

34. Lee to William P. Miles, Headquarters, January 19, 1865; Lee to James A. Seddon, Petersburg, February 8, 1865, and Lee to John C. Breckinridge, Petersburg, February 19, 1865, in D&M, 885–86, 890, 904–5; Lee to Mary Lee, Petersburg, February 21, 1865, in D&M, 907; Lee to Mary Lee, Petersburg, March 18, 1865, MC.

35. Lee to Jubal A. Early, Headquarters, March 30, 1865, in *OR*, 1:49 (2), 1174–75.

36. Lee to Davis, Petersburg, March 14 and 26, 1865, in D&M, 915, 917.

37. Ibid., Richmond, April 20, 1865, in D&M, 938.

38. Lee to William H. Platt, Richmond, May 16, 1865, Civil War Times Collection, United States Military History Institute, Carlisle, Pa., quoted in Noah Andre Trudeau, " 'A Mere Question of Time': Robert E. Lee from the Wilderness to Appomattox Court House," in Gallagher, *Lee the Soldier*, 554.

39. Lee, General Order Number 9, Headquarters, April 10, 1865, in D&M, 934–35. According to Emory Thomas (367), Lee's remarks were probably ghostwritten by Charles Marshall of his staff and then edited by Lee, but the sentiments were certainly Lee's.

40. For two meditations on the meanings of Lee's refusal to surrender inwardly, see Robert Penn Warren's brilliant essay, *The Legacy of the Civil War* (New York: Random House, 1961), and Thomas L.

Connelly and Barbara L. Bellows, *God and General Longstreet: The Lost Cause and the Southern Mind* (Baton Rouge: Louisiana State University Press, 1982).

10–The War He Refused

1. Lee to Custis, Coosawhatchie, S.C., January 4, 1862, in D&M, 100.
2. Lee to Fitzhugh, Savannah, February 16, 1862, VHS.
3. Mary Lee to Charlotte Wickham Lee, Richmond, July 11 and 19, 1862, VHS.
4. Lee to Mary Lee, Fredericksburg, December 7, 1862, in D&M, 354.
5. Ibid., December 16, 1862, in D&M, 363.
6. Ibid., December 21, 1862, in D&M, 378–79, and January 8, 1863, VHS.
7. Ibid., Camp Rapidan, November 11, 1863, in D&M, 622.
8. Ibid., Camp, January 24, 1864, in D&M, 661.
9. Ibid., Petersburg, September 18, 1864, in D&M, 855.
10. Lee to Lieutenant Colonel J. Critcher, Fredericksburg, May 26, 1863, in *OR*, 1:25 (2), 826.
11. Augustus S. Montgomery, Washington, May 12, 1863; Z. B. Vance to Jefferson Davis, Raleigh, May 21, 1863; Lee to Vance, Headquarters, May 26, 1863, and Lee to James A. Seddon, Headquarters, May 26, 1863, in *OR*, 1:18, 1067–69, 1073.
12. Lee to Davis, Petersburg, July 6, 1864, in *Lee's Dispatches,* 367–68.
13. Ibid., Headquarters, September 20, 1863, in *OR*, 1:29 (2), 763, and June 26, 1864, in D&M, 807.
14. M. N. Love to his mother, August 6, 1864, Love Papers, Petersburg National Battlefield Archives, quoted in Power, 139, spelling and capitalization modernized. Power (135, 139–40) quotes many Confederate responses to this massacre, a very few of which decried it.
15. Lee to Grant, Headquarters, October 1 and 3, 1864, and Grant to Lee, Headquarters, October 2 and 3, 1864, in *OR*, 2:7, 906–9, 914, 1009.
16. Lee to Grant, Headquarters, October 19, 1864, in *OR*, 2:7, 1010–12.
17. Grant to Lee, Headquarters, October 20, 1864, in *OR*, 2:7, 1018–19.
18. George W. Fitch to Major William Innes, Nashville, January 3, 1865, in *OR*, 2:8, 19–20; Grant to Lee, City Point, Va., March 14, 1865, and Lee to Grant, Headquarters, March 23, 1865, in *OR*, 2:8, 393, 425.
19. Lee to Davis, Headquarters, September 2, 1864, in D&M, 847–50.
20. See, for example, Lee to Governor Francis W. Pickens of South

Carolina, Headquarters, Coosawhatchie, S.C., January 2, 1862, in *OR,* 1:6, 395; Lee to D. H. Hill, New Market, Va., August 7, 1862, in *OR,* 1:11 (3), 667; Lee to James A. Seddon, Headquarters, March 25, 1863, in *OR,* 1:25 (2), 684.

21. Lee to Seddon, Headquarters, September 17, 1864, in D&M, 853–54; Lee to Seddon, September 20, 1864, in *OR,* 1:42 (2), 1260–61; Special Orders no. 234, Richmond, September 21, 1864, and Seddon to Lee, Richmond, September 22, 1864, in *OR,* 1:42 (2), 1268–70. Lee also pushed this project on General Braxton Bragg, who was fighting far to the west (*OR,* 1:42 [2], 1292–93).

22. Major General J. F. Gilmer to Lee, Richmond, November 21, 1864, in *OR,* 4:3, 829–31; Lee to Gilmer, Petersburg, November 21, 1864, in *OR,* 4:3, 838–39.

23. Lee to Seddon, Chaffins Farm, October 4, 1864, and Headquarters, December 11, 1864, in *OR,* 1:42 (3), 1267, 1134; Lee to Governor William Smith, Headquarters, February 9, 1865, HL.

24. P. R. Cleburne et al. to Commanders of the Army of Tennessee, January 2, 1864, quoted in Robert F. Durden, ed., *The Gray and the Black: The Confederate Debate on Emancipation* (Baton Rouge: Louisiana State University Press, 1972), 53–65, at 58. Durden's collection of primary documents remains an invaluable source for gaining an understanding of the strange debate over black Confederate troops. Also see the astute analysis by Craig L. Symonds in *Stonewall of the West: Patrick Cleburne and the Civil War* (Lawrence: University Press of Kansas, 1997), 181–201.

25. Message to the Senate and House of Representatives of the Confederate States of America, Richmond, November 7, 1864, in *OR,* 4:3, 797–99, reprinted in Durden, 101–6.

26. Major General Howell Cobb to Seddon, Macon, Ga., January 8, 1865, in *OR,* 4:3, 1009–10, reprinted in Durden, 185.

27. Lee to Honorable Andrew Hunter, Headquarters, January 11, 1865, in *OR,* 4:3, 1012–13, reprinted in Durden, 207–9; also see Hunter to Lee, Richmond, January 7, 1865, in *OR,* 4:3, 1007–9.

28. Lee to Ethelbert Barksdale, February 18, 1865, quoted in Durden, 206–7.

29. W. Albright, diary, March 16, 1865, Albright Papers; J. F. Maides to his mother, February 18, 1865, Maides Papers, both in the Southern Historical Collection, University of North Carolina, Chapel Hill, both quoted in Power, 268, 311.

30. Lee to Davis, Headquarters, March 10, 1865, in D&M, 914, and March 24, 1865, in *OR,* 1:46 (3), 1339.

31. Lee to secretary of war, Headquarters, March 27, 1865, in *OR*, 1:46 (3), 1356–57; Charles Marshall to Lt. General R. S. Ewell, Headquarters, March 27, 1865, George Washington Campbell Papers, LC. Lee dictated this letter to Marshall.

32. Marshall to Ewell, Headquarters, March 30, 1865, MHS, dictated by Lee; Lee to Davis, Petersburg, 3 P.M., April 2, 1865, in D&M, 927. For thorough discussions of black military experiences in Virginia, see Ervin L. Jordan, Jr., *Black Confederates and Afro-Yankees in Civil War Virginia* (Charlottesville: University Press of Virginia, 1995), and James H. Brewer, *The Confederate Negro: Virginia's Craftsmen and Military Laborers, 1861–1865* (Durham, N.C.: Duke University Press, 1969).

33. Lee to Davis, Headquarters, August 1, 1863, in *OR*, 1:27 (3), 1069.

34. Ibid., January 20, 1864, in *Lee's Dispatches*, 131–33; Lee to secretary of war, Headquarters, August 14, 1864, in *OR*, 1:42 (2), 1175–76.

35. Lee to Jeb Stuart, Headquarters, March 12, 1863, in *OR*, 1:25 (2), 664; Lee to War Department, Headquarters, March 21, 1863, in *OR*, 1:25 (1), 66.

36. Lee to Stuart, Orange, Va., August 18, 1863, in *OR*, 1:29 (2), 652.

37. Thomas L. Rosser to Lee, Headquarters Valley District, January 11, 1864, endorsed by Stuart on January 18 and Lee on January 22 and forwarded to the War Department, in *OR*, 1:33, 1081–82; Lee to General Samuel Cooper, Headquarters, April 1, 1864, in D&M, 689; Lee to Davis, Headquarters, January 20, 1864, in *Lee's Dispatches*, 131–33.

38. Lee to Davis, Headquarters, June 26, 1864, in *Lee's Dispatches*, 259–60; Lee to secretary of war, Headquarters, June 26 and August 9, 1864, in *OR*, 1:40 (2), 689, and 1:43 (1), 990–91.

39. Remarks written some time between 1865 and 1875 by R. L. Montague, ex–lieutenant governor of Virginia, quoted in *Reminiscences*, 295.

40. *Alexander*, 512, 530–33; Lee to Davis, Richmond, April 20, 1865, in D&M, 939. Mosby's men, perhaps eight hundred in number, did take to the Virginia mountains, vowing to fight on, until, on April 21, Mosby disbanded them. For more analysis of the potential of guerrilla warfare, see two recent collections: Daniel E. Sutherland, ed., *Guerrillas, Unionists, and Violence on the Confederate Home Front* (Fayetteville: University of Arkansas Press, 1999); and Kenneth W. Noe and Shannon H. Wilson, eds., *The Civil War in Appalachia* (Knoxville: University of Tennessee Press, 1997). See

also, among other works, Stephen V. Ash, *When the Yankees Came: Conflict and Chaos in the Occupied South* (Chapel Hill: University of North Carolina Press, 1995); Philip Shaw Paludan, *Victims: A True Story of the Civil War* (Knoxville: University of Tennessee Press, 1981); and Fellman, *Inside War.*

41. Lee to John Mackay, City of Mexico, October 2, 1847, VHS.

42. For a thorough analysis of Washington's inclusion of guerrilla warfare, see Mark V. Kwasny, *Washington's Partisan War, 1775–1783* (Kent, Ohio: Kent State University Press, 1996). John Shy has written that Washington "never seriously considered" adopting guerrilla war, an idea from which he "would have recoiled in horror. . . . A strategy of that kind would change the war for independence into a genuine civil war with all its grisly attendants—ambush, reprisal, counter-reprisal. It would tear the fabric of American life to pieces" and perhaps throw power to a military junta. And Don Higginbotham adds that both sides "preferred orthodox warfare, with guerrillas seen only as auxiliaries" and that "it is impossible to imagine the Americans as terrorists [who] hate their opponents and all they stand for. . . . Terrorism rips apart the vitals of the community." With all due respect, these two authors seem to have projected their own conservatism onto the Revolutionary War, which was a very nasty civil war as well as an anticolonial one, one that in many places did indeed tear the social fabric asunder, as Shy himself discusses concerning the Carolina backcountry. The history of terrorism and guerrilla warfare in the Revolution remains to be written. It was true that Washington hated such wild disorder and that Lee emulated his spirit, but Washington profited militarily from much of what he never quite accepted. Shy, *A People Numerous and Armed: Reflections of the Military Struggle for American Independence* (New York: Oxford University Press, 1976), 161, 212; Higginbotham, *War and Society in Revolutionary America: The Wider Dimensions of the Conflict* (Columbia: University of South Carolina Press, 1988), 156, 158; and in contrast, Kwasny, as well as Fellman, *Inside War.*

11–Cincinnatus

1. Lee to Armistead L. Long [Richmond, ca. May 1865], in *Recollections,* 170. For a full discussion of Lee's postwar years, see Charles B. Flood, *Lee: The Last Years* (Boston: Houghton Mifflin, 1981).

2. Lee to Fitzhugh, Near Cartersville, July 29, 1865, in *Recollections,* 177–78.

3. Ibid., Lexington, October 30, 1865, VHS.

4. Ibid., Lexington, June 8, 1867, in *Recollections*, 259–60.

5. Lee to Rob, October 26, 1867, and March 12, 1868, in *Recollections*, 281–83, 305.

6. *Recollections*, 407.

7. Lee to Rob, October 26, 1867; Lee to Caroline C. Stuart, Lexington, July 4, 1868, W&L.

8. Lee to Mildred, Savannah, February 26, 1862, in *Reminiscences*, 388–89.

9. Ibid., Fredericksburg, December 25, 1862, in D&M, 381, and Petersburg, November 6, 1864, in *Reminiscences*, 139.

10. Ibid., Lexington, January 27, 1867, in *Recollections*, 252–53.

11. Lee to my precious life [Mildred], Lexington, December 21, 1866, in *Recollections*, 247–48.

12. *Recollections*, 283.

13. Entry for August 21, 1888, and end of journal [1905], Mildred Lee Journal, VHS.

14. The comment on William Price comes in a letter from Custis to Mrs. Seddon Jones, August 20, 1895, W&L. For an insightful analysis of the bleak last years of the Lee children, see Coulling, 181–96.

15. Lee to Mrs. W. H. F. Lee, Culpepper, June 11, 1863, in D&M, 512; Lee to Robert M. Stiles, Richmond, May 19, 1862, GHS. After the war, more sons were needed to replace those lost, and so Lee wrote to Miss Sallie S. Wright, "Guided by your intuitive sense of propriety . . . you have done what I have exhorted all our young ladies in Virginia to do since the war. Select a brave young soldier, marry him at once, and make him happy" (Lexington, June 22, 1866, Tulane University Library, New Orleans).

16. Lee to Mary Lee, Camp Rappahannock, November 1, 1863, in *Recollections*, 112.

17. Lee to Annie, Coosawhatchie, S.C., December 8, 1861, in D&M, 91; Lee to Miss Jennie Washington, Camp, April 12, 1864, UVA.

18. Lee to Mary Lee, Camp, February 6, 1863, in D&M, 401.

19. Lee to Agnes, Petersburg, November 20, 1864, VHS.

20. Lee to Miss Margaret Stuart, April 7, 1864, W&L.

21. Lee to my dear daughters [Margaret and Caroline Stuart], Camp, September 8, 1863, VHS.

22. Lee to Carrie Stuart, Camp Rapidan, November 21, 1863, VHS.

23. Lee to Charlotte Lee, Richmond, April 20, 1862, VHS.

24. Lee to Mrs. Fitzhugh Lee, Dabb's, June 22, 1862, in D&M, 197.

25. Lee to James H. Caskie, Cartersville, August 30, 1865, W&L.

26. Lee to my precious little Agnes, Lexington, March 28, 1868, VHS. Precious little Agnes was twenty-seven at this time.
27. Lee to Miss Bessie Johnston, White Sulphur Springs, August 23, 1869, UVA.
28. "Nettie" to dear Gen. Lee, Darlington, February 12, 1869, VHS.
29. Lee to Belle Stuart, Richmond, May 2, 1868, VHS.
30. Lee to Julie G. Cheatham, Lexington, March 21, 1866, SH; Lee to Markie Williams, Lexington, April 7, 1866, *"To Markie,"* 68.
31. Lee to Miss Laura Mason Chilton, Lexington, November 22, 1869, MC.
32. Lee to Markie Williams, Lexington, November 5, 1866, ML.
33. Ibid., April 9, 1868, and February 5, 1869, ML.
34. Markie Williams to Agnes, Philadelphia, October 15, 1870, VHS.
35. Lee to my beautiful Lottie, Lexington, September 27, 1867, VHS. See similar letters in the same collection for November 2, 1868, and August 12, 1870. Rob married Lottie only after his father's death.

12–Barbarians in the Garden

1. These maxims, which come from a variety of sources, are quoted in Freeman, 4:278, 296.
2. Lee to an unnamed student, quoted in Freeman 4:278; Lee to John B. Baldwin, Lexington, December 15, 1865, VHS.
3. Lee to Rev. Churchill L. Gibson, Lexington, January 24, 1866, W&L.
4. Lee to Messrs. S. G. M. Miller, J. L. Logan, T. A. Ashby, Committee, Washington College, December 9, 1869, in *Reminiscences,* 170.
5. Lee to Fitzhugh, Arlington, May 30, 1858, and January 1, 1859, in *L&L,* 93, 96.
6. Lee to Fanny French, Lexington, April 6 and 29, 1866, VHS. Lee wrote in a letter of advice to the newborn Robert E. Lee Mooty of La Grange, Georgia, "Listen to your parents; obey their precepts; and from childhood to the grave, pursue unswervingly the path of honor and of truth. Above all things, learn at once to worship your Creator and to do His Will, as revealed in His Holy book." Lee to Robert E. Lee Mooty, Lexington, May 29, 1866, VHS.
7. Lee to Mrs. F. S. Cater, Lexington, April 2, 1869, VHS.
8. Lee to Colonel J. W. Lapsley, Lexington, June 5, 1866, VHS.
9. See, for example, Lee's letter of April 20, 1868, to an unnamed father, in *Recollections,* 296–97.
10. Anonymous story in *Recollections,* 332.

11. Lee to Hon. Lewis E. Parsons, Lexington, March 8, 1867, W&L. Parsons was one of a group of Southern senators elected in 1866 under Andrew Johnson's Reconstruction policies whom the Radical Republicans in Congress refused to seat.

12. Lee to Rev. B. B. Blair, Lexington, January 7, 1870, W&L.

13. Lee quoted in Flood, 146–47; on the 1869 restoration, see *L&L*, 107.

14. Address of R. E. Lee, November 26, 1866, in *L&L*, 421–22.

15. The best account of this is in Flood, 150–51.

16. Thomas, 388–89; Flood, 176–83.

17. Lee to George Sargent, Lexington, February 15, 1868; Lee to J. M. Platt, Lexington, February 13 and 27, 1868, W&L.

18. New York *Independent*, April 16, 1868, quoted in Thomas, 388, and Freeman, 4:354–55.

19. Address of R. E. Lee, Lexington, March 30, 1868, and Lee to J. B. Strickler, Lexington, May 10, 1868, in *Recollections*, 300–301. See Thomas, 389, Flood, 183–84, and Freeman, 4:358–60.

20. Lee to Colonel John W. Jordan, Lexington, November 20, 1868, and Lee to Mrs. E. Neel, Lexington, January 29, 1869, W&L.

21. On January 26, 1871, Mary Lee wrote to Mrs. John Tyler, who was living in the North, "I heard your sons were coming back to Virginia to live. . . . I suppose you have greater facilities where you are of educating your children though if they are as hot little Southerners as the rising generation here—they will not imbibe yankee notions very readily." Tyler Family Papers, LV.

13–SOUTHERN NATIONALIST

1. U.S. Congress, testimony of Robert E. Lee, February 17, 1866, *Report of the Joint Committee of Reconstruction*, 39th Cong., 1st sess. (Washington, D.C.: Government Printing Office, 1866), 129–36.

2. Lee to Mary Lee, Lexington, October 3, 29, and 30, 1865, VHS.

3. Lee to Rob, Lexington, June 19, 1869, VHS.

4. *Recollections*, 168; Freeman, 4:199.

5. Lee to Fitzhugh, Lexington, October 30, 1865; Lee to Rob, Lexington, October 18, 1866, VHS.

6. Lee to Colonel Joseph H. Ellis, Lexington, December 31, 1869, VHS.

7. Jack P. Maddex, Jr., *The Virginia Conservatives, 1867–1879* (Chapel Hill: University of North Carolina Press, 1979), 181. In general, see Maddex's discussion of what he calls the "immigration panacea" (178–83). On postwar Virginia politics, also see Jack

P. Maddex, Jr., "Virginia: The Persistence of Centrist Hegemony," in *Reconstruction and Redemption in the South,* ed. Otto H. Olsen (Baton Rouge: Louisiana State University Press, 1980), 113–55; and Richard Lowe, *Republicans and Reconstruction in Virginia, 1856–70* (Charlottesville: University of Virginia Press, 1991).

8. Lee to Rob, Lexington, March 12, 1868, *Recollections,* 306. Lee served actively on the board of directors of the Virginia Central Railroad, and in this sense could be considered an advocate of economic development, but only in the context of his larger vision of Virginia modernized along white lines. See, for example, Lee to J. B. Baldwin, Lexington, February 26, 1866; Lee to M. G. Harmon, Lexington, December 17, 1868, W&L.

9. Lee to W. H. Nettleton, Lexington, May 21, 1866, in *Reminiscences,* 251; Lee to Mrs. Emily Hay, Lexington, February 13, 1870, W&L.

10. Lee to Emily Mason, May 20, 1866, MC.

11. Lee to unknown, Lexington, December 18, 1868, in *Reminiscences,* 269–70.

12. Freeman, 4:302.

13. Lee to A. M. Keiley, Near Cartersville, September 4, 1865, in *Reminiscences,* 204.

14. Lee to John Letcher, Near Cartersville, August 28, 1865, in *Reminiscences,* 203.

15. Lee to Jubal Early, Lexington, October 4, 1866, VHS; Lee to Davis, Lexington, February 23, 1866, in *Reminiscences,* 212.

16. Lee to Charles Carter, Lexington, April 14, 1867, VHS; Lee to David Cabell, Lexington, February 25, 1867, Custis-Lee Family Papers, LC; Lee to Francis S. Smith, Lexington, April 5, 1866, SH.

17. Lee to Markie Williams, Richmond, June 20, 1865, and Lexington, December 20, 1865, *"To Markie,"* 62–63, 66.

18. Matthew Fontaine Maury to Lee, Mexico, August 8, 1865, typescript in VHS.

19. Lee to Capt. M. F. Maury, Near Cartersville, September 6, 1865, in *L&L,* 389; Lee to unknown, quoted in Freeman, 4:208.

20. Lee to Colonel Walter H. Taylor, Richmond, June 17, 1865, typescript in MC; Lee to General E. G. W. Butler, Lexington, January 25, 1867, typescript in DU.

21. Lee to Cassius F. Lee, Lexington, June 6, 1866, typescript in VHS; Lee to Chauncey Burr, Lexington, January 5, 1866, in *Reminiscences,* 210.

22. Lee to General George W. Jones, Lexington, March 22, 1869, MC.

23. Lee to Gen. P. G. T. Beauregard, Lexington, October 3, 1865, in *L&L,* 390.

24. Lee to General George W. Jones, Lexington, March 22, 1869, MC; Lee to James May, Lexington, July 9, 1866, in *L&L,* 391.

25. Lee to Sir John Dalberg (Lord Acton), Lexington, December 15, 1866, typescript in DU.

26. Lee to Judge Robert Ould, Lexington, March 29, 1867, quoted in Freeman, 4:313–14; Lee to Mrs. ———, Lexington, May 21, 1867, in *Reminiscences,* 225.

27. Lee to Giles B. Crook, Lexington, June 11, 1869, VHS; Lee to General Dabney H. Maury, Lexington, May 23, 1867, VHS.

28. Lee to Fitzhugh, June 8, 1867, in *Recollections,* 260.

29. Lee to James Longstreet, Lexington, October 29, 1867, in *Recollections,* 268–69.

30. The fullest discussion of Mahone remains Nelson M. Blake, *William Mahone of Virginia: Soldier and Political Insurgent* (Richmond: Garrett and Massie, 1935).

31. Quoted in Freeman, 4:301–2.

32. Lee to William S. Rosecrans, White Sulphur Springs, August 26, 1868, VHS, quoted partially in Freeman, 4:375–77.

33. Lee to an unnamed clergyman, June 20, 1865, in *Reminiscences,* 196.

34. Lee to my dearest Markie, Lexington, December 1, 1866, *"To Markie,"* 71–72.

35. Lee to my precious Annette [Carter], Lexington, March 28, 1866, W&L; Lee to General E. G. W. Butler, Lexington, October 11, 1867, ML.

36. Lee to Edward Lee Childe, Lexington, January 5 and 22, 1867, January 16, 1868, February 11, 1869, and March 8, 1870, SH.

37. Mary C. Lee to Mrs. W. H. Stiles, Richmond, July 5, 1862, typescript in GHS.

38. Mary Lee to Mary Meade, Lexington, October 12, 1870, VHS.

39. Mary Lee to Mrs. R. H. Chilton, n.p., March 10, 1867, typescript in MC; Mary Lee to Cousin Ellen, Lexington, February 2, 1867, MHS.

40. Lee to Fitzhugh, Lexington, December 2, 1869, in *Recollections,* 374.

Epilogue–Hannibal's Ghost

1. Lee to Edward L. Childe, Lexington, February 7, 1867, SH.

2. Lee to my dear Markie, Hot Springs, August 27, 1870, *"To Markie,"* 90–91. In contrast, former Union general Philip Sheridan, at-

tached to the German General Staff during the Franco-Prussian War, encouraged his hosts to be ruthless in crushing French guerrilla resistance and later celebrated the Prussian victory.

3. Lee to Childe, Hot Springs, August 22, 1870, SH.

4. Lee to Edward A. Pollard, Lexington, January 24, 1867, VHS. *The Lost Cause* was published by E. B. Treat and received several respectful reviews in the North. It was one of the opening rounds of the propaganda war accompanying the Southern white resistance movement to Reconstruction, in which Southerners bested Northerners. For a full discussion of one great postwar military-literary feudist, see Fellman, *Citizen Sherman,* 316–40.

5. Lee to Childe, White Sulphur Springs, July 10, 1868, SH. Hamley's book (Edinburgh: William Blackwood, 1866) went through several subsequent editions.

6. Lee to H. D. McConaughy, Lexington, August 5, 1869, typescript in W&L.

7. Mary Lee to Cousin Ellen, Lexington, February 22, 1867, MHS; Mary Lee to Virginia Long, Lexington, November 20, 1870, typescript in W&L.

8. Marvin P. Rozear, E. Wayne Massey, Jennifer Horner, Erin Foley, and Joseph C. Greenfield, Jr., "R. E. Lee's Stroke," *Virginia Magazine of History and Biography* 97 (April 1990): 291–308; narrative by William Preston Johnston, in *Reminiscences,* 446–59, at 451; Freeman, 4:492.

9. Connelly, 94.

10. Address of J. A. Early to the Surviving Officers of the Army of Northern Virginia, Lynchburg, October 24, 1870, in *Reminiscences,* 334.

11. Address of Jefferson Davis to the Surviving Officers of the Army of Northern Virginia, Lynchburg, October 24, 1870, in *Reminiscences,* 340–41.

12. Connelly, 90–91.

Index

About the Author

Michael Fellman lives in Vancouver, British Columbia, where he is Professor of History at Simon Fraser University. He is author of five previous books on nineteenth-century American culture: *Citizen Sherman: A Life of William Tecumseh Sherman; Inside War: The Guerrilla Conflict in Missouri during the American Civil War; Making Sense of Self: Medical Advice Literature in Late Nineteenth-Century America* (co-author); *Antislavery Reconsidered: New Essays on the Abolitionists* (coeditor); and *The Unbounded Frame: Freedom and Community in Nineteenth-Century American Utopianism.*

About the Type

This book was set in FF Celeste, a digital font that its designer, Chris Burke, classifies as a modern humanistic typeface. Celeste was influenced by Bodoni and Waldman, but the strokeweight contrast is less pronounced, making it more suitable for current digital typesetting and offset-printing techniques. The serifs tend to the triangular, and the italics harmonize well with the roman in tone and width. It is a robust and readable text face that is less stark and modular than many of the modern fonts and has many of the friendlier old-face features.